Promises, Promises

Promises, Promises

Essays on Literature and Psychoanalysis

ADAM PHILLIPS

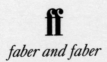

faber and faber

First published in 2000
by Faber and Faber Limited
3 Queen Square London WC1N 3AU

Photoset by Wilmaset Ltd, Wirral
Printed in England by Clays Ltd, St Ives plc

A CIP record for this book
is available from the British Library

ISBN 0-571-20297-7

2 4 6 8 10 9 7 5 3 1

for Brian Worthington and John Carey

To understand oneself is the classic form of consolation;
to elude oneself is the romantic.
Santayana, *The Genteel Tradition in American Philosophy*

. . . if the word 'inspiration' is to have any meaning,
it must mean just this, that the speaker or writer is
uttering something which he does not wholly under-
stand – or which he may even misinterpret when
the inspiration has departed from him.
T. S. Eliot, 'Virgil and the Christian World'

. . . the difficulties of theory have more to do with its
quest for explicitness.
Kate Soper, *Troubled Pleasures*

Contents

Preface

'I regard writing not as an investigation of character,' Evelyn Waugh said in an interview, 'but as an exercise in the use of language, and with this I am obsessed. I have no technical psychological interest. It is drama, speech and events that interest me.' Psychoanalysis is, of course, an investigation of character and, both as theory and practice, an exercise in the use of language. As a therapy it investigates character in language in order to make people happier, and find their lives more interesting. But it also is, and has, a technical psychological interest. It gives us the opportunity, unlike what was once called Literature, to see exactly what that might be; and why, if at all, that might be a better thing to have than a psychological interest or, more simply, an interest in the uses of language. What does it say about the various projects of psychoanalysis that they require – unlike the infinitely more various projects of literature – the kind of interest Waugh doesn't need, to be the great novelist that he is? The pieces in this book provide, among other things, an impressionistic approach to these questions. They wonder, with Waugh's shrewd distinctions in mind, what the language of psychoanalysis, and the languages of literature, might be good for – and what they've got to do with each other.

Waugh's writing, obsessed as it is with mothers (the nursery, drinking and so on), and malice, and development (knowing, or in the case of Waugh's characters, not knowing, what to do when), and madness (which is referred to in *Decline and Fall* as people 'not quite in their right minds'), is a historically exact, and illuminating parallel text to the best years of British psychoanalysis. In 1926, Melanie Klein gave her first lectures in London, in 1928, Waugh published his first novel, *Decline and Fall*; in 1964, Waugh published his last book, *A Little Learning* and in 1965, Winnicott published the last great book in this particular tradition, the less catchily titled, *The Maturational Processes and the Facilitating Environment*. Like Waugh, British psychoanalysis was more interested in depression than anxiety, and like British psychoanalysis Waugh could not escape a religious revival. If British psychoanalysis is, among other things, redescribed Christianity, Waugh's novels are the wittiest and most devastating contemporary account of what this Christianity – in Waugh's case, Catholicism – was called on to deal with. Like the psychoanalytic writing of this period, in which Waugh had no discernible interest – though he has many telling asides and references to it – his novels and his travel writings are about people's strange inability to get on with themselves and other people; about the uncanniness of separation, thoughts for the times on war and death.

I cite Waugh here only to illustrate something entirely unsurprising: that psychoanalysis, like all cultural inventions, is of its time and place – as contingent as graffiti – and that what it is apparently about overlaps with other contemporary social practices. Read in isolation from its cultural context – as it is in most psychoanalytic training – it can seem to be rather more of a specialism, rather more of a privileged language than it in fact is or could ever be. Psychoanalysis cannot make any useful sense if it is not seen as entirely of a piece with its culture, however adversarial it is, or claims to be.

Though psychoanalysis has always run the risk of seeming to be merely another 'luminous, self-justifying, self-sufficient, synoptic vision' – in Richard Rorty's words about the system-building philosophies – read closely it is rather more of a grab-bag of its culture and history than a vision or a system. In the language-schools that are called psychoanalytic training institutions there are forlorn attempts to purify the dialect of the tribe, but psychoanalytic writing (and practice) of every persuasion still sounds a bit like religion, a bit like metaphysics, a bit like anthropology, a bit like science. And a bit like what was still called in the earlier days of psychoanalysis, literature. Indeed, it has been to literature that psychoanalysts have turned when they have grown weary of their supposed system, of their technical psychological sentences.

When literature is not being quoted by psychoanalysts to back up the validity of their 'insights' – the Kleinian literature, for example, is littered with pious references to Wordsworth and Keats and George Eliot as pre-Kleinian Kleinians – it is used by them as a kind of refresher course in language. Indeed, the uses of literature in psychoanalytic texts, starting with Freud himself, betray a certain unease, a troubled and complicated relationship to writers and writing that has been integral to the history of psychoanalysis. Is the psychoanalyst a rival or a collaborator in some putatively shared cultural conversation; or should the analyst be trying to diagnose or interpret or even cure these so-called artists? What these 'artists' – and particularly writers, I think – tend to stand for in psychoanalytic writing is the possibility of an eccentric life, a life apparently untrammelled by system or convention. The writer, unlike the psychoanalyst, is the person who has not been dominated by someone else's vocabulary. Though sometimes enviously pathologized (or infantilized, or idealized, which comes to the same thing) the writer, and the whole notion of literature, have been productive problems for psychoanalysis, keywords in its evolving sense of itself. It is, though, something of a curiosity – to do with fantasies of

xiii

cultural prestige and anxieties about psychoanalysis as a performing art – that psychoanalysis has been so keen to affiliate itself with literature when, as one of the spoken arts, it is more akin to improvised drama (and to Brechtian theatre in particular). But then the image of Freud as not only a clinician but also as a great writer has always haunted the profession he invented; as though all psychoanalytic theory should aspire to the condition of literature, and clinical work, ideally, should be good material for the aspiring writer.

If psychoanalysis as a therapy is always encouraging people to go public on themselves – to speak – psychoanalysis as a profession has been notably reclusive. Though this is gradually beginning to change, it has been difficult for the so-called common reader to get an intelligible sense of what might be going on in psychoanalysis. Writers are allowed to have (and to want) audiences, psychoanalysts have only been allowed to have colleagues. But the integrity of analysts is not guaranteed by their never being seen. The cultivated privacies of psychoanalysis – that are essential to its practice and diminishing for its theory – obscure the politics of psychoanalysis, and its practitioners. Psychoanalysis as part of group life rather than a refuge from it – psychoanalysis as a foil for psychobabble – has to find languages that people are intrigued enough by to want to learn, without being so impressed by them that they lose their own voices (not to mention their minds). Psychoanalysis, at its best, should be a profession of popularizers of interesting ideas about the difficulties and exhilarations of living. And, as a so-called treatment, it should be more about living day-to-day as oneself than about being initiated into a sophisticated or prestigious theoretical system. Listening to what people say, which is more or less what psychoanalysis consists of, should be above all a reminder of fellow feeling.

The best advertisement for psychoanalysis has always been

good clinical work, not polemical defences of the truth or efficacy of psychoanalysis as a science or an art. But outside the consulting room there is only gossip and writing, and especially now the genre that has best combined them, journalism. It may be that journalism – either in the form of book reviews for non-specialist papers, of which there are several in this book, or the writing of articles for newspapers – will be the best way of going on writing the psychoanalysis of the future. By testing itself in a wider arena – both in the market-place, and whatever other places that can be found – psychoanalysis might recover those 'democratic vistas' that have eluded it for so long, at the level of training and clinical practice. Minority interests, like psychoanalysis and literature, can no longer take themselves for granted as (economically) viable vocations, and this may be no bad thing in so far as it prompts people to refashion what they are doing and what they think they are doing; to work out just what it is about contemporary life that is worth resisting or celebrating. Ideally, it should make psychoanalysts people who are only practising psychoanalysis until something better turns up.

The version of psychoanalysis that I want to promote in this miscellaneous book is more committed to happiness and inspiration (and the miscellaneous) than to self-knowledge, rigorous thinking, or the Depths of Being. It values truthfulness but not truth; and as a clinical practice it prefers small gains to revelations. It assumes that there is nothing wrong with anyone, that no one is 'ill', but that everyone is doing the best they can with what they have got. It starts from the belief that children have to learn to be kind, and be free enough to have fun (to lose themselves in whatever makes them curious and makes them feel alive); and that everyone of whatever age who comes for psychoanalysis comes, one way or another, to talk about these two things. Such Panglossian values are proffered (and preferred) in reaction to a profession that has become too eagerly complicit with the grim seriousness of the predicaments it has sought to understand; and that has become, in its slavish quest for academic respectability, more metaphysical and more committed to so-called 'research' as it has lost confidence in what it *really* has to offer, which is often quite simple. Psychoanalysis does not need any more abstruse or sentimental abstractions – any new paradigms or radical revisions – it just needs more good sentences. So the practitioners of this version of psychoanalysis will always be glad to come off rather badly when they are compared with other 'social scientists'. They will be short on facts – though not scornful of some of them – but they will be able to describe in an interesting way whatever happens to impress them. They will have little real foundation for these impressions other than their enthusiasm for them. This version of psychoanalysis would favour a theory as much because it sounded good, as because it might work (i.e., make a difference worth having if a way was found of putting it into practice); so it would think of theories as more like songs than instructions. It prefers the economy of assertion over the tedium of proof; and believes that a theory is only ever as good as its consequences, as the actions and the imaginings to which it leads, and the world which it aspires to make. From this point of view William James is every bit as great a psychologist – whatever that is – as Freud; and the practising analyst's time is better spent reading the philosopher J. L. Austin than the psychoanalyst Melanie Klein (ideally, one would read both). This is a 'literary' psychoanalysis only in as much as I think that reading what used to be called Literature is probably a better preparation for the practice of psychoanalysis than the reading of anything else (political history would be a close second). The ethos of psychoanalysis would be greatly improved if it was more widely acknowledged that one can no more institutionalize psychoanalysis than one can institutionalize poetry. You can teach poetry, but you cannot teach someone to be a poet. The same is true of psychoanalysis. More people are harmed, though, by bad psychoanalysis than by bad poetry.

Coming, as they say, from what was then called Literature as a student in the early 1970s, to psychoanalysis in the late 1970s, has made me wonder what I thought psychoanalysis could do for me – or what I wanted psychoanalysis to do for me – that Literature could not. And, of course, what I might have been using Literature for that made psychoanalysis the next best thing – or rather, the other best thing. This book comes out of these questions. As a newly qualified child psychotherapist working in a child-guidance clinic and what was then called a school for maladjusted children (in South London) I would read psychoanalytic theory written by academic intellectuals with their rebarbative jargon and think: 'these people' have no idea of the intractability of people's problems, of the sheer scale of people's unhappiness. But then I would read the professional literature written by clinicians and I would think: 'these people' are so mired in the intractability of people's problems, so overwhelmed and impressed by people's suffering –and by their own psychoanalytic training – that they have no imagination left. The drawback of the intellectuals' ideas was that they didn't have to work, and the drawback of the clinicians' ideas was that they did.

Of course, in actuality, the contrast was never as stark as I was making it. And now, in fact, much of the most interesting psychoanalysis is written by people outside the profession (it has become clear just how much psychoanalysis has been wasted on psychoanalysts). But this 'contrary' (in Blake's sense) that it suited me at the time to believe seems in retrospect to have been simply another version of something that turns up again and again in both the practice and the theory of psychoanalysis. It is the opposition between the Dreamer and the Pragmatist: the Dreamer who wants only to free-associate and to follow his words wherever they may go; and the Pragmatist who wants to solve his problems. The Pragmatist wants to achieve things, the Dreamer wants to experience them; the Dreamer wants the analyst to help him get back into his own delirium, the Pragmatist wants the analyst to help him sort himself out. The Pragmatist wants to know what to do, the Dreamer wants to see what happens. In order to be this useful profession of improvisers and popularizers, psychoanalytic writing will need to be a place – as indeed, literature has always been – where people can voice both enthusiasms with comparable vigour, where neither the Pragmatist nor the Dreamer can become a refuge from each other. Where, for example, it can be fully acknowledged that one doesn't necessarily say or write something because one believes it, but to find out whether one believes it. At their best both these old-fashioned things, psychoanalysis and literature, can inspire us to live more justly pleasurable, more morally intriguing lives, as complex Dreamers and Pragmatists. The pieces in this book go on making and breaking the links between two figures – and these once discernible 'disciplines' – with this in mind.

I have dedicated this book to the two people who changed my life by the way they taught me literature at school and university; and who taught me more about psychoanalysis, without ever mentioning it, than many of my psychoanalytic teachers did by mentioning nothing else. By teaching me to read they taught me how to listen.

Poetry and Psychoanalysis

Even if we wish to deny the common man his religion,
we clearly do not have the authority of the poet.
Freud, *Civilisation and its Discontents*

1

These days, when we are not being told that psychoanalysis is or is not a science, we are, perhaps unsurprisingly, being told that it is an art. And since, as a talking cure, its medium is mostly language, the arts with which it bears most obvious comparison are the literary arts. In the anxious quest for reassuring analogies – to work out what psychoanalysis is *like*, which has been such an integral part of its history – literature, after science, has seemed the most promising. It has been to writing and not, in some ways perhaps surprisingly, to the more oratorical arts that psychoanalysis has turned. When Freud suggested that his studies in hysteria seemed rather more like short stories, or was writing to Wilhelm Fliess about the inspiration he found in Sophocles and Shakespeare, he was acknowledging right at the beginning of what would become psychoanalysis, something like a divided duty, a splitting of affiliations. The psychoanalytic theory he found himself writing was science that sometimes sounded like literature. The form chosen was the scientific treatise, the genre endorsed by the profession he wrote for; but the so-called content smacked of poetic drama, or fiction. The two cultures of Science and Art

1

that were to polarize so dramatically during the twentieth century were sufficiently differentiated – understood to be at odds with each other – that Freud couldn't help but be perplexed by the ambiguity of his own work.

It is perhaps an appropriate irony that just now, when the status of literature as a definable discipline is most in question in the universities – when the very description of what literature is, is up for grabs – that those psychotherapists who aren't keen on science should be wanting to place psychoanalysis in the literature department, as it were. Once again, psychoanalysis finds itself aspiring to be like something that may not exist. It has always seemed difficult to accept that there may be neither an abject nor a glamorous sense in which what we loosely call psychoanalysis is peculiarly difficult to place, and the puzzles accruing from this might add rather than detract from its value. We should perhaps be suspicious of professions that are in the business of helping people to locate themselves, being too assured in their location of themselves. (It has always been difficult for psychotherapists to avoid putting the answer before the question.) The uncertain status of psychoanalysis is the point and not the problem. Indeed, psychoanalysis has become one useful site for contesting the relative merits of the arts and the sciences; both what they might be good for, and what we should do with our belief in them. And, of course, the extent to which they might be complementary and not solely antagonistic. Every time psychoanalysis goes over to one side or the other – aspiring stringently to be a science, or eloquently to be an art – it loses its place as a discipline in which the question can remain interestingly undecided. It seems obvious that we need both the so-called sciences and the so-called arts to help us with our predicaments. So in discussing what psychoanalysis uses poetry for – how psychoanalysis and poetics might be related – the other conversation that would complete the triangle would be between science and poetry (poets have never been by definition hostile to science). When Keats famously said that Newton had destroyed the poetry of the rainbow by reducing it to a prism, he was also implicitly acknowledging that Newton had fed him one of his best lines.

What psychoanalysis has done to and with poetry – though not what it has done *for* poetry – has been the subject of endless theorizing and commentary. What I am more interested in is what, it has been assumed by psychoanalysts, poetry might be able to do for psychoanalysis; what poetry seems to offer – or disrupt – in psychoanalytic theory and practice; what the poetic has represented for the psychoanalytic, if one can put it so generically. The poet, in a psychoanalytic context, was initially cast as an inspiring but also irritatingly usurping presence. Psychoanalysis has always been mindful of the poetic pasts that might have preceded it, of the literary influences that might have prefigured its figures of speech. 'At the beginning I was utterly at a loss,' Freud wrote in *Civilisation and its Discontents*, 'and the first clue that I had came from the philosopher-poet Schiller who observed that the mechanism of the world was held together by "hunger and love".' It was from Schiller, Freud says, that he got his first description of what he took, initially, to be the two basic instincts: sex and self-preservation. But as often as Freud refers to what he got from the poets, in a spirit of gratitude and admiration, he refers rather more dispiritedly, even enviously, to the poet's apparent easy access to profound psychological truth. After quoting some lines from Goethe's *Faust*, Freud writes: 'One may well sigh when one realizes that it is nevertheless given to a few to draw the most profound insights, without any real effort, from the maelstrom of their own feelings, while we others have to grope our way restlessly to such insights through agonizing insecurity.'

3

For the inspired poet it's a breeze, for the analyst it's a slog. The poet doesn't work; though the poet and the psychoanalyst seem to have a shared project. The poet is at once the source of profound insight and a rival in terms of the methods for acquiring such insight. 'The genuine poet', Ella Sharpe, one of the early British analysts wrote, endorsing Freud, 'is an intuitive psychologist.' So which is the best thing to be, and why? If we are in search of profound insight, whatever that is, the question might seem answerable. What is being asserted here is that poets and psychoanalysts have a shared aim (or object of desire), but different means for attaining it. But what makes Freud, or Ella Sharpe, believe that the poets' project – all poets at all times – has been the search for profound insights? One could feel that poets are being recruited, perhaps a bit desperately, as allies. Clearly for those people who like poetry, or who like the idea of poets (which is not the same thing), their transference to poets is a remarkable thing. Indeed, so remarkable is it that it is perhaps the one thing that could be said to unite the increasingly disparate schools of psychoanalysis. Freud, Jung, Lacan, Winnicott, Bion, Meltzer, Milner, Segal, among many others, all agree in their privileging of the poetic. Psychoanalysis may not have mattered quite as much as it would have liked to poetry, but poetry has certainly mattered to psychoanalysis.

Being a good poet makes you a good psychologist, it is suggested, one capable of 'profound insight'; but being a good psychologist doesn't seem to make people good poets. Indeed, it might be in a poetic sense, as it were, that one's reservation about psychoanalysis would be that one didn't like the language in which it was written, and spoken. And this would involve acknowledging that psychoanalysis can be no more and no less than the language in which it is represented. After all, one goes to psychoanalysis, as one might go to poetry, for better words. So it seems worth noting at the outset that psychoanalysts have claimed an affinity with poets that poets, contemporary with the advent of psychoanalysis, have not always claimed with psychoanalysis. So what does the psychoanalyst think she is affiliating herself with when she asserts a kinship between psychoanalysis and poetry? In what sense are analysts and poets on about or doing the same thing? And what are the consequences, for the actual practice of therapy, of believing that they are?

It is immediately noticeable that something has to be done to poetry to align it with psychoanalysis. In making poetry into a source of 'profound insight' or 'psychology' it usually has to be taken out of its historical context, and depoliticized. In the vexed relationship that the psychoanalytic profession has always had with poetics, it is striking how often, when poetry is invoked – and almost always to be celebrated – it is invoked ahistorically. When, for example, Meltzer proposes in an interview that psychoanalysts should be 'as poetic and precise as we can', we don't tend to wonder whether he means poetic like Chaucer or Donne or Whitman or Elizabeth Bishop, or whether he means the sonnet or the epic – as though the situating of poetic practice was virtually irrelevant; as though the poetic had a known referent beyond history or genre. Poetry seems to mean here something written or said with the most convincing kind of accuracy or insight. Poetry becomes the word for a specific kind of verbal rigour or a hoard of verbal wisdom, the best making of meaning that, at the same time, persuades us of the efficacy of meaning. So, by way of an initial assertion, I want to suggest that the idealizing of poetry in psychoanalysis – and not only there – is, among other things, a way of talking of our doubts about language, a scepticism – inevitable in a profession committed to language as therapy – about words and the value of meaning, about words as therapy.

5

The privileging of poetry and poets is a counter-force to the fear that language and meaning don't work. Or don't work in quite the ways we might want them to.

As we know, the privileging of poets and poetry in psycho-analysis has been complemented and rivalled by the privileg-ing of sciences and scientists. The analyst has always been able to say that the work of psychoanalysis, despite its evident flaws, aspires to scientific status. Many analysts, beginning with Freud, have been keen to assert, despite their voluble de-tractors, that they are scientists. It would seem to be a more complicated thing – a more obscure thing – for the analyst to say that she is a kind of poet. So my second assertion here is that the research scientist has always been an easier ego-ideal, or model, for the analyst, than the poet. Obviously the analyst can write poetry, or even make her psychoanalytic writing more poetic (whatever that means), but what would it mean for her to be more like a poet in her psychoanalytic practice? What exactly would she do, or do differently? What, for example, if she were to affiliate her practice with the poets, would count for her as a successful psychoanalytic treatment? We may have some idea of what a psychoanalytic cure might be from a scientific point of view, but what would be a cure for the poet-analyst?

As a prelude to this paper there are, then, two assertions: that the poet and poetry are used to sustain our belief in meaning, our belief, in Yeats's odd phrase that 'words alone are certain good'; and that the poet is a peculiarly difficult – and therefore peculiarly interesting – ego-ideal for the analyst. If the analyst were to aim to be more like a poet than a scientist, what would his work be like? What would he be wanting of and from the patient?

So the sub-title of my lecture might be: can psychoanalysis be anything other than a religion of words. As though psycho-analysis has replaced belief in God not with belief in sexuality,

or belief in emotional development, or belief in the unconscious, or indeed in any of the other core concepts, but rather
with belief in language. And something called poetry – or
literature – has become, then, the secular Bible for psychoanalysts.

2

Words are everything else in the world.
Wallace Stevens, 'Adagia'

It seems dull to begin at what one might pretend is a beginning.
But Freud's early paper, in its very title, 'Creative Writers and
Daydreaming' (1908), is an irresistible invitation of sorts. In this
paper Freud makes 'the assumption that a piece of creative
writing, like a day-dream, is a continuation of, and a substitute
for, what was once the play of childhood'. And the play of
childhood, in Freud's view by this time, like the dreams and
symptoms he had newly described, was a disguised representation of infantile sexual wishes. There is, Freud writes in this
paper, 'a path that leads from our discussion of phantasies to the
problems of poetic effects'. What distinguishes the creative
writer is that – like the dreamer and the playing child – he has
found a way of rendering unacceptable desires into shareable
form. 'Such phantasies, when we learn them,' Freud writes,
'repel us, or at least leave us cold. But when a creative writer ...
tells us what we are inclined to take to be his personal day-
dreams, we experience a great pleasure'. In this imaginative
alchemy, pleasure is wrested from aversion. To be a poet is to be
able to make the apparently impossible thing, an acceptably
pleasurable transgression. 'How the writer accomplishes this is
his innermost secret,' Freud writes, 'the essential *ars poetica* lies
in the technique of overcoming the feeling of repulsion in us

7

which is undoubtedly connected with the barriers that rise between each single ego and the others'. We disgust each other, Freud suggests, but through poetry we restore a sense of community; we are seduced into not only enjoying each other, but enjoying our hitherto repulsive ideas. It is also of some interest that Freud lapses into Latin to describe the means, the technique for doing this, as though the phrase *ars poetica* was a respectable euphemism for some unspeakable sexual practice. The arts of poetry for Freud are clearly highly charged. Through this 'aesthetic' 'altering and disguising' of his day-dream the creative writer 'enables us thenceforward to enjoy our own day-dreams without self-reproach or shame'. It is quite clear that whether for Oedipal – or what we might now call pre-Oedipal reasons – our day-dreams are guilty and shameful, and poetic techniques are required to perform the morally equivocal act of not merely making our desires acceptable to us, but positively pleasurable. The art of poetry, in other words, is the art of being happily unacceptable in public, of making known one's otherwise forbidden desires. The person referred to in this paper as the creative writer is an extraordinary double agent, a figure who doesn't fit easily into either of Freud's models of the mind. Clearly, the creative writer is not akin to the super-ego or the id; he could be described as the eloquent ambassador of the id, who has to some extent outwitted the moralistic clutches of the super-ego. But the creative writer is not sufficiently realistic in his perceptions, not perhaps sufficiently addicted to safety, to be merely another word for the ego. Or perhaps Freud's figure of the creative writer is the ego in its best, or most satisfied, version. The poet is our last hope for happiness faced with the scarcity of the external world, the depredations of the super-ego and the voraciousness of the id. The poet is the person who can get away with it.

But I think it is also worth considering that Freud is using this

8

paper to reflect on the profession he had invented. Is the analyst like the creative writer in so far as she too has the work of redescribing what the patient finds unacceptable, with a view to making it at least tolerable, if not also pleasurable? Or, to put it the other way round, is the aim of analysis to enable the patient to be more like this creative writer, able to make known his fantasies, and find them a source of pleasure, to make the patient the good-enough poet of his own life? Or, is the idealization of the artist to which Freud (and so many other analysts) has been prone – with its inevitable concomitants of envy, rivalry and suspicion – simply the consequence of the creative writer representing both an ego-ideal and a picture for Freud of the best possible version of what it is to be a person? After all, if the creative writer is doing what everyone does as a child and when they dream, then 'creative writer' is just another word for a person. The *ars poetica* are the arts of life. In his idealization of the poet Freud might be a late romantic; but by making the art of poetry a synonym for dream-work and children's play Freud was suggesting not that we should aspire to be poets but that poets are what we cannot help but be. Psychoanalysis becomes the science of poetry; or rather the attempt to render the poetry of the human in the language of science. What is *The Interpretation of Dreams* if not a formulation of the laws and logic of poetry? 'The poets and philosophers before me discovered the unconscious,' Freud said on the occasion of his seventieth birthday, 'what I discovered was the scientific method by which the unconscious can be studied.' It is a distinction that has not perhaps been sufficiently remarked upon. Poets and philosophers discover the unconscious; Freud discovers a method for studying it. What exactly is the difference? Did Freud turn *it* into a subject that could be studied? If the artists and philosophers didn't themselves study it, what did they do with it – perform it, enact it, show it? Is the

9

unconscious, as it were, pure poetry and philosophy, which Freud's scientific method enables him to reflect on, analyse, deconstruct?

There are two forms of practice: there are poets and philosophers, and there are psychoanalysts, with something called the unconscious in the middle, and they have different kinds of relationship to it. On the one hand, there is the poetry of the human – the unconscious in action – and on the other hand there is the scientific study of it. It is not clear – not clear to Freud himself maybe – whether the poet and the psychoanalyst are collaborators, or whether there is a sense in which the poet might aspire, or even evolve, towards the condition of the psychoanalyst, or vice versa. Is the dream better than the interpretation or vice versa? Whichever it is you can't interpret the dream without a dream.

It was Lionel Trilling in his great essay 'Freud and Literature' who most succinctly spelled out that Freud, whatever else he was, was a champion of the poets. 'For, of all mental systems,' he writes, 'the Freudian psychology is the one which makes poetry indigenous to the very constitution of the mind. Indeed the mind, as Freud sees it, is in the greater part of its tendency exactly a poetry-making organ ... it was left to Freud to discover how, in a scientific age, we still feel and think in figurative formations, and to create, what psychoanalysis is, a science of tropes, of metaphor and its variants, synecdoche and metonymy'. In a scientific age we still use language. Trilling's account makes psychoanalysis, as a science of tropes, sound like another word for linguistics; and it was, of course, Lacan, who promoted the consequences of just such a conviction. And yet what Trilling is doing here, in the American context of a burgeoning ego-psychology, in claiming Freud for the poets, is not necessarily a literary appropriation of Freud. Indeed, this may be a more or less sophisticated way of saying that people are language-using animals, and that these poetic arts, which can be scientifically studied, are just descriptions of how language works. Poetry becomes a description of what the mind does; it is a poetry-making organ. Freud showed us that people, as verbal language-using animals, were more poetic than we had recognized; indeed, people were, essentially, poets. And we are what we call poetic only because what we have to say is so unacceptable to ourselves and others.

The existence of poetic arts, the ubiquity of human poetry, proves just how much work has to be done on the stuff of instinctual life to make it viable. What Freud called the 'biological substrate' required imaginative acts of transformation to make the desires we need to communicate in order to survive, bearable for everyone involved. The demand on the mind for work is a demand on the mind for poetry. And poetry is the smugglers' art, repackaging contraband so it can be available on the open market. Human beings are disreputable poets, but fortunately they are subject to scientific redescription. Is science, then, a higher level of respectability? Certainly one doesn't tend to think that there is anything shameful or embarrassing about a theorem in physics, or a mathematical equation.

The Freudian mind might be a poetry-making organ, but this in itself is not a cause for celebration. Poetry may be our cultured natural medium, but something has to be done to the poetry. Poets, after all, are not famous for their mental health. If we describe the analyst as merely countering the patient's poetry with his own – psychoanalysis effectively as a bardic competition – we could quickly become puzzled. Biology is turned by people into poetry, but poetry clearly needs itself to be turned into something else. The scientific method of studying the unconscious, called psychoanalysis, has a purpose, a project. Poetry, in other words, is not sufficient; something has to be added to poetry to make a cure. In Freud's view, poetry in and of itself doesn't seem to make us feel better. Or, to put it less medically and more morally, our apparently innate poetry-making talents don't by themselves give us the lives we would prefer. One goes to an analyst to have one's poetry improved, but does this mean that the analyst speaks better poetry than the patient, or that – despite her having, exactly like the patient, a poetry-making organ – she has learned to speak some other language? Clearly, neither the analyst nor the patient can speak at all without using what Freud called the *ars poetica*, metaphor, synecdoche and metonymy. The picture that Freud presents, and that is so eloquently elaborated by Trilling, is that it is taken for granted that we are all poets. The question is, what, if anything, should be done about this?

And yet, of course, we are not all poets (or creative writers) in the more traditional sense of these words. We may all be, as Nietzsche famously wrote, 'artists in our dreams'; dreams and symptoms and children's play may be tropic. But to put it at its most minimal, we don't all *write* poetry even if we supposedly speak it and perform it; and perhaps even more to the point, there are no line endings in dreams, or children's play, or symptoms. Just as Freud is insistently promoting the human subject as essentially and ineradicably a poet, he also won't let us, or himself, forget, in his idealization of artists, that some people are what we call artists and some are not. Before the creative artist, Freud acknowledges ruefully, the analyst throws down his arms. There is apparently no contest; the creative artist is at once essentially human but also has got something the analyst just hasn't got. The artist represents for Freud the limits of psychoanalysis; faced with the artist and her work of art the analyst confronts the terminus of her explanatory ambitions. We see Freud both pitting himself against the so-called creative artist and using the artist as the exemplary human figure. We are all poets, but some are more poetic than others; and it is the difference that makes all the difference. It is, after all, evidently true that poets rarely seem to be envious of, or rivalrous with, psychoanalysts as a profession. Even in W. H. Auden's great elegy to Freud you never get the sense that Auden would prefer to be a psychoanalyst, or even to be Freud himself, than to be the poet that he was. What has the poet got that the psychoanalyst hasn't, and why is it better?

Psychoanalysis has always had an uneasy relationship to poetry and poets, uneasy, perhaps, in the sense in which Freud (and Strachey) used the word in Freud's great phrase, 'the laughter of unease'. If psychoanalytic writing has been more like incantation than poetry – characterized by the hypnotic repeated use of favourite words such as play, dependence, development, mourning, projective identification, the imaginary, the self, etc – it is perhaps reflective of this unease. We all cannot help but use language poetically, and yet there are people we call poets; we all, one way or another, speak and write, but that there are these discernible cultural objects called poems. It is as though some people are capable of, as we say, expressing themselves better than others and that we have somewhere agreed that this is a good thing to be able to do. Is the aim to be a poet or to be happy? Freud is in that long tradition of people who want to show us how impressed we are by words. And how we can't seem to get away from the idea of happiness.

3

The worse your art is, the easier it is to talk about.
John Ashbury

One of the things that distinguishes the words we call poetry is form; when prose is referred to as poetic we usually mean that the prose is unusually metaphoric, intensely evocative rather than overtly informative. But poetry – the form of writing that we can distinguish from prose so that we can call some prose poetic – is distinguished by its line endings. Poetry, T. S. Eliot said in a famous pronouncement, is a form of punctuation. Where ordinary prose ends according to the size of the page and the compositors' conventions, poetry adds a different kind of punctuation to the repertoire. What is added to the ordinary human poetry of language are formal constraints. Poets, unlike psychotherapists and their patients during sessions, write; and they impose line endings. Through reading other poets they acquire a sense of the available forms of their own and other poetic traditions.

Now it is, as Lacan has shown, an interesting, literary analogy for the practice of the analyst to say that she punctuates the sessions – with verbal interventions, or their omission, and by the endings of the sessions. 'The punctuation,' Lacan writes, 'once inserted, fixes the meaning'; 'changing the punctuation renews or upsets' the meanings that the patient asserts in his speech. The analyst's repunctuating of the analysand's speech 'shows the subject that he is saying more than he thinks he is'. If, rather absurdly, one was to speak quantitively, it is as though the point of the punctuation is to increase meaning, not to replace the patient's intended meaning but to add to it. The aim is to upset old meanings with a view to creating new ones. 'Psychoanalysis', Lacan writes, echoing Freud, 'should be the science of language inhabited by the subject. From the Freudian point of view man is the subject captured and tortured by language'. In this Lancanian sado-masochistic relationship with language, it is the function, in part, of the analyst's punctuation to show the patient just how captured and tortured by language he is. But Lacan, like every other psychoanalytic writer, can't get around the problem of hierarchy; the analyst upsets or renews the patient's meaning with a view to changing the patient for the better. Whether it is called in Lacan's language 'full speech' or becoming the subject of one's desire, there is an attempt to interfere with – for a higher good – the patient's words in the service of the cure. 'Literary art' which, Lacan writes in the Ethics seminar, 'is so close to the domain of ethics', like psychoanalysis, is punctuating for a purpose. The patient tries, consciously and unconsciously, to give his form to the session, and the analyst keeps changing the punctuation; the patient's sonnets are turned into free verse, his limericks are turned into elegies.

It is, of course, part of Lacan's literary art to persuade us of the interest of this analogy; because in actual fact punctuation is only a feature of written language. We can pause and change our intonation when we speak, and when we listen we might think of some hesitation, say, as a comma or a semi-colon; but there is no verbal inscription of punctuation. In psychoanalysis there is interruption and the ending of sessions. We have only to wonder what the equivalent in speech is of a line ending in poetry to find the analogy beginning to complicate. We may all, as it were, speak poetry, but it is that unusual thing, poetry without line endings, something akin to poetic prose. Poetry – at least in a psychoanalytic context – begins to mean something like verbal utterance suffused with meaning. In psychoanalysis there is always the risk that the wish for meaning will be usurped by the will to meaning.

So the poet becomes a figure for that person who can sustain our belief in the meaningfulness of language. And in this sense the poet could be conceived to be akin to the psychoanalyst; the patient coming to analysis to restore his confidence in words. Lacan believes – like every analyst, one way or another, after Freud – that it is worth speaking, and that some ways of speaking are better than others. And what are called the literary arts are somehow complicit with this belief. There are qualities of literary representation, capacities for symbol-formation, that themselves represent (or carry) the most cherished values of psychoanalysis across the whole range of what is otherwise a very contentious profession. 'The creative artist makes full use of symbols,' Klein writes in 'Some Reflections on the Oresteia', '... the greatness of Aeschylus's tragedies – and this might have a general application as far as other great poets are concerned – derives from his intuitive understanding of the inexhaustible depth of the unconscious...' The unconscious, at its best, is associated with powerful, resonant, full words; and once again in that familiar echoing of Freud, the poet is described as having an 'intuitive' understanding of the unconscious, the source of great poetry. Intuitive must mean here, of no discernible method, as opposed to the psychoanalyst's scientific exploration of the unconscious.

Whatever the differences between them, Lacan and Klein agree that some words are more revealing than others. And the paradigm for this – which, it should be said, could not be more traditional – is poetry, the literary arts. The poet, in some way, gets to in her poetry what the psychoanalyst gets to through his scientific method. At its most abstract it becomes a question of what the consequences are for the analyst of treating the figure of the poet as an ego-ideal. What, after all, does the name 'poet' signify given there are so many of them? If, as Lacan says, the literary arts are 'so close to the domain of ethics', what are the ethics of poets? What, to put it crudely, are poets generically transmitting as a system of ethics? The self-professed ethics of the scientist may be rather different from the self-professed ethics of poets, not to mention, of course, their unprofessed values, but such generalisations are meaningless. What, in short, are we valuing when we claim to value poets, rather than scientists, as our exemplary figures? If both Kleinians and

Lacanians, for quite different reasons, are suspicious of the patient's wish to identify with the analyst, they still have to persuade their patients to identify with their wish that they should not be identified with. For both Lacanians and Kleinians – if we talk about schools of psychoanalysis and not inclinations – the artist is still hero and heroine. Perhaps, above all, the poet. As poets struggle to find a place in contemporary cultural reality, psychoanalysts, implicitly or explicitly, are still promoting the poets as ego-ideals.

Psychoanalysis, the Kleinian Robert Caper writes in a recent book *A Mind of One's Own* – and he is representative in these views rather than exceptional – 'leaves us with a sense of insecurity about whether or not we can even define in words some of our most fundamental scientific notions, let alone communicate them to a broader public, or even among ourselves. I don't believe that the solution to this sense of insecurity lies in trying to make psychoanalysis more expressible in the scientific language we have. I think we would do better to try to change the language of science into something more psychoanalytic. At present only poets and artists are able to capture these kinds of experiences . . .' In this progress myth, an interesting variant of the common theme, it is suggested that, at the moment, scientific language cannot 'capture' psychoanalytic experience – only poets and artists can do that. But if we change the language of science into something more psychoanalytic, analysts, it is suggested, will at least be on a par with the artists and poets. It is a moot point, in the way Caper phrases it, whether this new psychoanalytic language will eventually supersede the language of poets and artists. What is clear, though, is that, as yet, these poets and artists can do something that psychoanalysts and scientists can't do, and that is, 'capture' certain kinds of experience. It is an odd and telling word – 'capture' them to what end? Or, what are they

17

imagined to be if they are in need of capture? But nevertheless there is here the valuing, if not the idealization, of language that is neither scientific nor psychoanalytic. What are psycho-analysts valuing when they value poets, and their language; and what are the consequences for psychoanalytic practice of choosing the poet as hero?

4

The organism is determined neither by its genes nor by its environment, nor even by the interaction between them, but bears a significant mark of random processes.
Richard Lewontin, *The Triple Helix*

It is obvious that when we are talking about poets and poetry we are talking about a remarkable diversity of voices. And the psychoanalytic canon of poets – the poets referred to or used by psychoanalysts in their theory-making – is notably restricted. And yet the figure of the poet, and references to something called poetry, do quite a lot of work, one way or another, in the way psychoanalysts theorize their practice. 'Artists' and 'poets' and 'poetry' are as much key words in the ways psychoanalysis reflects on itself, as the words 'infant', or 'mourning', or 'sex-uality'. So what do psychoanalysts feel themselves or their chosen discipline to lack, by their turning to poets and poetry? What does poetry seem to have or to be that psychoanalysts might want? Just as it is always a notable moment in the psychoanalyst's text, or indeed in her interpretation when she turns to Buddhism, or biology, or developmental research, it is the same with the quoting of poetry. It is as though, at that moment, there is a gap, an aporia, a space often unnoticed opens up that needs something else. At that moment something is required called poetry to do something specific. And of

18

course, at these constitutive moments of feeling at a loss – at this moment of deprivation, in Winnicott's language, when one might, as it were, steal something – the chosen object is of some significance. Whether it is Buddhism, or infant observation or poetry that comes to the rescue it makes a difference. It has consequences. Of course I am melodramatizing an ordinary occurrence into an emergency; we all have recourse to our preferred bits of the cultural field. But the point of making this crisis out of a drama is to suggest that, at these moments, we have recourse to – what we, in one form or another, quote – can always be fetishized.

When we describe psychoanalysis as scientific or artistic we have aligned it with a tradition – with a history – of human practices, aimed, presumably, at producing for us the kinds of lives we would prefer. So when, for example, the Sandlers conclude their last book, *Internal Objects Revisited*, with a quote from Byron, what are they doing? 'A source of severe resistance in analysis, one that often leads to a negative therapeutic reaction', they write, 'is our need to cling to the internal objects we have constructed. In this context it is perhaps appropriate to end this book by recalling the words of Byron's "The Prisoner of Chillon", relating what he felt when set free'. Here they are invoking, if not actually clinging to, poetry as a form of exceptional accuracy as being the best way of saying something. Analysts, I think, of virtually every persuasion, have some sort of belief in or commitment to poetry as a convincing, truthful, life-enhancing eloquence. The poet, in one kind of psychoanalytic language, is a highly valued internal object, and one who is often linked, I think, in some obscure way, with fantasies of freedom and independence: the poet represents the apotheosis (at least for some people) of self-becoming, of individuality, of difference wrought to a distinctive pitch through style. The poet, the fantasy of the poetic, is, as they say, carrying a lot for us, and yet poets, it is surely worth repeating, don't tend to be our models for mental health. Byron would not, I think, have been accepted for training at most psychoanalytic institutes.

When psychoanalysts evoke or invoke the poetic – not necessarily formal poems – it is often being intimated that the poetic is closer to the source of something or other; that our essence speaks in poetry. Or to put it in more familiar terms, that what we call the unconscious and what we call poetry are somehow linked. We may not all believe that the unconscious is structured like a language, but I imagine that many of us believe that poetry is a sign of the unconscious (of our knowingly and unknowingly saying more than we intend). When psychoanalysts talk or write of the unconscious they seem to be referring to something like a poet, rather than, say, describing the unconscious as itself a poem that has gone on inspiring more poetry. We should, I think, entertain a fable that Freud wrote a poem called the Unconscious, and like all poets he didn't know where it came from, so he said, as a kind of joke, that his poem 'The Unconscious' came from the unconscious.

But it is the psychoanalyst in the act of invoking the poet or poetry that I want to consider. And I want, by way of conclusion to use two inaugural moments – one explicit and one oblique – to show what might be at stake, what is being recruited and why, when the poets are wheeled on.

When I was training to be a child psychotherapist, about twenty years ago, something called 'not-knowing' was all the rage: a state of mind, at least at first sight, not difficult to achieve, especially as a student. But it became clear to me that 'not-knowing' – the analyst *not* jumping to authoritative conclusions – had become a virtue in psychoanalysis, reactive to what was deemed to have been an assumption of omni-science on the part of some analysts; that there were analysts who believed in the unconscious, indeed swore by it, but seemed to know their own minds, and the minds of their patients all too well. These were analysts for whom having the strongest convictions was in no discernible sense incompatible with a rigorous psychoanalytic critique of omniscience; and this 'not-knowing' was most prominently theorized, at least then, by Bion and Winnicott.

There were two important references – Bion using Keats's notion of negative capability, and Winnicott's writing of the patient's nonsense – one overt and often quoted, and one more understated but no less influential. What Bion and Winnicott wanted to say (wanted to add to psychoanalytic theory) needed a poet and the poetic to legitimate it, or to crystallize it or just to describe it. What was ironic about these two (linked) excursions into the literary arts was that both Bion and Winnicott were using poets and poetry to dismantle, or reconceive something that had been deemed to be essential, indeed, defining, of the practice of psychoanalysis: the making of sense through inter-pretation. The poets provided covert criticism of the analysts' will-to-intelligibility, and by doing so they reopened a question that was at the heart of psychoanalysis: *is not making sense good for us? And, what is making sense good for?* Or, to put it another way, is free association the means or the end of psychoanalysis? If, as Ferenczi once suggested, the patient is not cured by free association, but the patient is cured *when he can free associate*, free association itself must be a moral good. What Ferenczi, and virtually everyone after him found rather more difficult to describe was, what is so good about a life in which one is able to free associate. Either free association is in itself a consummate erotic pleasure, or the capacity to do it must be the means to a better life. What can the free associator do now that she couldn't do before, other than free associate?

When Bion and Winnicott started promoting 'not-knowing'

and nonsense – when they introduced, as it were, a bit of poetry into psychoanalytic theory – they were, I think, restoring the moral issue of punctuation to the psychoanalytic agenda. You can tell a psychoanalytic theorist from his bibliography, and there is perhaps an unintended irony in the fact that much psychoanalytic theory that preaches the value of otherness, and the disabilities of omniscience, should so often be quoting the same limited range of people. So it is notable when, in Bion's case, Keats makes it into his index (though interestingly, not under his own name, but under 'negative capability', his phrase).

Bion first gives Keats a place in the final chapter of *Attention and Interpretation*, published in 1970. But there are two interesting references in the selection of his writings published posthumously, and called *Cogitations*. The first one is a notebook entry of 1969, where Bion writes: 'The capacity of the mind depends on the capacity of the unconscious – negative capability. Inability to tolerate empty space limits the amount of space available'. And then later, in 1978, Bion speaks about visiting the Keats and Shelley museum in Rome with his wife. 'These poets and artists', he says, 'have their methods of recording their awareness of some sort of influence, stimuli that comes from without, the unknown that is so terrifying and stimulates such powerful feelings that they cannot be described in ordinary terms'. Once again there are two phenomena: what Bion calls 'ordinary terms' that are insufficiently descriptive, and whatever it is that poets and artists use; which of course are also ordinary words – there is very little specialist jargon in most poetry. But, nevertheless, the poets have their 'methods', which are unusually descriptive, and which are so good at describing the unknown and the potentially overwhelming – what in the eighteenth century might have been called 'the sublime'. It is when Bion needs to note something enigmatic about the capacity of the mind – about what it can contain – that he uses Keats's phrase as a kind of shorthand. But the notebook entry itself is interestingly constructed. 'The capacity of the mind depends on the capacity of the unconscious – negative capability. Inability to tolerate empty space limits the amount of space available'. Bion depends upon Keats's phrase to fill the theoretical space left by his sentence. And of course Bion made what one was unable to tolerate his special subject. Keats's concept of negative capability enabled him to tolerate something, made more mental space available. Poets become the people who can bear the influence of certain things upon themselves. Poets, Bion suggests, have a fuller language – words that can contain more – than ordinary terms. The poet is here elevated over the scientist and the ordinary language user. Keats is used by Bion, as we shall see, to help him describe his (Bion's) version, of the preconditions for meaningful language. The poet as the sustainer of our confidence in language; and therefore our confidence in psychoanalysis as being of any real value, given, just like poetry, it goes on only in words.

Bion begins his last chapter 'Prelude To or Substitute for Achievement' of his book *Attention and Interpretation* with this excerpt from Keats's 1817 letter to his brothers:

I had not a dispute but a disquisition with Dilke on various subjects; several things dove-tailed in my mind, and at once it struck me what quality went to form a Man of Achievement, especially in Literature, and which Shakespeare possessed so enormously – I mean Negative Capability, that is, when a man is capable of being in uncertainties, mysteries, doubts without any irritable reaching after fact and reason.'

Keats, as he says, is describing the qualities of a man of achievement, *'especially in literature'*; and it is Shakespeare who comes to mind, *the* man of achievement. And Keats is not necessarily objecting to reaching after fact and reason, but to the *irritable* reaching after these things. And Bion wants to translate Keats's elements of literary achievement into psycho-analytically instructive material. 'Any session', Bion writes, 'should be judged by comparison with the Keats formulation.' Keats's formulation, in short, becomes the arbiter, the criteria of judgement for the validity of a psychoanalytic session. What Keats's formulation, as Bion puts it, 'guards against', for the analyst, is his 'failure to observe' what is happening in the session and is, Bion writes, 'intensified by the inability to appreciate the significance of observation'.

The analyst's very impatience, one could say, becomes a kind of attack both on the analyst's own mind – his capacity to think – and on the patient's material. The analyst, Bion states, should aspire to be Keats's version of the man of literary achievement. If the analyst can be something like what Keats thinks Shakespeare was like then something good, or something better than something else, will come of it. Shakespeare wrote his plays, Keats wrote his poems, but what will the analyst produce? And the answer is, a good interpretation, good in Bion's sense of what a psychoanalytic interpretation should be. The analyst will be like a poet and her interpretation will be like poetry. But where is the patient, what is the patient making? The analyst may be wanting to be like Keats's Shakespeare, but what is the patient deemed to be like? If the analyst wants to be a poet, what does that make the so-called patient? Merely a user of ordinary terms, a bad poet?

If psychoanalytic sessions should be judged by comparison with Keats's formulation, that makes the analytic situation at best a school for poets, a 'singing school' in Yeats's phrase, and at worst the place where the aspiring poet/analyst can practise his art. But perhaps the main point here – certainly the one Bion wants to stress – is that of the analyst being like the great poet in his capacity to wait. And at the end of the waiting, that itself creates the space for attentive observation, there will be his poem, the good interpretation. Eventually all the associating, free or otherwise, will be interrupted; the raw material of the patient will have been contained, metabolized, thought about, and something like a poem will be made. But then of course, we are left with the question of what these great poems or good interpretations are for; what are they supposed to do for us? The aim, Bion writes, is for the analyst to use words to enable the patient to use words that will not be 'a substitute' for action but 'a prelude' to it. The analytic aim is to sponsor what he calls, taking up Keats's terminology, the 'Language of Achievement', which is both 'prelude to action and itself a kind of action'. Keats's negative capability, as the necessary prelude to the writing of great poetry becomes, in Bion's translation, the precondition for the therapeutic efficacy of psychoanalysis. Poetry, like a good interpretation, is language in action. The analyst is like the poet in that she aims for full speech, meaningful words, good language. What Bion calls the 'Language of Achievement'.

Achievement is an interesting word in this context. It is clear that for Keats the Achievement that he capitalizes is the making of great poems. It is not quite so clear, when we follow Bion's analogy through, what the comparable Achievements are in psychoanalysis. And to say the achievement would be the cure would be to beg the question. After all, Keats is only describing in his letter what he realizes makes a great poet; he is not saying anything here about why being a great poet might be a good thing to be (and I doubt Bion would have been enthusiastic about some of Keats's pronouncements about this; like, for example, the aim of poetry being 'to make all disagreeables disappear'). 'I have no faith whatever in poetry,' Keats wrote in another letter, 'sometimes I wonder that people read so much of it.' It is, I think, to sustain his faith in the possibility of a talking cure – of a cure made only of words – that Bion needed Keats; and that he needs effectively to aestheticize the analyst's work. It is the poet's description of a certain quality of attention that interests Bion; but as a practising analyst he has to add to this a belief in the curative power of such attention. Keats famously gave up medicine and became a poet; and believed most of the time that poetry was a force for good in the world. But the analyst has a more immediate pragmatic responsibility than the poet. The patient's poem called 'Free association' has to be turned into, given form, by the analyst's better poem called 'an interpretation'. But what makes some poems better than others? And is the implication of Bion's analogizing that ideally the patient, too, should aspire to a negative capability of his own? Should the patient become, through internalization, or identification, the poet of himself, the poet of his own life?

The picture is further complicated by the fact that Keats's description of negative capability also sounds like the pre-condition for free associating. Or rather, to be slightly more accurate, what Keats calls the 'irritable reaching after fact and reason' would be the saboteur of anything approximating to free association. The not-knowing that was to capture the imagination of so many analysts is also necessary for even the possibility of free associating. The patient associates and the analyst interprets; the patient's poem inspires the analyst's poem which inspires the patient's poem, and so on. Irritable reaching after facts and reasons is too impatient; eventually, though, Bion intimates, facts and reasons might emerge. But then again, if one was always capable of 'being in uncertainties, mysteries, doubts' what would ever qualify as a reason or a fact? Or indeed, why would facts and reasons be objects of desire? Keats doesn't want facts and reasons, he wants great poems.

Whether we call it free association or interpretation – or whether the analyst enables the patient's most rudimentary capacities for symbolization – the object of desire is full, meaningful words; Bion's Language of Achievement. But are these meaningful words in whatever direction they happen to lead us; or are meaningful words defined by their tropism towards the depressive position, or towards any of the other criteria for cure? Does the Language of Achievement have a known destination called, say, mental health? Once you bring on the poets you have a great diversity, a virtual anarchy of moral values. We know what Klein's definition of mental health is, but what kind of values, what versions of good lives do we find in, say, Blake, or Emily Dickinson, or Auden? By introducing Keats and his negative capability into psychoanalysis Bion inevitably invited us to be in uncertainties, mysteries and doubts about psychoanalysis itself. It is indeed instructive how few analysts seem to have been in a state of negative capability about Keats's formulation of negative capability. It is repeated like a mantra as though the poet's words were themselves beyond interpretation; when it is precisely poetry that invites interpretation. Poetry is words hospitable to interpretation, words wanting to be subject to multiple perspectives. Words that are inspiring because they resist fetishization, because they are not propaganda. What we refer to as the unconscious is any communication, any message to which we cannot remain indifferent. Good interpretations, like the poems that work for us, are at once irresistible and unpredictable in their consequences. Only dogma is a means to a known end. Only propaganda thinks it knows what it wants from us.

What Bion uses Keats to warn the analyst away from is premature or pre-emptive knowing – from propagandising. The poet's artful formulation about his art is used to hone the scientific skills of observation. This not-knowing, this negative capability, is the precondition for better knowing; whereas for Keats it is the prelude to great poetry. They are not the same thing. Bion's assumptions are clear: poetry is a kind of knowledge, a kind of truth, and this knowledge and truth is good for us. Our lives are better for it. Keats's version of scepticism is being recruited by Bion to protect him and other psychoanalysts from a larger and more daunting scepticism about the power of words, about the value of meaning. What Bion prefers to call, after Keats, the Language of Achievement, is, as it were, rich and earnest with purpose.

In *Playing and Reality*, Winnicott stresses 'a need for differentiation between purposive activity and the alternative of non-purposive being'. He broaches the possibility that for some people, at some times, it is the wish to make meaning, the belief in the value and need for meaning, that is the problem, that is insidiously defensive. 'In terms of free-association this means', he writes, 'that the patient on the couch, or the child patient among the toys on the floor must be allowed to communicate a succession of ideas, thoughts, impulses, sensations that are not linked except in some way that is neurological, or psychological and perhaps beyond detection.' The use of the word 'link' here may be a covert critique of Bion; but the point Winnicott is making is clear: 'There is room for the idea of unrelated thought sequences which the analyst will do well to accept as such, not assuming the existence of a significant thread ... according to this theory, free-association that reveals a coherent theme is already affected by anxiety, and the cohesion of ideas is a defence organisation.' This is not, of course, worlds away from Keats's 'irritable reaching after fact and reason'. But the analyst here is not waiting for meaning, or coherence, or an interpretation to evolve or emerge. And in elaborating his notion Winnicott alludes to that distinctively British genre of poetry that has never assumed the significance for British analysts that surrealism did for the French. There is, Winnicott suggests, a need for nonsense that is every bit as crucial – and sometimes more so – than our need for sense and meaning. In this scenario free association is an end in itself, and the need for meaning is linked to a kind of vigilant, and despairing self-holding. The need for meaning, the need for coherence, the need for purpose and achievement become desperate measures; traumatizing solutions to trauma. Poetry is alluded to here by Winnicott to warn us of the dangers of our need for meaning.

'Perhaps it is to be accepted', Winnicott writes,

that there are patients who at times need the therapist to note the nonsense that belongs to the mental state of the individual at rest without the need even for the patient to communicate this nonsense, that is to say, without the need for the patient to organize nonsense. Organized nonsense is already a defence, just as organized chaos is a denial of chaos. The therapist who cannot take this communication becomes engaged in a futile attempt to find some organization in the nonsense, as a result of which the patient leaves the nonsense area because of hopelessness about communicating nonsense. An opportunity for rest has been missed because of the therapist's need to find sense where nonsense is. The patient has been unable to rest because of a failure of the environmental provision, which undid the sense of trust.

This is at once a compelling implicit critique of nonsense poetry, which is by definition organized nonsense; and it is also suggestive in implying that there might be a defence against non-meaning, against nonsense, as well as a defence against meaning. This is not an attack on meaningfulness that Winnicott is sponsoring, but allowance of a need for nonsense. Psychoanalytic theory and nonsense poetry come together here to add something to psychoanalytic practice; the 'health', to use Winnicott's word, of acknowledging the need not to mean what we say. That the conferring or construing of meaning could itself be a trauma, an alienating demand, harmful to development.

I want to put together Winnicott's idea of organized nonsense and Bion's Language of Achievement not because one is right and the other wrong, but because they are complementary, and they both need poetry to say what is at stake for them. If the Language of Achievement and the need for the acceptance of nonsense dramatizes a debate in psychoanalysis, it is a debate about the nature and consequences of meaning, and so of what poetry might be good for in psychoanalysis, and how psychoanalysts might sometimes need poetry, in ways that poetry might not need psychoanalysis. A Freudian, or a Kleinian or a Lacanian poem would be a contradiction in terms.

I think it is worth pressing the crude, pragmatic question of what poetry is good for – or of what might be so good about poetry – because the question, what is so good about science is being answered all the time, and the question what is so good about psychoanalysis is being asked all the time, and not being answered very well. Poetry especially, and literature more generally, runs the risk of being literally shrouded in religious awe, by psychoanalysts in search of new ego-ideals. Once it dawns on people that Freud was a poetic writer – that psychoanalysis bears some intriguing and formative family resemblances to the wider field of poetics – then psychoanalysis ceases to be any kind of supreme fiction and can find a more promising place as one form of poetics among many others. And this is where, I think, that the larger and more daunting scepticism that I referred to earlier comes in. All poets – and Keats is a particularly illuminating example – have a fascinated ambivalence about their own vocation. A profession like psychoanalysis that gives so much responsibility to words, that makes language seem so promising must, by the same token, have profound doubts about, and obscurer hatreds for, language. And partly, of course, because these doubts and loves and hatreds will be themselves expressed in language. Psychoanalysis, like rhetoric, wants to persuade us that language can be persuasive and improve our lives. Psychoanalysis in all its versions believes that if we know more about how representation operates we will be better off (as though there is nothing else to our lives other than our representations of them). I think the valuing and the idealizing of poets and poetry among psychoanalysts might have a simple source: good poetry – the poetry that happens to work for us – makes words self-evidently compelling, self-evidently good. That is to say, they are an apparently instant cure for our pervasive scepticism about whether language works. Psychoanalysis needs such alluring reassurances.

5

Not-knowing for Bion – and often, though not always, for Winnicott – was in the service of better knowing. Accepting the patient's nonsense as nonsense is not deemed to be the be-all and end-all of analysis. Even though 'Life's nonsense pierces us with strange relation', as Stevens wrote in 'Notes Toward a Supreme Fiction', becoming increasingly nonsensical is not assumed to be the aim or even among the aims, of psychoanalytic treatment. The analyst, it is implied, like the so-called patient, is not supposed to not-know forever. But the terms themselves signify the essentially epistemological nature of the psychoanalytic project. When Bion and Winnicott promote the suspension or deferral of knowing, they are by the same token reminding us of the extent to which psychoanalysis is bound to a project of knowledge. Something will occur to someone, that can be spoken and will hopefully be of value. Something can be known about, and right knowing can make better lives. Whether one speaks of emotional experience, or of intellectual enquiry, these are rhetorical ways of describing preferred forms of knowing. Psychoanalysis, in all its versions, is part of those traditions that believe that knowing can do you good: knowing in words.

'Perhaps more shocking, and certainly more important, than any of Freud's or Wittgenstein's particular conclusions', Stanley Cavell writes, 'is their discovery that knowing oneself is something for which there are methods – something therefore that can be taught (though not in obvious ways) and practised'. Psychoanalysis is a method for self-knowledge, and each variant of psychoanalysis produces different versions or genres of self-knowledge. I am pressing this rather obvious point because though psychoanalysis is indisputably a method for self-knowledge, poetry is not. Poetry *can* be in the service of self-knowledge, but psychoanalysis is definitively in the service of self-knowledge, with all that that entails; that there is something we want to call a self (or a human subject), that it can be to some extent known (or known about), and that that knowledge can be good for us. Indeed, the acquiring of that knowledge – both the process of doing so, and the insights achieved – is the key to improving our lives. And each school of psychoanalysis has its distinctive version of the self-knowledge story. Kleinians are able to tell us elaborate, often rueful stories about their destructiveness, their sadness, and their sense of beauty; Lacanians can tell us ironic stories about the vagaries of their desire; Bowlbyans can talk poignantly about the impact of their separations and their attachments; and Winnicottians will probably stress their ruthlessness and spontaneity, or their lack of it. In each case, with the multiple variations produced by the idiosyncracies of personal history, specific forms of knowledge, specific languages are used to account for a life.

The writing and the reading of poetry can be used in the service of so-called self-knowledge, but poetry doesn't need to define itself as doing that – anymore than any other kind of literature does. Poetry can have other uses and inspirations, one of which can be, of course, a questioning of the moral value, or indeed the existence of such knowledge. 'The study of literature', the poet J. V. Cunningham wrote, 'is not in the ordinary sense to further the understanding of ourselves. It is rather to enable us to see how we could think and feel otherwise than as we do.' For psychoanalysis, to think and feel otherwise than as we do is dependent on self-knowledge. From a psychoanalytic point of view they are inextricable. So in talking about poetry and psychoanalysis – in putting them together – we may have to, as it were, disentangle some traditional equations. First, that so-called poetic language is a form of self-knowledge, or is productive of it; and secondly, that self-knowledge is the principal good that we seek.

Of course, it is misleading to talk about what psychoanalysis uses poets and poetry for – as though psychoanalysis was one thing, and psychoanalysts uniform. But it has nevertheless been my impression that when psychoanalysts refer to poets and poetry in their writing they tend to underestimate the great diversity of forms and voices; and their refusal to historicize – to historically situate the poetic – is the consequence of the refusal to historicize the unconscious. Clearly, the available forms of psychoanalytic writing are far more limited than the forms poetry can take; and that it may be easier to generalize about psychoanalytic writing than about poetry may itself be a source of some rivalry. But the rivalry and the collaboration between poetry and psychoanalysis – that is as old as psychoanalysis itself – is a distraction, I think, from something that is integral to the way psychoanalysts refer to the poetic in their writing.

33

As I have said, I think psychoanalysts invoke poetry and poets wherever their repressed scepticism about language and knowledge begins to come to light. *Knowing people in language is either impossible and/or no good: and knowing people is impossible or no good, or beside the point.* These, understandably, are the two daunting fears of psychoanalysis, the secret thoughts, the unavoidable scepticism that every therapist and every patient must at some times feel. Everyone would probably agree that language does something; but were we to go on from there and ask what it does and how it works we would soon become perplexed. And yet psychoanalysis depends on the workings of language. It has to believe in words, and have fantasies about what they can do. The poet tends to become the cure for that founding scepticism, rather than an additional way of enquiring into it. Psychoanalysis was unconsciously devised, perhaps, to find out something new about what people can do to and for each other with language.

If the relationship of philosophy to knowing is in some sense definitive of the discipline, the relationship of poetry to epistemology is far more ambiguous. Poets who are exclusively interested in epistemology are called philosophers; poets who are interested in words are called poets. And this, I think, is where psychoanalysis is most interestingly poised; not simply between science and poetry, but between poetry and epistemology. What would it be to be interested in words, but not necessarily in knowledge? To think of words as more like music than information? The great American poet James Wright said he wanted to 'say something humanly important instead of just showing off with language'. It should be the project of psychoanalysis to wonder about that distinction. And to wonder whether it is one.

Bombs Away

War cannot be negated. One must live it or die of it.
So it is with the absurd...
Albert Camus, *The Myth of Sisyphus*

It took bombs to deliver us.
J. B. Priestley, *Margin Released*

The year before war was actually declared – the possibility of war having been in the air, so to speak, for some time – T. S. Eliot had spoken of wanting to participate in some way in the war effort. He had hoped, in Peter Ackroyd's words in his biography of Eliot, 'for occupation in some form of National Service without that official status which might shut his mouth, and that he would be free to take part in any work for the future that was possible'. He ended up becoming an air-raid warden for the area of Kensington in which he lived, which involved watching for air raids and 'rehearsing the procedure for marshalling people in the event of an air raid, and practising his fire-drill by putting out bonfires'. This work, which seems so incongruous with our image of Eliot, did not shut his mouth. Despite being uncertain in September 1939 about whether he would write poetry again, within three or four months of war being declared Eliot started work on 'East Coker', the second of his *Four Quartets* which would eventually be published together in 1944. It is not always easy to remember – given the lack of explicit reference – that the

Four Quartets are war poetry, partly written in London during the Blitz. Although the poems are very much preoccupied with continuity and rupture – and indeed, with the idea of England and its Christian heritage – the landscape of the poems, though sometimes eerie and desolate, is not, as it were, bombed. The opening of the second section of 'Little Gidding' makes perhaps most obvious reference to the landscape from which the poems came:

> Ash on an old man's sleeve
> Is all the ash the burnt roses leave.
> Dust in the air suspended
> Marks the place where a story ended.
> Dust inbreathed was a house –
> The wall, the wainscot and the mouse.
> The death of hope and despair,
> This is the death of air.

Apart from its apocalyptic associations, 'This is the death of air' means also this is the death that comes from the air, the bombs that turn houses and lives to dust.

There is, of course, no reason why this or any other poem should be a documentary reflection of the world in which it came about. But what I want to look at briefly – by way of an implied comparison with the psychoanalysts – is one localized example of what Eliot, consciously or unconsciously, uses the war to do, and especially the air raids with which he and indeed all Londoners were much preoccupied during several of the war years. The word 'raid' is used only once in the *Four Quartets*, and it is in the passage in 'East Coker' in which Eliot is writing about writing poetry. The language of war is recruited to articulate something about articulation, but with the strangest implications: 'And so each venture'. Eliot writes about himself writing poetry:

Is a new beginning, a raid on the inarticulate
With shabby equipment always deteriorating
In the general mess of imprecision of feeling,
Undisciplined squads of emotion

In what in psychoanalytic language might be called the dream work of the poem, Eliot has turned the air raid into one of his pictures for the struggle to write poetry (air raids were effectively a raid on the inarticulate in that the victims couldn't speak nor be understood by the German bombers). In what sense is each new venture of writing like a raid on the inarticulate? Does a raid, as in a robbery, steal something back? To use the word 'raid' in this context could not help but bring with it the immediate history, the association of air raids, and by doing so, suggest something of the poetry of war. A poem is an air raid, a surprise attack, it conquers internal countries of inarticulacy. And this is not worlds apart from Freud's now famous slogan of usurpation, where id was there ego shall be.

This essay is about what British psychoanalysts – especially the increasingly important child analysts – used the war, wittingly and unwittingly, to articulate about the child's putative nature. And so it is about the conflict – not always articulated as such – between those who worked as if the unconscious, and therefore most starkly the child, was outside history, 'timeless', exempt from contingency; and about those for whom whatever was being described by the notion of the unconscious was utterly contingent, entirely a period piece; those for whom the war would confirm psychoanalytical theory, and those for whom it could not help but put it into question.

This essay is about, then, how the Blitz got into the poem that is psychoanalysis; and how the child in the Blitz is perhaps the dream-image – the emblem – of which most psychoanalysis after the war is the interpretation.* The child, from a psychoanalytic point of view, was living in a Blitz. In what was beginning to be called the child's 'internal world' there was always a war going on. But I want to begin with a clinical vignette.

A sixteen-year-old boy came to see me after the sudden death of his father because he found himself, as he put it, 'absolutely obsessed' by his father; for the first time in his life feeling really close to him, feeling the affinities between them. His presiding grievance with his father had always been that his father refused to really fight with him, to take him on. And this had been particularly strange to my patient, when he was a young boy, because his father was a war hero, with medals that he refused to show anyone, for bravery. How could he find out about his father's war if he literally refused to fight with him, when he quite explicitly, though gently, discouraged the boy from being rough. When it came to Oedipal conflict his father had been, as it were, a conscientious objector. My patient told me:

After the war, my father became obsessed by books about Germany: social histories, biographies of Nazis and German statesmen, memoirs of the period, all that stuff ... he believed – and he would often say this to my mother and I – that you had to find out what the enemy were really like so you could make yourself absolutely different ... my father developed a kind of private cult of inefficiency and gentleness ... he was a sort of hippy ... I was always trying to find the hard man in him. I did everything I could to make him an enemy.

* I think it is more illuminating to read psychoanalysts as poets – mostly, of course, poor ones – rather than failed or aspiring scientists; if we do this we need not worry about whether they are right or wrong, we can just argue instead about whether their words are persuasive, eloquent, evocative or beautiful. Whether they have made something haunting rather than true.

I said: 'I am trying to imagine a life – or a war maybe – in which you never know who the enemy is, never know how to find him'. And he said, 'if you never knew who the enemy was you wouldn't know how to be good, that's what my father believed'. I said, 'so the enemy makes you good, makes it possible for you to be good'; and he said, 'yes, gives you a picture of goodness'.

The complications of this attempt at generational unhaunting were obviously bemusing. From his experiences in the war – whatever kind of trauma they had been – the father was left still looking for the enemy. His obsession had been to understand and define the enemy as a negative ideal; he would never be like them: it would never happen again. His son also needs an enemy but comes up against something bewildering; the father who is an enemy by refusing to be one. For the father to refuse – or rather to try and refuse – to be the son's enemy could be a consummate act of unconscious Oedipal aggression. The son says to the father, I want/need to fight with you. The father says to the son; you need enemies in order to be good, but I won't be your enemy.

For the sake of this essay there are two emblematic things here. First, the need to locate, describe, understand the enemy. And secondly, as an inevitable corollary of this, the need for intimacy with the enemy (if you don't know who and where the enemy are they may be having a relationship with you without your knowing). For this man's father after the war, it seemed that, at least to his son, the most passionate relationship of his life was with the Germans; his wife and his son could rarely impinge upon this. For my patient his father reading books about Germany was a primal scene. (Indeed, one could think that the first couple that the child experiences – the child's first primal scene – is the mother's internal relationship to the enemy, the unacceptable within herself.) For my patient, after his father's death, found himself obsessed, once again, by his father's obsession: by the kaleidoscopic shifts between triangles: father, mother and son; father, mother and Germany; father, son and Germany and so on. In identification with his father he lived as if his partners and friends – the people about whom he was passionate, whose company he craved – were enemies. He lived, that is to say, as if knowing people was, unconsciously, a project of disidentification. He knew people in order to be unlike them.

In the critic Franco Fornari's book, *The Psychoanalysis of War* (1975) Fornari writes that, 'war serves to defend ourselves against the "Terrifier" as an internal, absolute enemy . . . in this manner we arrive at the incredible paradox that the most important security function is not to defend ourselves against an internal enemy but to find one'. As armchair psychoanalysts it is obvious to us that this solution – this security function – is a problem. But you can't fight a war, of course, as though it were the internal problem of the combatants. What do we imagine it would be like if, by magic, all the people in a war – in the middle of a battle – suddenly withdrew their projections, owned and acknowledged their personal terrifiers? Would they start attacking themselves?

In this cartoon there would be a stunned silence and then some people would go mad, some people would become sad or depressed and some people would feel a lot better; but how would they then see each other? What kind of relationship would they have next? What would they use each other to do?

In order to understand a lot of psychoanalytic theory we have to fast-forward it to the moment after the cure: the aftermath or the fall-out after the successful treatment. After my psychoanalytically cured war there would be more internal conflict – people would be really and most immediately up against themselves – but apparently less, or certainly different external conflict. Because we cannot bear the battle within, psychoanalysis tells us, we have our battles, whenever possible, outside.

I want to suggest in this essay that, in the first instance, the experience of the Second World War, in London, consolidated the psychoanalytic picture of the child that Melanie Klein had been developing since the twenties; because the child, the Kleinian child, was assumed to be already at war, though essentially with himself. But it was the unconscious dream work done on the war, the deferred action of that trauma – and of the Blitz in particular – that made of the child a site for contested accounts of both the nature of the child herself, and the child in the adult on which much of psychoanalysis depended. There was a war being fought, during and after the war, and not only between Klein and Anna Freud, to produce a privileged description of the child. As we shall see, the immediate experience of the Blitz confirmed much of Kleinian theory; the more gradual psychic processing of the experience – of both its practical consequences (the pragmatics of evacuation), and its emotional cost – produced a proliferation of competing descriptions, most notably in Britain from D. W. Winnicott, John Bowlby and W. R. D. Fairbairn.

If we cannot imagine psychoanalysis without the notion of war – psychoanalysis was partly made out of the materials of war, its casualties and its language – then the immediate experience of the Second World War seemed to put the finishing touches to a new description of the child that analysts had been struggling to articulate since before the First World War. If it was the workings and the provenance of the unconscious that Freud began with in *The Studies in Hysteria* (1895), in the Joke Book (1905) and the Dream Book (1900) and the *Three Essays on Sexuality* (1905) before the First World War – then we cannot help but notice that between the wars psychoanalysis changes. On the one hand it simply proliferates; there are more practitioners and theorists and psychoanalytic societies. Freud's work is translated and reprinted; psychoanalysis finds an obvious use for itself in understanding and treating the psychic consequences of war. But with the concepts of the repetition compulsion and the death instinct (in *Beyond the Pleasure Principle*, 1920) Freud produces a kind of psychic essentialism that, if we believe in these concepts, seems to have immense explanatory force. What now can't be explained by the war between Eros and Thanatos, and the drive to repeat? If the unconscious becomes more intelligible – a source of coherent narratives – it also begins to be usurped by a new figure called the child. For some psychoanalysts – most notably Sandor Ferenczi, Melanie Klein and Anna Freud – describing the child replaced describing the unconscious, or the dream work. Or rather, in their view, describing the child *was* to describe the unconscious. The child was, as it were, the unconscious *live*: you could see it in action. It had been found; in fact, you could virtually talk to it. With the advent of child analysis there was a growing sense that we could get closer to the source.

But in these new descriptions of the child – despite the great differences between Klein and Anna Freud with the ferocious controversies they inspired (see Pearl King and Riccardo Steiner's book, *The Freud-Klein Controversies 1941–45*, 1991) – the child had intelligible projects, the child had needs. It is infinitely more reassuring to have needs than to have an unconscious. (Need, one might say, could be defined: unconscious desire could only be tracked.) The war, *The Times* said, makes us 'think about essentials', in other words, makes description of need urgent. The psychoanalytic child that emerged from the Second World War in her various guises – Kleinian, Anna Freudian, Bowlbyan, Winnicottian – was equipped with, indeed constituted by, a discernible set of needs and was, in fact, equipped for a war of need. The child who came out of the Second World War had a variety of different wars inside her, depending on which psychoanalytic theorist you read.

'In the popular sociologies of the 1950s', Denise Riley writes in *War in the Nursery*, ' "we all know" that children need their mothers at all moments; and child psychology, ostensibly drawing on the "experiences of war" was scientifically reiterating "what everyone already knows".' The internal war that psychoanalysts had been refining in theory and practice between the wars came true, as it were, with the experience of the Second World War. What 'we all knew' about children after the war came, in part, from the complex relationship, the enmeshing, of war experience in Britain, and in London in particular, with the war which psychoanalysts increasingly believed constituted our being. For the psychoanalysts – and particularly the Kleinians – a war was another word for a person. So, what was the difference, if any, between the war outside and the war inside? And what were wars about, and so what did we need to cope with them? If the war with its bombings and evacuations, and mothers working, and fathers away indefinitely, showed people starkly what deprivation was for a child and so, by inference, what a child needed, then the child could tell us what a war was.

'If we accept the notion,' Winnicott writes in his 1940 paper, 'Discussion of War Aims', 'that basically in our natures we are like our enemies; our task is immensely simplified.' This, of course, is far from being a simple statement. The task he refers to is at once psychoanalysis, and the understanding of the war. This, one could say, is a virtual summation of psychoanalytic theory; basically in our natures we are like our enemies. Real wars, of course, make us believe we know what an enemy is:

someone essentially different from us. If there is so little difference between ourselves and our enemies we are clearly, as Freud suggested, a danger to ourselves.

I want to suggest that the Second World War was, so to speak, an ideal setting – and psychoanalysis was a more than suitable discipline – to ask, what is an enemy? And in child analysis it was as though one could be in on the beginning of the answer. Was what was increasingly being called development – or, in the Kleinian schema, more or less primitive positions – merely a process of locating the enemy and then of having a good enough relationship with it? Was child analysis – or indeed living a life – about winning wars, or finding suitable truces? In short, was a child someone in the process of locating the enemy; and where, if not from the adults, was the child going to acquire her sense of what she was up against? Acculturation, as the child analysts would formulate it after the war – and practise it in the consulting room – was teaching the child, and re-educating the child's mother to recognize the enemy.

In 1944, Earnest Jones, the founder of the British Psychoanalytic Society in London, who had been instrumental in the promotion of Melanie Klein's work in Britain, gave a lecture in America entitled 'Psychology and War Conditions'. Fresh, so to speak, from the Controversial Discussions in the British Society – the discussions themselves something of a war within a war – Jones used the opportunity of his lecture to explicitly reflect on the effect of war conditions in Britain, and more obliquely, on the war conditions in the British Society. Indeed, his title, which could have been Psychology *of* War Conditions, is itself suggestive of a necessary or even enabling link. Psychology, at least the psychology that is psychoanalysis, and war conditions go together.

In this paper Jones makes two related points. First, that it was only when we, the British, realized how evil the Germans were, that we began to feel better. It was, he says, with 'the apparently irresistible form of the Blitz-krieg', 'when we saw the Germans marching at will' into France, when we realized their 'invincibility', that they were so much more 'implacable' than in the last war, that we could then locate our resources, the good things that would protect us. 'At such a moment of mortal peril', he writes,

the country was seized with a united determination so admirably voiced by the genius of our prime minister, and it was this sense of unity that gave us the conviction that there was something we could believe in and trust, namely each other. This conviction was so strong as to be quite impervious to the pessimistic anxieties in the rest of the world concerning our fate.

It is the mortal peril – a clear sense, a vivid definition of the enemy – that turns the country into a strong positive group, providing what Jones refers to as the 'sense of unity'. The enemy, Jones implies, by the sheer force of the terror it inspired, made us a strong positive country, with a genius as a prime minister. In fact, Jones intimates, sheer horror of the Germans made us practically invulnerable, 'quite impervious to the pessimistic anxieties in the rest of the world'. What could be more inspiring than an enemy? How else, we might wonder in the light of Jones's fervent account, might we acquire such virtues and strengths? Without this much evil would there be this much good; would there be something that had the kind of unity that allowed us to call Britain a nation? Satan's dare in *Paradise Lost* (written after another war) – 'Evil be thou my good' – comes ironically true. Or to use Jones's preferred Kleinian language, though not in quite the way Klein intended, the Bad Object inspires the Good Object. We become good reactive to the defined presence of the bad. The moral question

45

here – redescribed in the new language of psychoanalysis rather than the old language of theology – is: what would we be without the Bad Object? The second and related point that Jones makes is that in his view – and this of course would fit with some of his psychoanalytic assumptions – the war made people feel better. 'There is no evidence I know of', he writes,

to indicate any increase in psychoneuroses in these five years (of the war), and there was a very general impression during the most dangerous period of the war that would explain this by the reciprocal relationship that exists between so-called 'real' suffering or danger coming from without and neurotic suffering; when fate inflicts suffering there is less need for the self-punishing functions of the neurosis.

What the war confirmed, and air raids in particular, was '... how very much easier it is for the human mind to tolerate external danger than internal dangers'. The war, Jones intimates, is just what a lot of people needed: 'the higher degree of single heartedness in this war', he writes like a man with a proof in his hands, 'results in a mental harmony that fortifies endurance against discomfort and distress'. Does Jones – and by implication, do psychoanalysts of his own persuasion – think that war is a good, indeed necessary thing? Or rather, does war between nations, or between opposing factions in psychoanalytic societies, function as a cure for the intolerable war going on all the time inside the individual? Being a person is virtually or potentially intolerable unless you are lucky enough to live in a time of war. Or putting it the other way round, what, from a psychoanalytic point of view, is peace?

In Jones's view here – echoing Freud but not exactly echoing Klein – external danger makes us feel better (Klein's implicit point is that it doesn't really make us feel better, it is a delusionary imitation of the problem). The defence of projection, coupled with either or both the neurotic need for self-punishment and the implacable danger of the death instinct, makes up a virtual instinct or need for war; which, paradoxically, is in the service of the individual's self-protection, and moral well-being.

This discussion about war reveals a battle of theoretical allegiance in Ernest Jones himself. In at least one reading of Freud, war – or at least the evacuation of the bad or destructive – is a necessity for psychic survival. This in a sense, is Freud as tragic realist. We are at war with ourselves and with culture. Real wars enliven us because they give us something to do – they give us both a target, and a performable project, a theatre – for our inner divisions; and they provide sufficient punishment, in terms of suffering, to make us more light-hearted. And yet, as Jones almost won't let himself notice in his lecture, this rather complicates the practice of psychoanalysis, especially Kleinian analysis with its essential project of enabling the patient to restore his destructiveness, to return the projections to their source, to facilitate the acknowledgement of a severe ambivalence in the service of entry into the depressive position. Or, to put it slightly more straightforwardly, if we are mad and bad, is psychoanalysis driving people mad by encouraging them to take their mad badness back inside themselves? Better out than in, or better in than out? Is psychoanalysis the alternative to war, or an art of war? If there is such a thing as mania – at least in Klein's description of it – then war is only ever going to be a temporary or provisional solution to inner depression and the madness that is an attempted self-cure for depression. And yet, as Jones is eager to assert – partly it confirms certain central psychoanalytic descriptions – the real war seemed to be every bit as curative for many people as he might have hoped psychoanalysis would be. War might be psychoanalysis's great rival. In fact, ironically, the real war, by validating some of Freud's still embattled ideas, could make psychoanalytic treatment itself a poor substitute for war. If war can do us good, and psychoanalysis can do us good, how should we choose between them? War and psychoanalysis might seem mutually complementary, each a proof, a validation of the other.

In child analysis it seemed as though we could find out, as it were, how wars started. Child analysts, in the unique setting of the war, were trying to find out what a good war was. 'Very notable', Jones wrote ominously in his lecture, 'was the adaptation displayed by children provided their parents showed no neurotic terror'. Here we have, in miniature, the child analyst's question; what does the child depend upon to sustain his or her emotional well-being? And who is in a position to decide – to provide the privileged descriptions of – emotional well-being or health?

The child analysts had a good war. But Jones, as a virtual but still ambivalent Kleinian, was at least in this sentence, putting a great onus on the parents, as Winnicott and Bowlby were to do after the war. 'Provided the parents showed no neurotic terror', Jones observed, the children adapted well during war time. But what kind of adult would it be who showed no neurotic terror during a war? Or, as it would soon turn into in theoretical discussions after the war, what kind of mother would it be who showed no neurotic terror in the war of child-rearing, the war in the nursery? No neurotic terror can only mean: bringing no personal history to the experience.

Psychoanalytic theory always runs the risk of de-historicizing wars; as though there is something more or less universal called war that has certain more or less generalizable psychic effects. As though, say, technological developments would make no material difference to the psychic experience of war. War, from the psychoanalytic perspective endorsed by Jones, is a great relief for two reasons; it places the enemy fairly and squarely outside. And it defines the enemy, gives it definition, tells us who they are, what they are like, how they work. 'It might be said', Freud wrote in 1915 in 'Thoughts on War and Death', 'that we owe the fairest flowerings of our love to the reaction against the hostile impulse which we sense within us'. We are in this sense, dependent on the enemy, either within or without, to react against; to free us to construct our goodness, our virtues.

The experiences of the war in London – both the immediate experience of air raids, rationing etc. – and the second-hand experience of media reports and rumour – were the raw material, the day residues, out of which child analysts in London elaborated psychoanalytic theory to redescribe the enemy within. The war provided a ready-made set of representations out of which the Bad Object could be constructed – and reactively the Good Object. The good mother would be one who could absorb and process the infant's air raids – who would be undestroyed by his bombs; she would never mastermind an implacable invasion. In other words, by looking at one of the many experiences of the war that dominated people's lives – the air raids on London – we can glimpse something of the inevitable contingency – and historical occasioning of the theorizing of unconscious fantasy, the sense in which psychoanalytic theory is always local history, and the way it attempted to privilege its descriptions by apparently exempting them from the specificities of history. We can see something of what happens when Freud's privileged description of the instinctual war that constituted the individual met the experience of a real war. Bombs, and the real possibility of invasion, seem, in retrospect, to have been just what child analysts needed to extend their account: the invasion by mothers, by their separateness or their intrusiveness; the invasion of the mother by the child; the child invaded by his instinctual life and needing maternal protection. These were the images that would organize psychoanalysis after the war; and the fathers who were mostly absent during the war would be mostly absent from the theory.

So, what did child analysts use the experience of war to do, what was the work of inner transformation, the dream work, coming up with in terms of theory and practice? What was it like doing child analysis under the threat of invasion, in the expectation of air raids?

In 'On The Theory of Anxiety and Guilt', written in 1948 – a summation of her then present position – Melanie Klein explains how the war had vindicated, indeed proved the validity of her most cherished theoretical conviction. 'If external danger is from the beginning linked with internal danger from the death instinct', she writes,

no danger situation arising from external sources could ever be experienced by the young child as a purely external and known danger . . . This was clearly shown in the analysis carried out in war time. It appeared that even with normal adults anxiety stirred up by air raids, bombs, fire, etc. – i.e. by an 'objective' danger situation – could only be reduced by analysing, over and above the impact of the actual situation, the various early anxieties that were aroused by it.

War, she is quite clear, is fundamentally an internal problem; 'over and above the impact of the actual situation' – over and above being where the air raids came from – there are what she calls the 'various early anxieties' that are aroused. War reminds us, like a prompt, of our early selves; and our early selves are terrorized by the mysterious workings – the 'silence' Freud called it; and a silent war is indeed a terrifying notion – of the death instinct inside us. And because Klein takes the insidious ineluctable death instinct so seriously war cannot, in fact, provide sufficient relief. No danger for the child, or for the adult, can be 'purely external and known' because of its link with the death instinct. The Germans, with the air raids and their bombs and their threats of invasion, were merely reminders of a far greater danger within; a surplus or excess of inner danger that the enemy simply hinted at. Our fear, one might say, echoing Freud, is always in excess of the object's capacity to satisfy it. This, for Klein, was what analysis during the war had 'clearly shown'. It had clearly shown something that was terrifying partly because it could never be clearly shown, was already beyond representation.

From Klein's point of view, paradoxically, the war worked for people – made them feel better – for two reasons, which needed to be carefully distinguished: one, as it were, genuine, and one spurious. For 'many people', she writes, the excessive anxiety produced by the war, 'led to a powerful denial (manic defence) of the objective danger situation, which showed itself in an apparent lack of fear'. War, that is to say, inspired in people the attempted self-cure of mania, the flight into invulnerability that itself spells our horrifying vulnerability to the death instinct. This, for Klein, is, as it were, the bad gain of the war; that as it mobilizes primitive terrors, it mobilizes primitive defences. But the good gain of the war, she writes, was that there were other cases in which,

the relative stability of children in spite of war-time dangers was not determined so much by manic defence as by a more successful modification of early depressive and persecutory anxieties, result-ing in a greater feeling of security regarding both the inner and external worlds, and in a good relationship with their parents. With such children, even when the father was absent, the reassur-ance gained from the presence of the mother, and from home life, counteracted the fears stirred up by objective dangers.

Instead of the internal, false solution of mania, these children, in Klein's view, could allow themselves to depend on, to gain reassurance from, their family. What Klein calls, rather vaguely, 'the good relationship with the parents', 'the reassurance gained from the presence of the mother, and from home life', counteracts and modifies the death instinct by showing comfort and reliability in action. The child sees that destructiveness can't destroy everything, that there are goodnesses sufficiently resilient to withstand the bad. That, in moral terms, virtue has a place because it works. The outside world is our only consolation for – our best refuge from – the internal world.

So, for Klein, the Second World War had been such a problem for people because it linked them with their earliest anxieties. It jogged their memories of their primitive selves. And it had made people feel better either spuriously, by restoring their primitive defence of mania; or more realistically, in her view, by making possible good external reassurance. Group spirit, the pooling of human resources, courage and resilience in action, all showed the children – and the adults – that they could be successfully protected, if not secured, from the death drive within. And at a different level, the war provided a reassurance for Klein herself by apparently validating her controversial theoretical convictions. The war inside is always worse than the war outside. The war inside is ahistorical and beyond contingency; the war inside is the truth of our being; the war outside is merely history. The enemy outside is a weak impersonation – an accident of history – compared with the enemy within. The war outside ghost-writes the internal drama. The historical reality of the war, confirmed for Klein and her followers, the fundamentally ahistorical nature of the internal world. Wars were contingent: Eros and Thanatos, and the theories that promoted them, were not. Because the real psychic war was always already going on – the war before the war was already happening – there is a sense in which the war did not impinge on Klein; it was not a difference that made a difference.

It was, as it were, a confirmation not a new experience. The extraordinary and virtually unprecedented threats of air raids, of bombings, were easily assimilated into the theoretical apparatus; but they were often assimilated rather than transformed. The dream work of theory did not make them strange (or disclose their actual strangeness). In the conventional symbolic they were merely the most recent – the most up-to-date, contemporary, representation of the death instinct (or of related primal scene material).

When Richard, for example, the ten-year-old hero of Klein's *Narrative of a Child Analysis* (1961) conducted during the war, drew pictures of bombers in his sixteenth session and told Klein the shameful secret that he had dirtied his pants the previous night, she had no problem interpreting that 'the thought about the secret had occurred at the moment when he had recognized that in the drawing he was the bad German bomber', and she added that his big job was felt to be the bombs. 'His fear lest he might bomb his family with his faeces might have been the cause of his dirtying his trousers last night ...' and so on. Klein, in a sense, doesn't need Richard's personal associations to bombs, because she already knows what they are. They are exempt from dream work. Dream work – the process of inner transformation – is the making of history. Richard, one might say, in the context of Klein's treatment, can't make enough history out of his bombs. 'The outbreak of war', Klein writes in the introduction to the case history,

had greatly increased Richard's difficulties ... the war stirred up all his anxieties, and he was particularly frightened of air raids and bombs. He followed the news closely and took a great interest in the changes in the war situation, and this preoccupation came up again and again during the course of his analysis.

A trauma is that which is beyond, or resistant to psychic transformation. The preoccupation that comes up again and

53

again. When Richard's personal and contingent bombs meet Klein's ahistorical death instinct theory; when, that is to say, Richard's material is met by Klein's theoretical preoccupation that comes up again and again in the treatment, it is as though both Klein's and Richard's personal history become secluded, set aside (they were in actuality safely away from the war, in a village). The meaning of bombs and air raids is self-evident – or rather the penumbra of possible, evolving personal meanings is foreclosed. Bombs, like the death instinct itself, are outside history.

The theory of the death instinct – that for Klein found its ultimate confirmation in the war – was itself like a trauma. And like all trauma, it appears to stop time. In so far as a trauma is not subject to inner transformation, it insulates one from history; it makes history impossible. Or to put it more straightforwardly, for those psychoanalysts who believed in the death instinct – and it was, and still is, one way of telling analysts apart – the war could seem, in one sense, rather unreal. Margaret Little, one of Winnicott's analysands, reported that at the first scientific meeting of the British Society she attended during the war, there were:

bombs dropping every few minutes and people ducking as each crash came. In the middle of the discussion someone I later came to know as D. W. stood up and said, 'I should like to point out there is an air-raid going on', and sat down. No notice was taken and the meeting went on as before.

'No notice was taken and the meeting went on as before.' This, one might say, is a formulation of the problem; how could you make the war real for the psychoanalysts of the British Society, get them to notice it, or pay attention to it, so that the meeting is interrupted? What kind of conversation would it be that could prevent the contingent historical situation – an air raid during the war – from stopping the meeting? In this emblematic moment – farce that presumably could have ended in tragedy – Winnicott in his polite English way, points out that there is a war going on; nobody takes any notice and 'the meeting went on as before'. Winnicott, of course, would go on reminding the Klein group that there was a real war outside – that the real world had its real dangers – but the air raids did not impinge upon the meeting. So my question is, what is it about psychoanalysis – its theory and its practice – that meant, despite the air raids, despite the bombs, that the meeting went on as before? Another way of saying this might be to ask why, in the reported analyses of children during and immediately after the war – the accounts, say, of Klein, Winnicott and Milner – the analysts always know what bombs stand for? From a psychoanalytic point of view there was nothing enigmatic – nothing requiring associations – about this historically unprecedented experience when it turned up, as it inevitably would, in children's play material.

In his *London at War: 1939–1945* (1995) Philip Ziegler makes it clear in some detail that, as he puts it, 'the population of London as a whole endured the Blitz with dignity, courage, resolution and astonishing good humour', that Londoners effectively manufactured and lived out their own myth of themselves during the war, which made possible what seems, at least in retrospect, a spectacular accommodation to a terrifying predicament. Though in part clearly government propaganda, there were, in Ziegler's view, two main elements in the myth of the Blitz, 'the comradeship and sense of unity which it inspired among Londoners and the cheerful good humour with which it was endured'. The war in London, as many people acknowledged, brought out the best in people. Indeed, what was so remarkable about the Blitz was how surprisingly, or apparently, untraumatized most people were by it: the myth of the Blitz was the truth about the Blitz. Melanie Klein's daughter, Melitta Schmideberg, published a long paper with lots of clinical examples in the *International Journal of Psycho-Analysis* in 1942 entitled 'Individual Reactions to Air-Raids'. What she demonstrated at great and tedious length was that reactions to the air raids weren't that individual. 'There were far fewer dramatic reactions to the raids than had been expected,' she writes in the summary of her paper:

It is true that a number of cases of raid shock have probably escaped observation and that many of those who could not stand the raids left for the country. But the majority of the population adapted itself to the new Blitz reality. It did so by acquiring new standards of safety and danger and by gradually learning to take the bombing as an unpleasant but unavoidable part of life. Fearlessness was usually based on the secret conviction 'I cannot be hurt' – an emotional denial of the possibility of being hurt and regression to the narcissism of the baby. Adaptation was helped by identification with those less frightened than oneself and 'projection' of the frightened part of oneself on to more timid people. Activity, providing a sublimated outlet for aggressiveness and countering the feeling of helplessness, was a help. Rational fears were increased by irrational ones. Yet the Blitz situation also provided ample libidinal, sadistic and masochistic satisfaction. The condition of certain neurotics improved.

In this psychoanalytic account – not dissimilar from many others – it is as though war brings out the best in people's defences. Denial, regression to narcissism, identification, sublimation: people reaped the full benefit of their psychic repertoires. The Blitz provided unique opportunities for the satisfaction of perverse or component instincts of masochism and sadism ('the condition of certain neurotics improved'). The Blitz enlivened people because it freed them to perform gratifying defences and forbidden instincts.

Air raids, as a specific version of the war, were successfully, indeed triumphantly adapted to by the people of London. 'In 1940–1941', J. B. Priestley wrote, 'for once we felt free, companionable, even – except while waiting for the explosions – light-hearted. It took bombs to deliver us.' Air raids, in a quite different sense, were easily assimilated into psychoanalytic theory and practice. The Blitz appeared to in no way modify or indeed falsify psychoanalytic theory ('the meeting went on as before'). In fact, it confirmed it in most of its particulars. For the people of London the war disclosed unprecedented resources of communal feeling and personal resilience. For the psycho-analysts – especially for the Klein group – the war was reassuring proof. War was no surprise. War becomes, with the experience of the Blitz, that most paradoxical thing: the trauma that is apparently easy to incorporate. 'The majority of the population', Schmideberg writes, 'adapted itself to the new Blitz reality'. The new Blitz reality is an unintendedly inter-esting phrase in this context (inviting us to construct a new Blitz reality principle). For some psychoanalysts the new Blitz reality was apparently not that new.

And yet, of course, the trauma of the Blitz, the new Blitz reality, was inevitably subject to those personal processes of history-making that psychoanalysis calls dream work and deferred action, and that were to issue in disguised form after the war as theories of the mother–child relationship. And I think it is in psychoanalytic descriptions of the child after the war, and indeed prompted by the war, that the psychic transformation of war experience is most vivid. The child is, and comes to represent, the person most vulnerable to devastating interruption: from inside by the instincts, from outside by the nurturing environment; the mother who is, herself, an independent subject. The child is addicted to routine, to reassurance, to attachment, to going on being, to continuity of care: in this post-war story the radical antitheses of the new Blitz reality. When the new Blitz reality is not the child's death instinct in action – the bombed familiar cityscape an image of the child's depredations in and on the mother's body – it becomes the traumatic mother: tantalizing, invading, unpredictable, implacable, retaliating, impinging; unable to metabolize the infant's bombs, that are called projections. Air raids destroy the familiar landscape, rupture attachments, create the need for evacuation. For Winnicott, being dropped, in the psychic sense, is the primal catastrophe. A dropped baby is a bomb. For Bowlby the new Blitz reality and its consequences proved how much children needed their mothers. When the new Blitz reality was not being used as a picture of the child's internal world, it was being used (and exploited) as a kind of negative ideal of mothering. Mothers mustn't Blitz their children; mothers must be like Londoners during the war – flexible, good-humoured, resilient, generous. The child's invasion bringing out the best in them.

In the attempt to legitimate itself, some psychoanalytic theory has attempted – wittingly or unwittingly – to dehistoricize the child, to assume that the child's material in the clinical session is merely a local example of a universal and trans-historical predicament; that, in the terms of this essay, bombs and air raids are nothing special, are not being used to articulate some recalcitrant piece of secret personal history. But whether we like it or not, it is always the dream work that is putting history back in the picture. It is always free association that is linking us to our unprecedented specific pasts. In psychoanalytic theory and practice after the war there are bombs everywhere. What some of the analysts forgot was that children take history personally.

Clutter: A Case History

1

All psychoanalyses are about mess and meaning, and the links
between them; about the patient's and the analyst's relationship to disorder, and their mostly unconscious fantasies of
what disorder might entail, something orgiastic, something
violent, something inchoate, something longed for and feared.
If our lives have a tendency to get cluttered, apparently by
themselves but usually by ourselves, most accounts of psychoanalysis have an inclination to sort things out. A kind of
pragmatic clarity is considered a virtue in psychoanalytic
writing; it always has a how-to ingredient as though its genre
was the instruction manual. The raw material of psychoanalysis – the unconscious desire that is personal history – may
be wildly unreasonable, but there are eminently sensible
vocabularies for summing it up.

Psychoanalysis, in the more empirical British tradition and
the more ego-psychological American tradition, aims to clarify
things; it is impressed by the lucidity it promotes without
acknowledging that this supposed lucidity is itself an effect of
language. Psychoanalytic theory – and indeed, its highly

ritualized practice – has an aversion to clutter. Its categories of pathology are always fantasies of disorder (there is, for example, a well-known diagnostic category called a character disorder, as though character could be anything else). Psychoanalysis, of course, wants us to be interested in – indeed, wants us to reappropriate, to re-dream – whatever we are keen to get rid of. And yet, in all its versions, it promotes the intelligibility of system; it repudiates chaos.

So, in the inevitable to and fro we might prefer between idealizing order and idealizing disorder, clutter has rather an ambiguous status. It has the paradoxical implication of being something which may have no intrinsic or discernible order or pattern, and yet of being something that people make, wittingly or unwittingly, determinedly or helplessly. It invites us, in other words, to do something puzzling, or even uncanny; that is, to make meaning – as in, just say something about – the absence of pattern. Clutter, like all the orderly disorders we can describe in language, tantalizes us as readers of it. We can't be sure who the joke will be on if we say something intelligible or persuasive about it.

It is obviously unpromising to try and imagine representation without structure, or games without rules (if clutter was a game how would you learn to play it?). And yet our virtual passion for learning rules – if only by breaking them – lures us into situations where we can't apply them. All the now infamous psychoanalytic categories – hysteria, obsessionality, narcissism – are, among other things, parodies of rule-making. The obsessional neurotic, for example, in classical psychoanalytic theory, has an addiction to the clutter of order to conceal his instinctual life from himself. Winnicott's 'false-self personality', in his words, 'collects demands' to clutter up his life: to baffle and evade his desire, to protect but to starve his true self. If psychoanalysis is necessarily about the inevitable passions of losing and finding, about the terrors of the absence of meaning and desire, it is worth wondering how clutter is made, and what clutter can be used to do. It is, as everyone knows, a lot of work that makes a lot of work. Looking, say, at the clutter of one's desk it can sometimes seem the apotheosis of that wish that Freud saw as so insidious, the wish to frustrate oneself. But as the psychoanalyst Michael Balint once remarked, talking about defences, anyone who is running away from something is running towards something else. By the same token, when we are talking about clutter we should remember, anything that stops something happening is making something else possible. That if you lose something you might find something else in the process of looking for it. Indeed, this may be the only way you can find something else.

So in this case-history of clutter, my first image, my emblem for the story, is the picture that mothers – not so often fathers – frequently conjure up for me of their adolescents' bedrooms. When they want to give a full account of how impossible their child is, the adolescent bedroom is *the* symptomatic scenario. This story is set in the cross-fire between the parents' view of the adolescent's bedroom, and the adolescent's view of the adolescent bedroom. The adolescent, it should be noted, rarely complains about the parents' bedroom.

2

The person I want to write about, a painter in his early thirties, referred himself to me because he thought he was becoming 'mildly agoraphobic'. It was, he said, difficult to be sure because, obviously, he spent most of his time at home painting. He was not, he thought, a loner but had, ever since early adolescence, a passion for painting. He had a world of friends and a girl-friend; he knew something about psychoanalysis and it was clear to him, as far as he knew, that he did not especially have relationship problems. As he said, what 'people call relationship problems should just be called relationships'. I couldn't help agreeing, while also assuming that he was locating something about desire – about his link with other people – in his apparent symptom. His mild agitation about going out, and in particular the way he found himself steering clear of wider open spaces like parks and the countryside, had made him wonder, as he put it, 'what there was out there that he didn't want to see'.

Since, perhaps unsurprisingly, he thought of his fear in visual terms I asked him if he could see any links between this fear and his work. When I asked him this in our first meeting a curious thing happened. He said, 'When you asked me that, I suddenly had a very strong image of that famous photograph of Francis Bacon's studio. And I remembered thinking when I first saw the picture, "How could he find anything in all that mess?".' Then he paused and said, as an afterthought, 'And his pictures are so uncluttered'. I said, entering for some reason into a seminar on Francis Bacon, 'Yes, it's odd, isn't it? The paintings are uncluttered but rather claustrophobic.' And he replied, rather amazingly to me, 'You feel like the figures can't get out, but Bacon got them into it so presumably he could get them out.' There was a pause then, and I had so much to say that I couldn't think of anything to say. It was as though we had suddenly done a lot, and there was too much already. The word I want to use now, is clutter; but as it turned out, a sense of impossible excess was to be integral to this man's predicament, and hence the predicament he would put me in. What I did say was: 'Are you worried that I might get you out of painting?' And he replied, 'I will be in a mess if I come here with agoraphobia and you cure me of painting!' As is often the case, I think, when people fear that psychoanalysis will destroy their talent – and symptoms are a talent, if only for survival – they are often having to manage a very powerful wish to be cured of it.

One of the things this man had struggled with since adolescence was a great fear of – and intimidation by – other people's envy of his talent. One of the ingredients in what he began to call his 'space fear' was that when he went out people would know what he had just painted and would want to attack him or spoil it, or stop it being finished. He was, as it were, staying at home to protect his children. We established, in short, that he had only begun, or begun again, to feel hemmed in as he became successful. It was to be perhaps his only revelation in the treatment that it is possible to make envious attacks on oneself, that no one is more envious of one's gifts than oneself.

A lot of our conversation was about how space works, how one can make it work, how one finds the space one needs, and how often making the right space is the point, all else follows from there. The frame makes the picture; as he said, 'without it you wouldn't know where to stop, or start'. We could link this with the unframed quality of life outside his flat. And by the same token we talked a lot about the filling of space – indeed that one can make space by filling it, as though space was simply an idea to house things in – and of the difference between filling space and filling time. He had never thought of himself as someone who filled time; but of course, being a painter, meant he was, in a sense, filling space all the time.

Psychoanalysis only begins, in any sense, to work when people begin to be impressed by their symptoms. It was the links between his present, apparently mild symptoms and the initial dilemmas my patient found himself in when he began painting as a fourteen-year-old boy that brought the analysis to life. Faced with an empty canvas, in short, he would 'clutter it all up', and then he wouldn't be able to do anything with it. In his very eagerness, the way he painted stopped him painting. It was as though painting was too exciting, or too illicit, or too something, and he needed the clutter to stop what he thought of as the real painting happening. After all, what would he find himself painting if he didn't clutter up the canvas? The earliest sexual fear he could remember himself having – and it was painting that turned up for him when sexuality did – was of premature ejaculation. There was something he desperately wanted and something he had to get out of as soon as possible. And someone he must refuse to satisfy.

It is perhaps one of the most useful, indeed pleasurable Freudian insights that the way we defend ourselves tells us, in disguised form, what it is we desire. If clutter was the obstacle to desire, it was also an object *of* desire. In clutter you may not be able to find what you are looking for, but you may find something else instead, while you are looking for it. Clutter may not be about the way we hide things from ourselves but the way we make ourselves look for things. It is, as it were, self-imposed hide and seek. I may clutter up my canvas, or my studio to stop myself working – to sabotage the process – or I might do it to force myself to work in a different way. The problem with not being able to bear frustration is that you never notice the paradoxical nature of your acts: to frustrate one version of the self is always to gratify, to promote, to re-find another version.

One of the reasons that Bacon had been so important to my patient – apart from the fact that he was powerfully effected by the paintings, even as a child – was because he had, in fact, shown him the way out of this problem of cluttering up his canvases. In an interview he had come across with Bacon, the artist had spoken about his now famous untechnique of, at a certain point, throwing paint at the canvas. When my patient had first read this, he said with his own almost unwitting irony, 'everything fell into place'. Not only did this idea fit with a whole nexus of then adolescent intellectual passions – Gide's gratuitous acts, Breton's random writing, the chance and indeterminacy of John Cage's compositions; in other words, a passion for loop holes, for ways of abrogating self-control in the service of contingencies – but it also fitted in with one of his own techniques for the uncalculated, which I imagine was an adolescent reworking of a childhood game. Little children often like dropping things behind them as a way of making them disappear. My patient, aged about fourteen, had invented a new way of dressing in the morning. For obvious and not insignificant reasons he could only do this during the holidays, when he wasn't going to school.

He invented this new method one morning when he couldn't decide what to wear. So he took a lot of clothes out of his cupboard, dropped them over his shoulder behind him, and took what came to hand, irrespective of whether it matched, or indeed, of whether he liked it. But as important was the fact that his method depended on accumulation, that is to say, in his view, it got better the longer he did it. The more clothes that piled up over time on the floor of his room the better it was. When he bought new clothes he would drop them on the floor, pick up the bundle of clothes, and drop it over his shoulder so they would be properly mixed in. To begin with, his, as he called them, 'bohemian parents' were amused by this – after all, the art of family life is to not take it personally – but eventually his mother cracked. 'But you can't find anything in this room', she would say to him quite sensibly; to which he would reply, in one way or another, that that was the point. The clutter he created meant that things found him (he would say to his mother, 'our clothes should come and find us', which seemed rather profound to me). Sometimes, he acknowledged to himself, it was extremely frustrating not being able to find something that he was looking for, but this was more than compensated for by the way he could both discover things he didn't know he was looking for and, of course, that he would find himself wearing such apparently unusual combinations of clothes. Of course, as he now conceded, it wasn't all quite as random as he then liked to think – he was, after all, still selecting his clothes, but from a different way of organizing them.

Part of the freedom of being fourteen – or at least the freedom one has to fight for, is the freedom to sleep-walk; the freedom, that is to say, to do things in one's own way. This is why psychoanalysis can be so disruptive for adolescents – indeed, for anyone – because at its worst it forces a pattern. It can make the links that should be left to find their own way. It had never occurred to my patient, until we started talking, that there was a link between the problem he was having with his painting and what he called his 'mess-dress' method. By, as he put it, cluttering up his paintings it was as though he couldn't paint; by cluttering up his room he could dress in his own way. One was apparently a problem, one was a solution. Something that worked for him in one area of his life, was felt to be a kind of sabotage in another area. It is often true in psychoanalysis that solutions can be found by mapping one area of a person's life on to another, apparently disparate one. When it came to dressing, clutter was useful to him; it was exactly what he needed, and so he deliberately made a mess. When it came to painting it seemed to take him over, he was making it but he couldn't get away from it. Ordinarily one might think, one person's clutter, is another person's . . . what? Pattern, beautiful object, whatever. For this man, from one psychoanalytic point of view, there was an unconscious project to keep these two selves separate. The self that dressed and the self that painted had to be kept apart. When he dressed he could make, at least from his point of view, a good mess. When he painted he made a bad one.

Clearly, a lot could be made of this, in psychoanalytic terms. The analyst doesn't merely tell the so-called patient what he thinks of him, he shows the patient what he thinks of himself. In this splitting of himself he managed to keep the destructive mess away from his parents; 'no one', as he once said to me, 'gets hurt if you fuck up a painting ... except yourself'. Or you could think that his elaborate quasi-obsessional ritual of spontaneous dressing, exactly the same as cluttering up his canvases, was in fact an anxiety about allowing himself to fantasize, to really elaborate the thought of his desire. Faced with a wardrobe or a canvas he might start imagining – owning up to – dreams of what he wanted, who he wanted to be, what of himself he might want others to want. If paint, like clothes, was for him then, at an unconscious level, a covering up, then what were the catastrophes associated with nakedness? What would he have been doing, what would he have been thinking about, if he had neither got dressed nor painted? If one was to be a crude old-style Freudian, in other words – not an uninteresting thing to be – one might think of clutter as a reaction formation against some simple crudities. Think how cluttered – how complicated and confusing – one's mind or indeed one's conversation can become faced with someone we desire.

All of this, to some extent, and at different times, seemed pertinent to my patient. But I want to consider here some more specific questions. First, what is a good mess? Which might mean from whose point of view is it good (or bad) and what are the unconscious criteria for deciding? In one mood I might think despairingly, 'This room is too cluttered'; in a different mood I might take it for granted, find it rather cosy, be impressed by being the kind of person who lives in creative chaos, and so on. In other words, what makes clutter work for us, and how does it work when it does? A good life, one might say, involves making the messes you need.

So, how does clutter work for us? After all, we may be able to tolerate, and even enjoy our own mess, but nothing tests our feeling for other people more than our feelings about their mess. Indeed, our relationship to what we think of as the other person's disorder, or their disordering of us, is a picture, a synecdoche of our relationship to them. Where we experience other people as disorder can be where we experience them as other. In this sense, clutter *is* other people, they get in our way. It's always worth wondering when we think someone is ruining our life what we imagine our life uncluttered by them would look like. I think all this is relevant because our relationship to clutter – what we identify as clutter, when we use the word – has a history. And personal history is always co-constructed, is always made in the context of relationship. So we may wonder, at the start, with whom did we first experience what we think of now, or even thought of then, as clutter? How did we learn it, and how were we taught it? Two different things.

My patient, growing up, as he said, with 'bohemian parents', had clearly spent some of his childhood longing for what he thought of as 'an ordinary home' like some of his friends had. Of course his friends found his home, crowded as it usually was, with things and people, incredibly exciting. 'We are ram-shackle but we are comfortable', his mother would apparently say, sounding like someone from an Edwardian or Bloomsbury novel. What my patient thought of as an ordinary home was one in which meals were regular and on time, and one in which the adults made more time for the children. It was only by going to other children's houses that he began to realize that there were other worlds. But as he remembered it, it was as though other people's 'more normal' homes crystallized something that he had always sensed but never quite realized, that he experienced his life as something of an obstacle course. A lot of things seemed to get in his way. The freedom of his parents' household could be sometimes just a mess for him.

At home there had been both too much space – the space created or imposed upon him by his parents' own absorbing preoccupations, which left him, he thought, too much to himself – and too little space; the house seemed cluttered with its unpredictable population of people and its various artefacts. And this was another ingredient of his present agoraphobia. Outside, with all that space, and no one keeping an eye on him, what might have happened to him? Which was the passive version of a more frightening question, what might he have done? The neglect he had felt at home had left him feeling uncontained; this was then, in adulthood, displaced on to the outside world, as a fear of freedom.

When he cluttered up his canvases as an adolescent he was inevitably doing several things at once. At a documentary level it was a representation of the clutter he experienced his home as – a clutter that could preclude his freer expression of himself. What he had, to some extent, suffered passively at home – his parents' chaos – he now actively inflicted on his canvas. There was a strong Oedipal current here – that is what the parents do, they prohibit, they baffle one's desire.

None of our parents gave us enough freedom; gave us the freedom we needed and deserved, the freedom to make them our partners. But also the clutter at home suited him – he could exploit it as part of his defence against his own desire. He could become addicted to the obstacles to his desire rather than to the objects of his desire. He could protect himself from his own delirium of wanting. The rage of frustration can be more comforting than the derangement of desire.

But, as is often the case, the solution is as interesting, as inventive, as the problem. When, following the lead of another father, Francis Bacon, my patient started throwing paint at his canvases he was, as he put it, 'making a mess of the mess'. It wasn't, exactly, that he needed to unclutter his canvas, but rather that he needed to find a different way of cluttering it up. What mattered then was simply that it worked. His coming for psychoanalysis meant we could think about – in relation to his presenting symptom – what made this new kind of clutter work for him. 'While you're working in a certain way', Bacon said in an interview, 'you try to go further in that direction, and that's when you destroy the image you had made; an image that you will never retrieve. That's also when something unexpected suddenly appears: it comes with no warning . . . What's most surprising is that this something which has appeared almost in spite of oneself, is sometimes better than what you were in the process of doing.' Bacon is saying, whatever destroys the image takes its place; that the act of ruining something produces something else. That the spoiled thing can not only – though not always – be better than the original thing, it can also be, indeed can't help but be, utterly unpredicted; in that sense, unique, unprecedented: that only by absolutely losing something – 'an image that you will never retrieve', as Bacon says – do you get the surprising thing.

Chambers Dictionary defines clutter as 'a clotted or confused mass: a disorderly accumulation: confusion . . . to clog with superfluous objects, material etc'. What Bacon suggests – without superstition – and, indeed my patient found, was that the disorderly accumulation of throwing paint, the act that could clog the picture with superfluous material, could also disclose something new; something that paradoxically was closer to one's heart by being beyond one's design. Clutter, as chaotic accumulation, could be both a thwarting and a source of revelation. One might think of the difference as being two different kinds of unconscious work, the good mess and the bad mess – the mess that can be used, and the mess that stultifies. It may be a more productive distinction than the one between clutter and pattern. Our vocabulary of disorder, by virtue of being a vocabulary and implying a grammar, is always glib.

In her wonderful book *On Not Being Able to Paint*, Marion Milner refers to a kind of personal aesthetic she discovered for herself through what she called 'free drawing', the visual equivalent of free association, the kind of doodling one might do in an idle moment:

One thing I noticed about certain of my free drawings was that they were somehow bogus and demanded to be torn up as soon as made. They were the kind in which a scribble turned into a recognizable object too soon, as it were; the lines drawn would suggest some object and at once I would develop them to make it look like that object. It seemed almost as if, at these moments, one could not bear the chaos and uncertainty about what was emerging long enough, as if one had to turn the scribble into some recognizable whole when in fact the thought or mood seeking expression had not yet reached that stage. And the result was a sense of false certainty, a compulsive and deceptive sanity, a tyrannical victory of the common sense view which always sees objects as objects, but at the cost of something else that was seeking recognition, something more to do with imaginative than common sense reality.

Milner counsels us to be wary of the pre-emptive imposition of pattern, of the compulsive sanity of reassuring recognitions. Of what we might be doing when we are too keen to clear up clutter. Clutter, that is to say, may be a way of describing either the deferral that is a form of waiting, or the waiting that is a form of deferral. Our eagerness for recognition can be a self-blinding.

Winnicott's Hamlet

*This unfortunate aphorism about art holding the
mirror up to nature is deliberately said by Hamlet in
order to convince the bystanders of his absolute insanity
in all art-matters.*

Oscar Wilde, 'The Decay of Lying'

1

In a famous letter of 1936, Freud wrote to the writer Arnold
Zweig refusing Zweig's request to be Freud's biographer.
Freud, as one cannot help but notice, protested rather too much:

> only today ... can I settle down to write you a letter, alarmed by the
> threat that you want to become my biographer – you, who have so
> much better and important things to do, you who can establish
> monarchs and who can survey the brutal folly of mankind from a
> lofty vantage point; no, I am far too fond of you to permit such a
> thing. Anyone who writes a biography is committed to lies,
> concealments, hypocrisy, flattery and even to hiding his own lack
> of understanding, for biographical truth does not exist, and if it did
> we could not use it.
>
> Truth is unobtainable, mankind does not deserve it, and in any
> case is not our Prince Hamlet right when he asks who would
> escape whipping were he used after his desert?

The 'threat' of a biography seems to have put Freud in
something akin to a panic. As he justifies his resistance to the
whole idea he gets himself into a quandary about truth.
Biographical truth doesn't exist, and *if it did* it couldn't be

used. Truth is anyway unobtainable, and even if it was, mankind doesn't deserve it. This has the kind of implausible, distraught logic that Freud taught us how to enjoy.

And then there is Hamlet; 'and in any case', Freud writes in a final flourish, 'is not our Prince Hamlet right when he asks who would escape whipping were he used after his desert?'. What is Hamlet doing here; what is Hamlet being used for?

In Act II, scene 2, Polonius introduces the actors to Hamlet who gets them to recite something he has heard before in preparation for the Murder of Gonzago. Impressed by the recitation, Hamlet says to Polonius:

HAMLET: ... Good my lord, will you see the players well bestowed? Do you hear, let them be well used; for they are the abstracts and brief chronicles of the time: after your death you were better have a bad epitaph than their ill report while you live.

POLONIUS: My lord, I will use them according to their desert.

HAMLET: God's bodykins, man, much better; use every man after his desert, and who should 'scape whipping? ...

Freud's allusion to this scene in his letter clearly has its own oblique accuracy. The letter shares a nexus of preoccupations with the scene in the play which it refers to. If Freud, like everyone else, gets the biography he deserves he won't come out of it very well. If Polonius treats the actors according to their deserts they will, in Hamlet's view, merely be treated punitively, with insufficient regard. Actors, Hamlet believes, are the most truthful historians: 'they are the abstracts and brief chronicles of the time'. As though they were biographers Hamlet warns Polonius of the risk of not valuing them. 'After your death you were better have a bad epitaph than their ill report while you live'. In the scene, like the letter, there is something about who deserves what, something about what it might be to provide an accurate account, something about truthfulness. The actor, like the biographer, has to imagine what it is like to be someone else. Like psychoanalysis – one version of the biographical truth that Freud is so interestingly sceptical about – acting and biography raise a question about what it is to know someone. Hamlet will use the actors in the play to expose an unpleasant truth; to, as it were, recover some biographical information; to get at the truth about his mother, his father and his step-father – and so, of course, himself.

In his 1964 paper, 'The Concept of the False Self', delivered at a symposium entitled *Crime, A Challenge*, Winnicott gave Polonius a walk-on part. 'I think you will agree', he writes,

that there is nothing new about the central idea. Poets, philosophers and seers have always concerned themselves with the idea of a true self, and the betrayal of the self has been a typical example of the unacceptable. Shakespeare, perhaps to avoid being smug, gathered together a bundle of truths and handed them out to us by the mouth of a crashing bore called Polonius. In this way we can take the advice:

> This above all: to thine own self be true,
> and it must follow, as the night the day,
> Thou canst not then be false to any man.

You could quote to me from almost any poet of standing and show that this is a pet theme of people who feel intensely.

Once again, here, the play *Hamlet* is being used to tell us the truth about truth; in this case the almost tautological truth of the existence and importance of the true self. There is, as it were, a true account in you of who you really are; something in you that you can be true to. There is something there to, in Winnicott's case, 'betray', and in Freud's case, misrepresent. You, or someone else, can be your own worst biographer.

It is, of course, part of the rhetorical function of quoting like

74

this, to assume that the meaning, the interpretation of the quote is self-evident. Polonius's speech both in and out of the context of the play is, as Winnicott intimates, rather more complicated than it seems. 'Perhaps to avoid being smug,' Winnicott suggests, Shakespeare put this 'bundle of truths' into the 'mouth of a crashing bore called Polonius'. There is an interestingly implied relationship here between truth and smugness and, perhaps linked to this, the constitution of an elite group with a shared preoccupation: 'You could quote to me from almost any poet of standing', Winnicott asserts, 'and show that this is a pet theme of people who feel intensely.' It is nowhere suggested in *Hamlet* that Polonius is a poet of standing or, in Winnicott's sense, a person who feels intensely. Crashing bores promoting true selves or crashing bores being used by Shakespeare, *the* poet, to promote true selves? At its most minimal, one could say, *Hamlet* is about what the rhetoric of truth and falsehood can be used to do. 'Your noble son is mad,' Polonius tells Gertrude, 'Mad call I it; for, to define true madness, / What is't but to be nothing else than mad?' (Act II, scene 2, 92).

Hamlet the character makes a mockery, in a sense, of Polonius's advice to his own son Laertes, 'to thine own self be true'. And by the same token, Hamlet himself predicts what critics of the play will want to do to him; 'Why look you now, how unworthy a thing you make of me. You would play upon me; you would seem to know my stops; you would pluck out the heart of my mystery ...' (Act III, scene 2, 386). Hamlet says this to Guildenstern, as though there was a heart, a centre, to be plucked, a self to be true to. As if it was that simple. A famous, formative book on *Hamlet* by Dover Wilson is called *What Happens in Hamlet*, something psychoanalysts – including Winnicott, as we shall see – have been notoriously keen to work out; as indeed, are most of the characters in the play;

what's happening in Hamlet, they keep wondering, mostly to put a stop to it. What's happening in my mother, Hamlet keeps wondering, what's happening in Claudius?

Freud, who also didn't want his mystery plucked out by a biographer, or didn't believe it could be – two wishes or fears not always easy to tell apart – wrote in his 1904 paper, 'Psychopathic Characters on Stage' that: 'After all, the conflict in *Hamlet* is so effectively concealed that it was left to me to unearth it'. Through his new-found understanding of the Oedipus complex, as described in *The Interpretation of Dreams*, Freud had solved the problem of *Hamlet*: 'it was left to me to unearth it'. Biographical truth: the 'idea of a true self' which, Winnicott says, 'poets, philosophers and seers have always concerned themselves with': the Oedipus complex. And Hamlet as a magnet for the Essences, for all the strong descriptions of the heart of the mystery. And, of course, perhaps the most sacred idea of all: that a person is a mystery, and the mystery has no heart, no centre to it.

As we know, throughout his life Freud was interested in the mystery of who Shakespeare was, keen to work out the pertinent biographical truths. When it came to Shakespeare, Freud seems to have made an exception. Shakespeare – along, perhaps, with Sophocles and Dostoyevsky – was the ultimate, mysterious knower of what Freud thought of as probably universal, transhistorical non-contingent deep truths about human nature. But then, of course, if this was the case, the question arose of what exactly psychoanalysis had to contribute ('I have nothing to say', Gore Vidal once remarked, 'only something to add'). 'The poets and philosophers before me discovered the unconscious,' Freud said on the occasion of the celebration of his seventieth birthday. 'What I discovered was the scientific method by which the unconscious can be studied.' All Freud added, he claims, was science; add scientific method to Shakespeare and you get psychoanalysis. What might Freud have meant? We could imagine, for example, that a group of people called, say, Sophocles, Dostoyevsky and Shakespeare – or Winnicott's 'Poet, philosophers and seers' – spotted a bird called the Unconscious and produced beautiful, persuasive, dramatic descriptions of it; and then a group of people calling themselves scientists came along – the word 'scientific' was first used in English in 1589, about twelve years before *Hamlet* was performed – and did what?

Or, after the scientists had described the bird, what did it look like? What could we do with it, or to it now, that we couldn't do before? I'm suggesting this not to disparage science but to show on the one hand something tiresomely obvious, that psychoanalysis is, among other things, the site for two contested kinds of description that go under the allegorical names of Art and Science. But perhaps more interestingly, if, as Freud said on more than one occasion, 'The poets and philosophers before me discovered the unconscious' before science – whatever that is, and clearly it isn't one thing, any more than art is – how did they do it? What did they know, or how did they know what they knew? Unmethodically? Unempirically? Unfalsifiably? Or would it be better to say that they simply used different historically circumstantial languages, other vocabularies: their own preferred, wholly contingent sentences? From this point of view, to be psycho-analysed, or to train to be an analyst, would be to learn a language. Or, to put it another way, when psychoanalysts quote Shakespeare, within the language of their own discipline, what are they doing? Whether Shakespeare inspires the anxiety or depression of influence – if the works of Shakespeare are some kind of secular Bible – he, in a certain sense, confronts psychoanalysts with what they've got to add: and what they know differently.

'I am not so ashamed', Winnicott wrote to Ernest Jones in 1952, 'about saying that Shakespeare knew as much as a psycho-analyst as although I agree that the word "knew" is wrong at any rate it is a point of interest for discussion and not a mistake ...' 'Knew' is an important pun here; what is new about psychoanalysis? Or, to move the story forward, what is new about Winnicott compared to Freud? It may all be in Shakespeare but is it – psychoanalysis – all in Freud? You can't, after all, find words like transference, primary process, dream work, masochism, repetition compulsion, castration, Oedipus complex anywhere in Shakespeare. There is, at least, a notable change of vocabulary. To say something sounds Shakespearian is quite different from saying that something sounds Freudian. If I'm reading Freud and write a thought in the margin, I am writing psychoanalytic theory; if I'm reading Shakespeare and write a thought in the margin, I'm unlikely to be writing poetry, and so on. Indeed, that we put Shakespeare and Freud together is itself of interest; that some link suggests itself between psychoanalysis and Shakespeare ties a knot for us. But what is the subject they have in common? Why would it have occurred to Winnicott to feel *ashamed* about 'saying that Shakespeare knew as much as a psychoanalyst' (he might conceivably have been ashamed if he'd put it the other way round, i.e., a psychoanalyst knew as much as Shakespeare). What did he expose that was so inappropriate, so untimely, so humiliating? Was it an affront to Jones that Shakespeare might be more important than Freud, that psychoanalysis was not *that special*, that the question of knowing goes to the heart of something psycho-analysts are inevitably troubled by? 'Although I agree that the word "knew" is wrong,' Winnicott writes, concessionally making no concessions, 'at any rate it is a point of interest for discussion and not a mistake...'

When Shakespeare turns up in psychoanalysis, it is often *Hamlet* – and when *Hamlet* turns up, the play is usually used to say something about knowing and truth, about its difficulty, its impossibility, its uncertain status and definition. One thing that is new about Winnicott is that after Winnicott we can ask, what are psychoanalysts using *Hamlet* for, what are they using it, and Hamlet as a character, to do? (If I was to give this essay the kind of psychoanalytic title I don't like, I would call it 'From Dream-Work to Object-Usage'.) But to get from Freud to Winnicott – to get from Freud's Hamlet to Winnicott's Hamlet – we have to go via Ernest Jones's book, whose title *Hamlet and Oedipus* (1949) also leaves too little to be desired. Jones, as he says in his opening paragraph, does not 'share the shyness or even aversion displayed by the world at large against too searching an analysis of a thing of beauty, the feeling expressed in Keats's lines on the prismatic study of the rainbow'. What Jones refers to, with not enough aversion, as 'Keats's lines on the prismatic study of the rainbow' are not Keats's lines exactly, but the poet Haydon's account of Keats's and Lamb's lines in the 'immortal dinner' of 1815 to celebrate his painting, Jerusalem. Haydon writes:

Wordsworth was in fine cue and we had a glorious set-to – on Homer, Shakespeare, Milton and Virgil. Lamb got exceedingly merry, and exquisitely witty ... (and) in a strain of humour beyond description abused me for putting Newton's head into my picture – 'a fellow', said he, 'who believed nothing unless it was as clear as the three sides of a triangle'. And then he and Keats agreed that he had destroyed all the poetry of the rainbow, by reducing it to the prismatic colours. It was impossible to resist him and we all drank Newton's health and confusion to mathematics.

What Jones implicitly pathologizes as Keats's (and Lamb's) 'shyness or even aversion' Winnicott was to speak up for but not, paradoxically, by mocking scientific method in any sense.

Hamlet, as Jones unconsciously intimates, is the rainbow, with, as Haydon writes, 'Jerusalem towering up behind us as a background'.

2

> *To read Freud and Abraham on the subject of mourning*
> *and melancholia alongside* Hamlet *is to be impressed*
> *again with the majesty of human achievement. Science*
> *and Art here fit exactly; they are completely wedded.*
> Ella Sharpe, *The Impatience of Hamlet*

> *Freudian literary criticism of Shakespeare is a celestial*
> *joke; Shakespearian criticism of Freud will have a hard*
> *birth, but it will come since Freud as a writer will*
> *survive the death of psychoanalysis.*
> Harold Bloom, *The Western Canon*

The figure often rather loosely described by Freud and the early analysts as the 'creative artist' seems to be used as a kind of limit factor for the reach of psychoanalysis; someone the analyst can define herself against. The artist was both a challenge, a provocation to analytic method, but also the occasion for a certain humility and self-doubt. 'Before the problem of the creative artist,' Freud wrote in 'Dostoyevsky and Parricide' (1928), 'analysis must, alas, lay down its arms'. It is a curious image; does analysis lay down its arms as an act of worship (like not going into church with your machine-gun) or as an act of acknowledged defeat? The creative artist has won, though what exactly the battle is for is not entirely clear (truth, perhaps: the best description of character, or of what it is to live a life?). From a psychoanalytic point of view, it seems, the creative artist both could not be understood *and* knew things in

80

a way that could not be understood. As though the artist had a secret method called 'who he or she happened to be' that was too enigmatic to be known. Or, more simply, unlike a neurosis or a dream, not subject to knowing. Something for which the method of psychoanalysis was inapplicable. But somewhere, as Freud intimates (and Jones concurs with his point about Keats), there is a war between psychoanalysis and the artist. Can the analyst do to the artist or his or her work, what Keats and Lamb thought Newton had done to the rainbow, 'destroyed all the poetry of the rainbow, by reducing it to the prismatic colours'.

Freud's comment is, I think, a wish that reveals a fear; a fear about what the analyst in Freud had done to the creative artist in Freud. This fear, as Jones's book *Hamlet and Oedipus* makes clear, was not a problem for Jones. 'Experience has shown', he writes, 'that intellectual appreciation in particular (of art), is only heightened by understanding.' Whenever experience is appealed to – 'Experience has shown', Jones writes, when experience shows us nothing we don't make it show – we know something is up. For Jones, art – in this case, *Hamlet* – is there waiting to be understood. Understanding is referred to, not as a self-evident good; Jones has some doubt about its value in relationship to art, but no apparent doubt as to its meaning. From Jones's point of view, we all know what understanding is, and psychoanalysis is, for him, a specially powerful modern form of it.

There is something Hamlet (the character) doesn't understand that Freud and Jones do. Twice, rather intrusively in his book, Jones uses the unusual Miltonic word 'transpicuous' (which means 'to see through'). I read Freud's infamous remark, 'Before the problem of the creative artist, analysis must, alas, lay down its arms', as saying – here understanding doesn't fit; here faced with a work of art that works for us we are unavoidably provoked to wonder about what we call understanding and explanation; that here we've got the wrong tools, so we lay down our arms and wonder what else, if anything, to use. When it comes to art, psychoanalysis runs the risk of falling into the mainstream, promoting 'understanding' when understanding itself is the problem. Winnicott, as we shall see, does not stage his Hamlet as someone lacking insight, but as someone caught, in Winnicott's odd language, between being and doing (perhaps it is enough to say simply that Winnicott's hiding and being seen is quite different from being understood and misunderstood). So the question becomes not do we want a scientific or an artistic understanding – whatever those may be – but, what do we use this word to do? What does understanding do for Hamlet?

For Jones there is *'one* underlying main theme' in *Hamlet*, though he delays as much as Hamlet in telling us what it is; but unlike Hamlet, this is because, I imagine, we already know what it is. It takes Jones as long to confirm his father, Freud, as it takes Hamlet to avenge his father (Jones's not uninteresting book could have been entitled, 'Why Freud was right'). 'The main theme of this story', Jones writes, 'is a highly elaborated and disguised account of a boy's love for his mother and consequent jealousy of and hatred towards his father'. This, of course, explains Hamlet's fabled delay and, as Jones remarks, the question of Hamlet's 'so-called "simulation of madness"' has also now been cleared up. 'Before the advent of the new science of psychopathology (psychoanalysis) such discussions were bound to be little better than guesswork and now possess only an historical interest'. It is the simplest of progress myths: from Shakespeare – from *Hamlet* – to Freud. 'It is the essential difference', Jones writes, 'between prehistoric and civilized man; the difficulties with which the former had to contend came from without, those with which the latter have to contend really come from within. This inner conflict modern psychologists know as neurosis, and it is only by study of neurosis that one can learn the fundamental motives and instincts that move men. Here, as in so many other respects, Shakespeare was the first modern'.

Once again, Shakespeare and *Hamlet* are being used to tell a truth story; a this-is-the-way-it-really-is story. What is not in doubt in Jones's history of mankind is that there *are* 'fundamental instincts and motives that move men'; and that, of course, by definition, these can be learned about. Hamlet, unfortunately, was estranged from his own centre; 'Hamlet is stunned by the effect of internal conflict', Jones writes, '... into the essential nature of which he never penetrates'. The essential words here are 'essential' and 'penetrates'. In Jones's book, *Hamlet* becomes the site for the bemusing and familiar relationship between the unknowing knower, Hamlet (and Shakespeare) and the knowing knowers, Jones, and Jones's version of Freud.

Hamlet and Oedipus was published as a book in 1949 – though some of the work it contains dates from 1923; now it seems an absurdly naive book. Indeed, it is easy to read it – as I have been doing – a bit like Jones reads *Hamlet*. From the position of the knowing knower. I am as much ahead of the game here as Jones thought he was. Reading Jones reading *Hamlet*, in other words, raises the question – that seems a psychoanalytic question – what are the alternatives to reading or listening as the knowing knower? How can we describe this persuasively without wheeling on glib assertions of the wonders of 'not-knowing', or bad readings of Keats's negative capability?

I said earlier that the title I didn't want to give this essay was 'From Dream-Work to Object-Usage'. One way of describing why Jones's book is poor, why Jones's *Hamlet* is so dull, is that Jones hasn't dared to *use* the play, in Winnicott's sense; to make something sufficiently his own with it. It hasn't been dreamed enough. His reading is just *not strange* (it's not what the critic Harold Bloom would call 'a strong misreading'). Something is clarified but nothing is perplexed.

So in the language I have been speaking there is the unknowing knower – who Freud and Jones call the Creative Artist; the knowing knower, who we can caricaturally call, at least in the context of Jones's book, the psychoanalyst; and then there is the Dreamer, the Unknowing knowing knower. And this brings us, finally, to Winnicott's *Hamlet*, and his extraordinary reading of 'To be or not to be' as about his sense of being and doing, of masculine and feminine elements. A triumph, one might say, of what a cultural cliché – women are, men do – can be used for. Through crude identification we can live and speak the clichés about gender in the culture; through dream-work and object usage we can make something more idiosyncratic and strange out of what we find.

3

Shakespeare wished to impress upon us the truth that action is the chief end of existence.
Coleridge on *Hamlet*

Immature poets imitate; mature poets steal.
T. S. Eliot, 'Philip Massinger'

I want to call unacknowledged borrowing another way of describing dream-work. 'Mature poets steal', as T. S. Eliot remarked, and, of course, unacknowledged borrowing is a nice way of talking about theft and indebtedness, two issues that were of particular interest to Winnicott. We are all, as it were, anti-social in our dreams, able only to steal what belongs to us.

84

In dream-work we steal – from the dream-day, from the past – without ourselves or the world knowing. Dream-work, as Freud describes it, adds a nuance to the phrase 'property is theft'. Dream-work is daylight robbery.

Winnicott's reading of *Hamlet* owes an unacknowledged debt to Jones's work, to which he makes no reference (acknowledged borrowing, one might say in the light of Eliot's remark, is a failure to transform). We can, perhaps, go some way to understanding Eliot's remark – and indeed, Winnicott's concept of the anti-social tendency – by noting that Jones acknowledges his debt to Freud insistently, and fails to significantly rework Freud's reading of *Hamlet*; Winnicott acknowledges neither Freud nor Jones, and finds for himself a really odd redescription of Hamlet's Oedipal dilemma. Hamlet's puzzle – which is Winnicott's puzzle – about the difference between being and doing is not the same as the conflict about incestuous wishes. For Freud and Jones, it is a question about what Hamlet can bear to let himself know, whether he can face the truth of either his own wish to kill his father, or of the fact of his mother's sexuality. Winnicott's distinction between being and doing – in Winnicott's view Hamlet doesn't have a conflict, he has an absence, a dissociation of alternatives – is, it should be noted, about truthfulness but not about knowledge. It isn't that there is something crucial that Hamlet refuses to know, it is that an alternative way of being is not available to him; the difference, in psychoanalytic language, between repression and dissociation.

Not incidentally, I imagine, the other main reference to *Hamlet* in Winnicott is in a talk given in 1950 to psychology and social work students entitled, 'Yes, but how do we know it's true?'. In this paper Winnicott describes two stages people go through when learning psychology. 'In the first stage', he writes:

they learn what is being taught about psychology just as they learn the other things. In the second stage they begin to wonder – yes, but is it true, is it real, how do we know? In the second stage the psychological teaching begins to separate out from the other as something that just can't be learnt. It has to be felt as real, or else it is irritating or even maddening.

The first stage of learning can be called identification; the student becomes like somebody who knows these things. In the second stage, something akin to dream-work and object-usage goes on. Each student, consciously and unconsciously, makes something of their own out of it all, finds the bits they can use. As in Winnicott's description of object-usage the students attack the subject with questions and find out what survives. As in Freud's account of dream-work they find themselves turning the most unlikely bits into something surprising. That is to say, they make the subject fit in with their own unconscious projects. They use it for self-fashioning.

It is in describing people using their own real, in his sense, knowledge, that Winnicott brings in *Hamlet*, and once again truthfulness is at issue:

Perhaps you have been teachers, or you have actually been parents, or you have had charge of people in an office or a factory. Every day you found yourselves surprising yourselves, acting or not acting in a way that exactly fitted the situation, as much as Hamlet's speech 'To be or not to be' fits into the exposition of the theme of the play exactly. When you were so placed you could have stood a great deal of digging down into the psychology of your fellow human beings and of yourselves.

These professional people 'surprising [them]selves, acting or not acting in a way that exactly fitted the situation' is as integral to something – call it, the emotional environment – as 'To be or not to be' is to the play *Hamlet*. The implied image is of a good fit; a non-compliant emotional attunement. 'To be or not to be' may fit with Winnicott's sense of the play *Hamlet*, and yet the character Hamlet – and in this famous soliloquy, particularly – is radically at odds with his world; indeed, cannot find a way to act or not act that fits the situation (acting, and the nature of action being, of course, two of Hamlet's – and Winnicott's – insistent preoccupations). Once again, Hamlet is used to say something apparently self-evident, that soon becomes enigmatic. It is, after all, a curious example for Winnicott to have chosen in this context, given how many well-placed speeches there are in Shakespeare. Whatever else it is about, Hamlet's soliloquy concerns whether it is better to be alive or dead; and the reasons he comes up with for staying alive are not cheering. With uncanny consistency, Hamlet turns up again, in British psychoanalysis, to complicate questions of truth and knowledge. In 1966, Winnicott was to return to Hamlet's soliloquy, to redescribe the Freudian story of bisexuality as to do with acting or not acting, doing and being.

It is after a discussion entitled 'The Male and Female Elements Contrasted' that Winnicott brings on *Hamlet*. The pure female element, Winnicott writes, 'has nothing to do with drive (or instinct) ... it leads us to *being*, and this forms the only basis for self-discovery and a sense of existing ... when the girl element in the boy or girl baby finds the breast it is the self that has been found. If the question is asked, what does the girl baby do with the breast?, the answer must be that this girl element is the breast'. The male element by contrast is, 'object-relating backed by instinct drive ... The classical statement in regard to using, finding, oral erotism, oral sadism, anal stages, etc. arises out of a consideration of the life of a pure male element'.

What are we to make of this? Winnicott *seems* to be trying to describe two attitudes, two ways of relating to an object, that exist in sequence: first being, then doing. One can *be* the object – Winnicott likens this to primary identification – or one can do something to it; one can be absorbed, immersed or one can use for some purpose. And the object, of course, can be a person; or, indeed, a work of art. To call these male and female elements may be neither here nor there; they *don't* need to be gendered, perhaps, to be of interest. Or rather, one question might be, what has Winnicott's language added to Freud's notion of bisexuality: or is calling being and doing male and female elements merely compliant with both the psychoanalytic tradition and gender clichés in the culture?

To illustrate his idea Winnicott brings in *Hamlet*; 'I am reminded of the question', he writes, 'what is the nature of the communication Shakespeare offers in his delineation of Hamlet's personality and character?'. But we know by now that when Hamlet comes on, things always get more difficult. Hamlet is deemed by Winnicott – rather explicitly articulated in the soliloquy – to have drastically, indeed terminally, separated his male and female elements. When his father was alive, they 'lived together in harmony'; but after his death, his female element utterly dissociated from his male element, Hamlet is at sea. 'Hamlet is depicted', Winnicott writes, 'at this stage as searching for an alternative to the idea, "To be".' Hamlet's male element, Winnicott says, was 'unwelcome', 'threatening to take over his whole personality'; he staged the play within the play, 'to bring to life his male element which was challenged to the full by the tragedy that had become interwoven with it'. Rather than contest Winnicott's – for me, at least – alternately baffling and intriguing interpretation, I want to ask what Winnicott's Hamlet is for; what is Winnicott using Hamlet to do for him here? Perhaps Winnicott, like Hamlet, was also 'searching for an alternative to the idea "To be" '. Or, in a complementary sense, searching for a description – within the rather awkward context of psychoanalysis – of an alternative to the instinct-driven self. Psychoanalytic theory, one might say, is all about doing; so what else is there? If you don't kill your father – or revenge his death – what ways of being, what kind of life is open to you? Do you then need to kill something in yourself? Instead? Or, to take this in a slightly different direction, if being is another word for the female element, what is another word for being (and similarly, with doing)? In other words, is it possible to say what Winnicott is getting Hamlet to say, given that for Winnicott the whole soliloquy, after the first two words, is 'a journey that can lead nowhere'. Winnicott dismisses the whole of the rest of the soliloquy as the 'rather banal alternative, "... or not to be"' followed by, as he says, Hamlet going 'over into the sado-masochistic alternative', leaving 'aside the theme he started with'. The first two words, as a question, are real to Winnicott; after that it's all downhill. Hamlet, unlike Winnicott, cannot formulate an alternative to 'To be' because of his dissociation (for what Winnicott was calling around the same time the False Self, there was the opposite problem; the false self couldn't think of an alternative to that kind of frantic, spurious doing Winnicott called, in a memorable phrase, 'collecting demands'). One thing, anyway, is relatively clear: Winnicott was using Hamlet to stage what was, for him at least, an abiding opposition. Psychoanalysis had described for us the instinctual self – to use the wrong word – what other self was there? It is perhaps worth adding that we don't see Hamlet doing much pure being in the play.

Winnicott's Hamlet is neither paralysed by old-fashioned doubt, nor new-fashioned Oedipal conflict; he is dissociated. He is supposed to illustrate – though I don't quite see how – this dissociation of male and female elements. And yet one could think that Winnicott is using Hamlet to do something – to pose a problem – that is either, from a psychoanalytic point of view radically evasive because defensive, or radically subversive. What would it be like, Winnicott implicitly asks us to imagine, to be a person who couldn't imagine an alternative to being? After all, psychoanalysis is always asking us to imagine a person who cannot imagine an alternative to doing, to instinctual life. What if, say, the Oedipal crisis – as described by Freud and Jones's Hamlet – killed off the possibility of being, made it impossible; that like a secular Fall it, irredeemably, put being and doing at odds with each other; 'contaminated' them, to use Winnicott's word. Perhaps, Winnicott is suggesting, the tragedy of the Oedipus complex ineluctably dissociates being from doing. In this sense, one might say, Hamlet doesn't want to – can't bear to – think of an alternative to being; the possibility of being has already been lost. There is only doing for him now.

But I am as interested here in the accuracy, the evidence for Winnicott's reading of Hamlet's soliloquy as in what he can let himself do with and to, both the play itself, and to the previous psychoanalytic readings of Freud and Jones. The British psychoanalysts' reading of Hamlet is a tale of two footnotes. In the opening sentence of Jones's Preface to *Hamlet and Oedipus*, he writes that 'this essay was first written ... as an exposition of a footnote in Freud's *Interpretation of Dreams*'. Unacknowledged by Winnicott – and of course, he may not have read Jones's book – is a footnote in *Hamlet and Oedipus* which reads: 'This trait in Hamlet's character has often been the subject of comment ... Vining's suggestion that Hamlet really was a woman'. This *could* be linked to Winnicott's formulation that Hamlet was searching for an alternative to 'To be ...'; that is, an alternative to his own femaleness. That we can't be sure whether Winnicott knew of this is, I think, integral to his method, about which, in an infamous statement, he was quite explicit. 'I shall not first give an historical survey and show the development of my ideas from the theories of others, because my mind doesn't work that way,' he wrote in 1945, introducing his paper, 'Primitive Emotional Development': 'What happens is that I gather this and that, here and there, settle down to clinical experience, form my own theories, and then, last of all, interest myself to see where I stole what.'

This, one could say, is a perfect description of the dream-work. I gather this and that, here and there, during the dream day; settle down to clinical experience, i.e., go to sleep; form my own theories, i.e. have a dream; and then, of course, interpret it, track its sources, interest myself to see where I stole what; the dream-work method.

And then there is the object-usage method. 'I recall one Sunday morning calling on him,' Masud Khan writes (in *Through Paediatrics to Psychoanalysis*), 'with Professor Lionel Trilling's *Freud and the Crisis of our Culture*, and urging him to read it. He hid his face in his hands, paused, convulsed himself into visibility and said: "It is no use, Masud, asking me to read anything! If it bores me I shall fall asleep on the first page, and if it interests me I will start rewriting it by the end of that page."' The object-usage method entails destroying something in order to recreate it – as Winnicott does, silently, with Freud and Jones's reading of *Hamlet*. He uses them as he needs them. It is as if to say: without ruthlessness, no transformation; nothing ruined, nothing gained. A lot of the so-called 'envious attacks' described in the psychoanalytic literature are misrecognized attempts at ruthless transformation. It is not surprising that describing them as envious to the patient can be so dismaying.

Winnicott's Hamlet, then: from dream-work to object-usage. Two ways of reading: two ways of relating to an object. Two ways of doing something to oneself and an object. But how can we describe an alternative – in psychoanalytic language – to doing?

Winnicott's soliloquy begins, 'To do, or...'?

The Sexual Liberation of Fritz Wittels

While the patient's interest is to be freed of constraints
making his life a misery, the interest of the analyst ... is
conditioned by the way his work will be accepted by the
psychoanalytic community.

Heinrich Deserno, *The Analyst and the Working Alliance*

For anyone interested in the history of psychoanalysis, or
indeed, in how people start having new kinds of conversation,
The Minutes of the Vienna Psychoanalytic Society are an inexhaustible source of amusement and instruction. From 1906 to
1915, in his role as official secretary to the Society, Freud's keen
and earnest young student, Otto Rank, recorded the first
formal psychoanalytic discussions by the first men who
thought of themselves as psychoanalysts. A surprisingly
wide range of topics is covered in the three hefty volumes
published in America in the early 1960s: from, as perhaps one
might expect, masturbation and female assassins – 'Federn
comments that to slips of the tongue and the hand, we must
now add slips of shooting' – to works of philosophy,
psychology and literature. There are early moments of what
would become an influential new genre, psychoanalytic
seriousness – 'According to Bölsche, clothes are the cause of
nudity' – and glimpses of esoteric romance: 'the genitalia are
said to be the first gods, and religious feeling is derived from
the ecstasies of intercourse'. It is clear, despite the almost

Review of Edward Timms (ed.), *Freud and the Child Woman:*
The Memoirs of Fritz Wittels (Yale, 1995), from the *London Review of Books*

palpable presence of Freud in these pages – 'our great father in Vienna', as Wittels calls him in his memoirs, 'the greatest psychological genius of all time' – that a lot of these people were relishing the demands that they speak their minds, and on such diverse topics. A profession that encouraged people to say whatever occurred to them is bound to be interesting to observe when it wants to keep to the point.

Reading these ur-minutes is rather like reading a play within a play. The characters are coherent – they stick to their subjects, 'Urethral Erotism', say, or 'Psychic Hermaphroditism' – but their formal conversations are informed by a shared belief in digression. They often speak with great conviction about extreme irrationality, as though they have all just learnt a new language – which they have – and can't wait to speak it with each other. And far from being merely Freud's dramatic mono-logue this is a play whose minor characters are more and more intriguing. The person we think of as Freud would have been unintelligible without these others, many of whom we have never heard of, and whom Freud often disparaged as a group in his private correspondence. But among the more than support-ing cast, some are rather more insistent, more obviously ambitious and pressing in their claims, than others. Fritz Wittels, the author of this fascinating, terrible book – it would once have been called a 'symptomatic text' because it is so revealing by being so artlessly crass – stands out in the minutes for his aggrieved, rather hectoring omniscience. And for his choice of topics: Tatjana Leontiev (a Russian revolutionary who tried to assassinate a Tsarist official), 'Venereal Disease', 'Sexual Perversity', 'Female Physicians', 'The Natural Position of Women'. In the memoir, a bumptious *mea culpa*, he refers to the 'one-sided and unjust way in which I flourished the shining blade of psychoanalysis'. It is a portrait of the psychoanalyst as a young idealist, a bit too impressed with his new sword.

93

Wittels, in short, was a rampant misogynist, as he almost admits in his unendearingly naive way. He records the 'irony' of his earlier article against women doctors, 'inasmuch as I have changed my mind completely and for many years have been in favour of them. I love intelligent women who eventually may beat one in an argument.' As a born-again analyst, callow and idealistic, Wittels was something of a problem for the Vienna Society. Of his paper on the Russian revolutionary the minutes record that 'the speaker expresses his personal dislike of Leontiev and of all hysterics'. In one sense, he was owning up to something that the other analysts were inevitably troubled by. After all, psychoanalysis was about how complicated liking is; and the hysteric was the person who liked in baffling ways, who was adept at (unconsciously) asking for the opposite of what she wanted. But Wittels was rather too smug, too pleased with himself, with his hatred and his 'honesty'. 'One must not condemn the assassins so harshly and unmask them because of unconscious motives,' Freud said in response to Wittels's paper, 'the harshness of such a judgment would be repulsive.' Federn, one of the most incisive members of the Society, 'sees the error of those who, totally imbued with the Freudian way of thinking, ignore all other points of view'. It is precisely the way Wittels manages to ruffle the more powerful members of the Society that makes him such a significant figure. They want him to be kinder, less fanatical; and yet Wittels, in his revolutionary zeal, is taking psychoanalysis to one of its logical conclusions.

'The mission of psychoanalysis,' he writes in his memoir, 'is to make our hearts free from anxiety and guilt and free for joy.' But he was too ferocious a maker of hearts. Once her unconscious motives have been disclosed, the revolutionary will be free to be a sexually satisfied – and, more important for Wittels, satisfying – woman. Women, Wittels believed, must learn to 'wear the uniform of sexual satisfaction'. In the Vienna society he seems to speak up, as it were, for the bewildered hatred of women (and therefore of men) that is a potential agenda in any psychoanalytic theory. Psychoanalysis, one could say, has been an attempt to think through the terror of women (in both senses). Wittels's contributions to the Vienna Society, backed up by his memoir so ably edited and reconstructed by Edward Timms, make possible a reconsideration of some of the most contentious issues in psychoanalysis: the problem of the 'problem of women', and the disappearance of the idea of sexual liberation. And indeed the question of why sexuality should be so easily linked to ideas of liberation. It is clear from this preposterous, hair-raising memoir why Wittels was such an embarrassing shadow for Freud.

Wittels was showing the Vienna Society how easily the key psychoanalytic ideas about sexuality and the unconscious could be used as revenge – against women, against fathers and against the 'ill'. It was as though Freud's psychoanalysis could be liberating because it legitimated character assassination in the name of truth. For Wittels, as much of the memoir confirms, psychoanalysis was virtually a science of revenge. After he had delivered his paper on 'The Natural Position of Woman', Hitschmann quite accurately remarked that 'the speaker seems to be fighting a series of obstacles which he resents as impeding his sexual life; he fights: pregnancy, women who have become inaccessible because they are educated, then syphilis'. As with his more virulent paper on female doctors – one of the group noted his 'anger that women wish to study rather than to have sexual intercourse' – the audience was unsettled by what Wittels seemed to be using psychoanalysis for.

Wittels saw psychoanalysis – more boldly, he believed, than Freud himself – as unequivocally a source of sexual and therefore human liberation. It 'proclaimed an imminent revolution in our sexual mores', he writes in his memoir, 'of which Freud, strictly conventional in his private life, would have preferred to hear as little as possible'. This may be a case of the son beating (to use one of Wittels's words) the father at his own game, but it is also accurate. Freud was listening to something he didn't entirely want to hear about. On the other hand, Wittels's untrammelled eagerness, his ingenuous embrace of the freer sexuality promised by psychoanalysis, comes out in his writing as resentment of women's apparent unavailability. With the advent of psychoanalysis he can call it neurosis. If women weren't people we would all be free. For a woman to have a life of her own, he consistently implies, is a form of withholding. Before we condemn Wittels, however, we should consider whether we have never had this thought ourselves; and what we do with it once we have had it. Wittels, in other words, produces a particularly awkward distaste in the reader. And by the same token he makes us question whether, from a psychoanalytic point of view, we can come up with a version of sexual liberation that is not a covert revenge fantasy; or merely a wish to be liberated from women or, indeed, sexuality itself. Women, Wittels believes, were made for 'love', but 'civilisation' has distorted their sense of themselves. Freud, 'the Master', the 'magnificent healer', was the 'liberator of suppressed sex life – this was his destiny'. He had shown Wittels the way, in his writings. What Wittels calls in the memoir the 'fury of my revolutionary attitude' was inspired by Freud. As the members of the Vienna Society, including Freud himself, clearly acknowledged, Wittels may have been cross but he was also clever.

To talk now about sexual liberation seems cute, like talking about the withering away of the state, or loving Great Literature. And yet in the early days of psychoanalysis Freud himself clearly sensed the possibilities for sexual freedom implied by the kinds of theory he was making up. But he was discovering his version of sexuality in middle age (he was forty-nine when the *Three Essays on the Theory of Sexuality* were published). Ageing and the harshness of life – not to mention his temperamental suspicion of pleasure and mysticism, which are always inextricable – had the effect over time of eroding his sexual hopes for people. And psychoanalysis after Freud, always the province of the middle-aged, has made its grandest metaphysical claims for states of deprivation. But in his great early paper, 'Civilised Sexual Morality and Modern Nervousness' (1907), Freud says quite clearly that 'the injurious influence of civilization', as he puts it, is due to 'the harmful suppression of the sexual life of civilized people (or classes) through the "civilized" sexual morality prevalent in them'. His new psychoanalytic sentences were written, as Wittels recognized, in the service of a new set of acknowledgements about sexual possibility.

Freud's two radical propositions in this paper offer us what might be called an ambivalent utopianism, an idealism that is wholehearted only by being always divided against itself. First, he suggests, sexuality is ineluctably conflictual. There's no such thing as a free association. The Oedipus complex – and the later concept of the Death Instinct – make of sexuality an unappeasable war. For human beings, like and unlike other animals, sexuality always struggles against something else. Wittels passes over this point with unseemly haste. Freud's second proposition, though, is both more compatible with Wittels's wishes and more disturbing. 'In man,' Freud writes, 'the sexual instinct does not organically serve the purposes of reproduction at all, but has as its aim the gaining of particular kinds of pleasure.'

This was to be the real scandal of what Freud called infantile sexuality. Not only that it is a warm-up for adult life – and therefore that children are prototypically sexual creatures – but that infantile sexuality, with its sole aim of 'gaining particular kinds of pleasure', is the fundamental paradigm for erotic life. As Wittels writes towards the end of his memoir, 'before Freud, only the act for the purpose of propagation was called a sex act. Freud saw in our sexuality the god Eros, the constructive principle, in manifold forms. Beauty, fragrance, music, the mouth, the teeth, eyes, skin, muscles, all the mucous membranes have to play their role in this magnificent symphony.' Most small children adore the obvious pleasure of pleasure; what the adults politely call 'affection' is often irresistible to the child's profoundly sensual self. It is this, along with their intense, sometimes daunting suffering, that adults find most unsettling about small children; their suffering can make the adults distraught, but their erotic pleasure always makes the adults awkward and uncertain.

The counter-Darwinian implications of a human sexuality untied from procreation – or even anti-reproductive – seem to make an even starker conundrum of women's sexuality. Either, one might think, sex without procreation is an (envious) attack on women's (and men's) generativity; or else, given the availability of safe contraception, not to mention cures for sexually transmitted diseases, it is a story about sexual liberation; about the (sometimes cruel) giving and getting of pleasure that Freud referred to as the child's polymorphous perversity, and which 'civilized' notions of relationship merely obscure. For sex to be free it must issue in nothing but sensual delight, in appetite regained. We may all know that it can't be as simple as that, but we can still be puzzled about why it isn't. If Wittels is too gauche to be sufficiently puzzled in this memoir, he has nevertheless heard something in Freudian theory that has been too easily trivialized: the sheer scale of erotic inhibition, the contemporary loss of confidence in sexuality, suggests that we need to rethink what we are using our sense of our own complexity to do to our erotic lives. Psychoanalysis has always been about, among other things, the ways we price ourselves out of the market. *Freud and the Child Woman*, with its tabloid title – not, it should be said, the title Wittels gave it: it was unpublished at his death in 1950, but he had considered calling it 'A Story of Ambivalence', or slightly less catchy, 'The Story of an "Orthodox" Freudian' – is a tellingly brash document in the generally uninspiring psychoanalytic history of sexual liberation, of the way fantasies of sexual freedom turn into fantasies of sexual depredation.

Like most stories of sexual liberation, *Freud and the Child Woman* is mostly a story about passionate relationships between men; men who adore their own ideas rather more than they adore the women they involve in them. You would assume from this book that the story of Wittels's life was the story of his infatuation with three powerful men: Karl Kraus, then Freud, and then the eccentric Viennese analyst Wilhelm Stekel ('I have committed two crimes in my life,' Freud remarked, 'I called attention to cocaine and I introduced Stekel to psychoanalysis'). There are formulaic references to parents and siblings – psychoanalytically formulaic, 'meaningful' incidents and enigmas from childhood – and there is the inevitable *fin de siècle* Viennese nanny who casts her spell. The early parts of the memoir are, in fact, more evocative of Freud's Vienna than of individual people – the pervasive influence of Nestroy's plays and of gossip as a virtual art form. It was the ideological disarray that, in Wittels's view, made Vienna such a fertile source of ideas. 'From the beginning of the 19th century,' he writes, 'Vienna was an admixture of Catholicism, a centralized monarchy, and the ideals of the French Revolution which infiltrated society against the will of both the church and the government.' 'The Viennese might say of themselves,' Wittels asserts, 'those who are not ambivalent are not Viennese.' Freud, in that sense, had written from the heart of the city. There is barely a reference in the memoir to a wife or a child, both of which he had, or even of his wife dying; and the child-woman Irma, who gives the book its title, is a shady presence, despite Wittels's obvious wish to bring her to a kind of novelistic life. She is given only one chapter and what he says there makes it quite clear that she was a figment, the child of a *folie à deux* between Kraus and Wittels; almost literally a token, sometimes merely to regulate the homosexual anxiety between the two men, as Wittels seems to acknowledge with baffled dismay. 'Without Kraus she had no value for me, just as I had no value for Kraus without her.' Kraus, as he says, 'held me spellbound', his preferred way of being held.

'Irma was our laboratory,' Wittels writes proudly, and then proceeds to tell us how and why they treated her as one. Irma was seventeen, the youngest daughter of a janitor in the suburbs of Vienna. Kraus had seen her on the street and been struck by her resemblance to a woman he had previously fallen for, and who had cured him apparently of his natural puritanism. This woman, Annie Kalmar, who had died of pneumonia, was, in Wittels's words, 'promiscuous, passionate, gay, careless, a drunkard, intelligent without being educated'. She had made Kraus 'a violent preacher of the gospel of the whore'; Kraus believed that 'it was the duty of woman to surrender to everybody whose appeal she felt'. Irma, despite being what Kraus called only a 'torso' of his ideal, became his 'hetaera'. In other words, Kraus, who was educated, re-invented her as 'a miracle of a Dionysian girl born several thousand years too late'. 'According to theory,' Wittels writes – and it does sound as though these men needed a lot of theory to get themselves going – 'she could not be and should not be true to anyone'. Irma had fallen among thieves. When Kraus and Wittels took her to Venice she had only been interested in their hotel. 'Finally, when she was implored to cast at least one glance at the water glittering in the sunshine, she summarized her feelings with the question: "Any sharks in it?"' There were.

If Irma had fallen among today's 'helping professions' it would probably (and, I imagine, correctly) be assumed that she had been sexually abused as a child. But then today any 'excessive' interest in sexuality is likely to make people suspicious and consoling. But from a Freudian point of view, people, including the young, *are* excessively interested in sexuality, but are persuaded, or rather coerced, into not giving it too much importance. This is one of the things education is for. We would, for example, prefer to think of sexual abuse as implanting something alien in children rather than evoking something natural. One can, and should, disapprove of the sexual abuse of children without denying that it raises some unsettling questions about sexuality, about its uncertain measure in our lives. When Wittels gave his paper 'The Child Woman' (which he published in Kraus's journal, the *Torch*), he presented Irma herself as a kind of heroine of the polymorphously perverse, 'sadistic, lesbian and whatnot'. She is the exemplary alternative to our modern neurasthenia. The opposite of a hysteric, she articulates her desire unambiguously and directly. Unlike her civilized contemporararies, she is not crippled by ambivalence. She is 'a girl of great sexual attraction, which breaks out so early in her life that she is forced to begin her sex life while still, in all other respects, a child. All her life she remains what she is: oversexed and incapable of understanding the civilized world of adults. Nor does this world understand her.' At the meeting Wittels backs up his case – 'my flood of enthusiasm', as he calls it – by quoting Helen of Troy,

Lucretia Borgia, Manon Lescaut and Zola's Nana: but not, of course, the uneducated Irma. Her account of herself is oddly irrelevant to Wittels (and to Kraus, who soon tired of her), despite the fact that at the time he was writing and, indeed, giving the paper, he was having an affair with her. But then, in a sense, none of it had anything to do with her.

Freud, Wittels reports, was 'somewhat annoyed' by his paper. Wittels's attempt to marry Freud's psychoanalysis with Kraus's vicious and sentimental classicism was unpromising (later he would try, even less successfully, to get Freud and Stekel back together), but the fury of Freud's reaction suggests that Wittels had touched Freud's deepest fears about psychoanalysis. 'It was not his intention', he said, 'to lead the world to an uninhibited frenzy. On the contrary he wished to teach men not to satisfy their instincts in a thousand more or less neurotic disguises. They should consciously decide what to do and what not to do. Instead of repressing and lying to themselves they should consciously reject what they consider evil.' Wittels talks about 'the child woman' – 'one of my more important contributions to analytical psychology' – and Freud hears the Bacchae over his shoulder.

Freud was saying: make the unconscious conscious because only then can you make intelligent ethical decisions. Wittels, however, had already decided that polymorphous perversity, or Krausian promiscuity, was a self-evident good. For Freud, psychoanalysis prepared one to make a morality for oneself: for Wittels it gave one a morality, ready-made. In this sense Freud, despite his caution, was the revolutionary, and Wittels the timid idolator. 'We knew from Freud that repressed sex instincts made men neurotic to such an extent that an entire era was poisoned,' Wittels writes ruefully. 'What we did not know then was that former Puritans running wild would not help either.' He is ashamed now of his naive and dangerous disregard for the necessary constraints of civilized virtue ('love, fidelity and devotion'). And yet once again in the memoir Wittels is bowing, even bowing out. By exactly missing the point he was making another: psychoanalysis could not exempt itself from promoting its own preferred forms of life.

Freud was promoting sexual freedom but was terrified of the aggression it would bring in its wake. If it was so difficult to be sexual and kind, one could at least be truthful. For Freud, honesty with oneself was the profoundest satisfaction. But as Wittels couldn't help reminding him a little too gleefully, Freud's theory proposed less conventional forms of satisfaction: if it was our nature to be sexual in the ways Freud described, then it was against our nature to be honest. If these are the alternatives, as Wittels can't quite bring himself to say, then psychoanalysis is less amenable to our prejudices, radical or otherwise. Wittels may have simplified sexual pleasure, but Freud was too keen to demonize it. The real controversy was about honesty.

Wittels's description of the child-woman was an unconscious cartoon of men's rage about their need for women, of the impossibility of men's demands on women: 'impossible', partly because they are unarticulated (out of fear), and partly because they are demands for everything (and therefore inarticulable). The child-woman's supposed pleasure is to be endlessly desirous and available, in unconditional circulation. This is trivial and offensive as a male fantasy about women: it is far more interesting as the expression of a man's illicit wish for himself. We always disparage, or promote, in the other sex our repressed ambitions for ourselves. Like all caricatures, Wittels's interpretation of Freud's work brought some of its more disturbing elements into starker relief. If Freud knew that sexuality could not be simple, he also knew that it was integral to our sexuality to wish that it was.

What Wittels doesn't seem to have realized until too late was that his real passion was for revenge: in other words, for disappointment. Disillusioned by Kraus – 'the man who had called me the greatest German writer' – he wrote a satirical novel about him and Kraus took him to court. 'For some time,' he writes ingenuously, 'I was tempted to write a novel in the manner of *Don Quixote*, whose hero was a man who read so many detective stories that he lost touch with reality.' Wittels's confusion of himself with Kraus in the novel – *Ezekiel the Alien* – is almost too obvious to be properly embarrassing. 'The sexual philosophy' of his novel's hero 'was unmasked as an over-compensation for his ugliness. Unable to conquer honest women, he debased them all to prostitutes. His name, in the novel, was Benjamin Disgusting.' Wittels's consistent knack of misjudging his relationship with the reader is one of the most bemusing things about his memoir; and the kind of self he wants to use it to construct often invites ridicule. He makes the reader cruel. Freud, concerned that psychoanalysis would be tainted by association with this book, tried to dissuade Wittels. 'I shall summarize my verdict in one sentence,' Freud told him with pragmatic good sense. 'You lose nothing if you do not publish the book; you lose everything if you do. The novel is bad.' Wittels as self-styled (or rather, stylized) rebel was incorrigible ('I continued to throw my articles in the face of a bewildered bourgeoisie,' he writes bravely in the memoir). Kraus succeeded in stopping publication of the book in Berlin, but not in Vienna. By exposing the story of Kraus and Irma, poorly disguised, and with an obvious link to the whole ethos of psychoanalysis, Wittels had brashly retaliated against both his fathers, neither of whom had sufficiently valued him. He was now so important that he had to be dropped by them. After all, he boasted, how could Freud possibly tolerate 'obnoxious theories on sexuality publicly discussed, psychoanalysis stigmatized in the person of one of its foremost exponents'? Wittels, one might say, is brilliant in this memoir about how ambivalence makes us vulnerable, because we are always on the side of the enemy. His penchant for self-destructive acts is almost poignant. But 'The Scandal' – one of his chapter titles – seems to have been his preferred genre, with its heady mix of shame and triumphalism.

By the end of this brief memoir Wittels is virtually reconciled with Freud; mostly, he suggests, thanks to an analysis with Freud's arch-enemy Stekel, which consisted of bracing winter walks ('I have kept the impression, although my memory may be wrong, that my analysis in the snow yielded better results than on the couch'). And he has, with Freud's blessing, successfully established himself as one of the first psychoanalysts in America. His account of American antipathy to psychoanalysis is often sharp and well observed, though sanctioned, of course, by Freud's prejudice. 'These primitives,' Freud wrote to Wittels, 'have little interest in science not directly convertible into practice. The worst of the American way is their so-called broad-mindedness.' Wittels evidently thrived, and eventually died, in America, where he could finally become a pioneer. His memoir is a testament to the tyrannies of self-importance.

Edward Timms says that the Wittels archive in New York is 'one of the richest sources' for the study of *fin de siècle* Austrian culture, and the evolution of psychoanalysis in Vienna and America; and that 'a systematic assessment of his life and work is long overdue'. It is clear from this disagreeable memoir that this must be true, but that it might be a thankless task. There won't, I imagine, be a return to Wittels. And yet the whole ethos of these early analysts is still a prolific source of ideas; their new-found excitement reminds us of what it might be like to have discovered something irresistible and transforming. They give us a sense of just how psychoanalytic ideas can inform ways of life. After all, where can we go now for versions of sexual freedom? (If we want to read about the erotic, it would be perhaps to Bataille that we would go but not, ironically, to the psychoanalytic literature.) There is still a psychoanalytic book to be written about sexual liberation. Memoirs like Wittels's are a sobering reminder of what such a book could be like.

The Manicuring of Jacques Lacan

*What one objects to in the ironists is not their
diagnosis but their tone.*
T. J. Clark, *The Painting of Modern Life*

The suspicion about psychoanalysts that is currently fashionable creates an interesting dilemma for their biographers. The
biographer of a great analyst is always tempted to prove
something, to second-guess the dubious reader. Since psychoanalysis as a treatment is itself about the possibility and,
indeed, the value of biographical truth – psychoanalysis as the
biography that is supposed to improve the biography – we are
likely to want something specific from this callow new genre.
We want to know whether these people should have been
trusted, and why, and if we should go on trusting their so-
called followers. In other words, biographies of psychoanalysts
make us wonder what it is that makes a person trustworthy to
us, and what, if anything, this has to do with the significance
we give to their lives and their work.

By the conventional standards of psychoanalytic orthodoxy,
Jacques Lacan (1900–81) was a heretic. His notoriety was based
on his shortening of the psychoanalytic session – sometimes to
five minutes. His fame was based on his radical revisions of
Freud and his insistence on the ways in which language and
sexuality disrupt a life. Towards the end of his life, historian of
psychoanalysis Elisabeth Roudinesco tells us, Lacan 'usually

Review of Elisabeth Roudinesco, *Jacques Lacan*, translated by Barbara Bray,
(Columbia University Press, 1997), from *Slate*.

saw his tailor, his pedicurist, and his barber while conducting his analyses'. So what?

There is a tension in any biography between what the subject wanted to be – who he or she was always wanting to become – and what the biographer wants the subject to be. In this sober, incisive, and riveting book, a well-documented history rather than a novelistic evocation of the man himself, Roudinesco cannot conceal her dismay that Lacan was not better behaved, more temperate in his appetites, less baroque in his provocations. She wants him to be more poignant and less boastful.

It was, of course, about excesses – of desire, of meaning, of emptiness – that Lacan wrote so eloquently. For Lacan, a person was by definition in excess of himself, an excess to himself. He believed there was something fundamentally unintelligible about the vagaries of a life. But Roudinesco neither takes pleasures in nor makes intriguing sense of the fact that Lacan's theories 'denounced the omnipotence of the ego in general, though he himself asserted the supremacy of his own'. In doing this he was doing with some style exactly what Freud described everyone as doing (though not, presumably, merely doing what he was told). Lacan's writings are clearly, among other things, the confessions of a self-justifying megalomaniac – unusual in itself, because such people don't tend to explain themselves, or at least explain themselves with such intricate subtlety. But by the same token these are also the most inexhaustibly interesting and stylish psychoanalytic writings since Freud's. The Lacan characterized in this book as flamboyantly voracious for the Freudian triumvirate of women, money and power is, as Roudinesco suggests, a Balzacian hero: a triumph of appetite over class. This is a story of a man with an amazing talent for finding what and whom he needed to make himself what he wanted to be, the greatest analyst since Freud. This was, in the best sense, the most childish of ambitions.

As always, from the evidence available, there is no obvious reason why this particular family should have produced that particular psychoanalyst. Lacan's father owned a very successful vinegar distillery; the family were respectable bourgeois Roman Catholics. Lacan's adored youngest brother became a priest, and his sister spent most of her married life in Indochina – so clearly some distance was needed from what was otherwise a typical French family of a certain type. Very early, as one might have expected, Lacan wanted to be top of the class, though in fact he wasn't an especially talented boy. He had a precocious intellectual curiosity. He tended to read, as Roudinesco remarks, rather than play Cowboys and Indians with the other boys.

Of course, Lacan's life here is being read retrospectively, partly through the prism of his writings, whereas he was living it prospectively (we have to remember, given that Lacan's work was the theorizing of life stories, that he himself never knew what was going to happen next). If one of the dominant motifs of Lacan's early life is his contempt for his father, as it is in this account, then it can seem virtually inevitable that his early work was about the terrible cultural consequences of the 'weakening of the father imago' (there were no strong fathers anymore), and that much of his later work should be obsessed by what he called 'the-name-of-the-father' and the symbolic significance of the phallus. But psychoanalysis – and Lacan was particularly shrewd about this – has always been essentially a critique of straightforwardly causal accounts of how people become who they are. Indeed, what distinguishes psychoanalysis is that it can show us the ways in which a life is *not* merely the effect of its causes (biology, parents, etc.).

As Lacan progresses through psychiatry, the Second World War (as a doctor in France), surrealism, psychoanalysis, structuralism – Lacan's life was apparently a magnet for everything intellectually interesting happening in France. He was, for example, Picasso's personal doctor – he seems to have had a knack for finding useful fathers and brothers. His friendships with the writer and critic Georges Bataille, the philosopher Maurice Merleau-Ponty, the anthropologist Claude Lévi-Strauss and the linguist Roman Jakobson were formative in ways that he either fails to note or misleadingly acknowledges. Here Roudinesco is rather limitingly censorious, wanting Lacan to pay his debts rather than being amazed by what he could make of what he found in the work of these remarkable people. Lacan was apparently always dismayed by how little his mentors were influenced by him. In this book, it is Lacan's craving for recognition – his almost demonic hunger to be unforgettable – that drives him; and that, every so often, is gently pathologized by Roudinesco.

Roudinesco alludes to many mistresses, though always discreetly, in the abstract. Lacan's private life, however, was really a tale of two families. A first marriage, in his twenties, to Malou, the sister of a close friend, with whom he has three children; and then a second marriage to Sylvie, Bataille's ex-wife, with whom he has his adored daughter and acolyte Judith. The children of the first marriage are told nothing of the second marriage until they are young adults. So Lacan leads a bizarre double life. One of the most chilling scenes in the book is when Lacan, Sylvie and Judith stop at a traffic light in Paris and see two of Lacan's other children. They approach the car and Lacan drives off. Confronted with some of the more callous follies of this extraordinary life, the 'so what?' question becomes more and more pressing. And yet in much of Lacan's thrilling and sophisticated theorizing – that is haunted by France's experience of two world wars – he seems to be asking a simple question: why are people the animals that are so excessive in their aggression and their rivalry? Where Melanie

Klein takes our murderousness for granted, Lacan goes on being genuinely puzzled. He is continually shocked by, and therefore shocking about, human cruelty, whereas Klein is wanting us to be merely rigorously grief-stricken about it.

'An act always misunderstands itself,' Lacan wrote. Indeed, all Lacan's writing is an elaborate meditation on the ways in which – and the structures by which – we can never be transparent to ourselves. Lacan's life was a struggle against the institutionalization of knowledge and he flourished by creating havoc, both publicly (in a famous break with the International Psychoanalytic Institute) and privately (among some of his colleagues). He wanted psychoanalysis to be a science of self-deception, a proof against the old pieties. It would be strange to wish that he were more lovable, or honest, or familiar. His life is exemplary in the modern sense, not as a picture of virtue, or even as a struggle to live out some kind of personal truth, but rather as a question: how complicated can we allow people to be before we stop trusting them, or indeed listening to them?

The lesson of Lacan's daunting and exhilarating self-fashioning is that psychoanalytic heroes – from Freud onwards – always have a sado-masochistic relationship with both their admirers and their detractors (and of course with themselves). If there are to be usefully inspiring psychoanalysts in the future – rather than merely cult figures – they will have to stop trying to have new theories and aim instead just to write interesting sentences; and they should never teach their own work, only the work of others that they value (from a psychoanalytic point of view no writer can be the privileged authority on what he finds he has to say). And above all they must never involve themselves in formal groups – or so-called institutes of psycho-analysis – but simply, like most other people, just try and find people they like talking to (psychoanalysis should initiate people into the more difficult art of informality). When there are no more students, there will be no more masters. What Lacan's life teaches us, unlike his fabulous writing, is that prestige should not be the name of the game. The lesson of the master is the one we should stop listening out for. 'Experience', as Lacan wrote, 'is not didactic.'

Pessoa's Appearances

'True originality', Cocteau, Pessoa's contemporary, wrote, 'consists in trying to behave like everybody else without succeeding.' It was once characteristically modern to idealize originality, and to conceive of it as a form of failure. The fittest as those who didn't fit. If there is nothing more compliant now than the wish to be original – to find one's own voice, etc. – it is also assumed now that originality and success can, and should, go together. But for the European modernist writers of Pessoa's generation – he was born in Lisbon in 1888 and died there in 1935 – the question was still what has been lost when words like success or originality become ultimate values, when lives and writing are so eagerly judged by these criteria? The romantic concept of genius, after all – the apotheosis of essential originality – was itself a kind of elegy for a lost community. All the solitary disillusioned moderns – Baudelaire, Kafka, Eliot, Beckett – are preoccupied by their sociability: its impossibility, its triviality, its compromises, its shame. For these writers, ambition (or nostalgia) without irony flies in the face of the evidence; a successful life was a contradiction in terms, because the modernist revelation was that lives don't work. A certain revulsion was integral to their vision.

One of the many remarkable things about Pessoa's writing is

Reviews of Fernando Pessoa, *The Keeper of Sheep*, translated by Edwin Honig and Susan M. Brown (reissued by Sheep Meadow Press; originally pub. 1986); *The Book of Disquietude*, translated by Richard Zenith (Carcanet Press, 1996); and Eugenio Lisboa and L. C. Taylor (eds), *A Centenary Pessoa* (Carcanet Press, 1995).

the relative absence of disgust; he is not mostly repelled by other people, by modern life, by his own obscurity and frustration and failings; he is genuinely baffled. He is confounded not by what he sees, but by the way he sees things:

On writing this last sentence, which for me says exactly what it means, I thought it might be useful to put at the end of my book, when it's published, a few 'Non-Errata' after the 'Errata', and to say: the phrase 'this chance movements' on page so-and-so, is correct as is, with the noun in the plural and the demonstrative in the singular. But what does this have to do with what I was thinking? Nothing, and so I'll let it drop.

It is part of Pessoa's sophisticated innocence – his witting dismay – to assume he has made a mistake here ('and so I'll let it drop'). If a 'few' non-errata might put the whole book under suspicion, none at all should make us wonder. And that it is '*chance* movements' that he happens to use as the phrase to illustrate his point is not, as it were, accidental. To presume something is an error is simply to look at it from a point of view that makes it one. It was Pessoa's commitment to the unavoidable multiplicity of points of view within himself that constituted his poetic vocation. To be a poet for Pessoa was to be the various poets inside him: each of his 'heteronyms' as he called them, a corrective to the other, baring as they did, different strands of the poetic traditions he inherited. Pessoa, in other words, found a poetic solution for what is not always considered to be a poetic problem: the unburdening of the past. It has been a short step, as it were, from Rimbaud's 'I is an other' to multiple personality disorder.

The idea that one might be or have several personae or selves – that one is haunted, or has disparate voices inside oneself – is not, of course, a new one. What is new, or rather, culturally and historically specific, are the uses to which they have been put, or the functions they have been assumed to have. The double, the unconscious, oneself as a stranger, the multiple, are all ways of describing the breakdown of a consensus in a self conceived of as, at least, potentially more unified. Anything unaccountable, unbearable or divisive comes from, or is carried by, this other place (or person). But once the self has been described like this – and split in these various ways to make something more manageable – the question always arises of whether anyone is in charge, if any one self or version knows what's going on. As though there must be unity, an omniscient narrator somewhere: someone who actually does the splitting. Indeed, one of the curious things about, say, self-reproach or self-love is that it assumes that one part of the self is virtually omniscient, really knows best. One is not lacking in authority in these moments of abjection or smugness. Selves, in other words, are always split hierarchically, in terms of internal power relations: the strongest parts of the self supposedly causing (i.e. coercing) the weaker parts; being, in a sense, irresistibly persuasive.

As Octavio Paz says in his illuminating introduction to *A Centenary Pessoa*, an essential guide to and useful selection of Pessoa's work, the heteronyms the poet invented stopped his internal conversation degenerating into a monologue: 'Pessoa, their first reader, did not doubt their reality. In contradicting him, they expressed him; in expressing him, they forced him to invent himself.' Because he did not find his voice, but his voices, Pessoa never fell into the trap of knowing what he was doing; he didn't need to imitate himself in order to keep writing. Pessoa discovered that to sound like oneself could be a contradiction in terms. That the I, in effect, was like an anxious host who does all the talking for fear that no one else will speak. But Pessoa was not preaching the death of the author, he was just acutely aware of how the author got in the way of the writing. His four main heteronyms, among an estimated seventy-two – Alvaro de Campos, Alberto Caeiro, Ricardo Reis, and himself, the one called Pessoa – each a remarkable poet in his own right, used him like an unintrusive parent: 'I graded their influences', he wrote in a letter, 'recognized their friendships, heard, inside me, their discussions and divergences of criteria, and in all this it seemed to me that I, the creator of it all, was the least thing there. It is as if it all happened independently of me.'

Once this virtual revelation, or visitation had occurred – on the 8th of March 1914, 'a kind of ecstasy whose nature I cannot define. It was the triumphal day of my life ...' – Pessoa began to both fashion himself into, and accept himself as a kind of medium; a man without character, a setting for voices. 'Having accustomed myself', he wrote, 'to have no beliefs and no opinions, lest my aesthetic feeling should be weakened, I grew soon to have no personality at all except an expressive one. I grew to be a mere apt machine for the expression of moods which became so intense that they grew into personalities and made my very soul the mere shell of their casual appearance...'

This is not, of course, an unfamiliar account of writing poetry; but the poets who describe similar experiences – Blake or Keats in their letters say, or Eliot in his theory of poetic impersonality – seem always the strongest of characters, each of them formidably distinctive in their writing and, as far as one can tell, in their everyday lives. Pessoa, as *The Book of Disquiet* records with a kind of subtle astonishment, really experienced himself as having no personality, as a man without recognizable qualities, an absurd chaos of moods that it was simply implausible to try to unify into a person. For Pessoa, madness was not the failure to make sense – to make it all cohere, or fit together – but the attempt. As he wrote in a late poem in 1932, 'Rage in the Dark, the Wind':

The soul contains, it seems,
A dark where there hardens and
Blows a madness that comes
From trying to understand.

To be unselfpossessed was his project – 'Who believes he is his is astray. / I'm various and not mine' – that he never evaded by turning it into a fate. Pessoa doesn't go in for the smug (or triumphant) self-defeat of tragedy. He is melancholic, but he rarely affects the certainty of the doomed.

It is surely a disarming reflection of our cultural insularity that it has taken so long for Pessoa's work to become known. When Harold Bloom recently listed him among the twenty-six authors who comprise, for him, the fabled Western canon, *Time* magazine implied that this was a symptom of Bloom's slightly pretentious interest in 'academic obscurities'. It will certainly be a shame if Pessoa's work is swiftly shrouded in academic obscurities given Pessoa's 'relevance' to virtually everything academically topical. But the sheer fascination of Pessoa's poetic vocation – and the quality of the writing with its unheard-of tones of voice that keep breaking through in the entirely convincing translations here – makes Bloom's choice a characteristically inspired one. As all the pundits so also well collected in *A Centenary Pessoa* agree – Borges, Steiner, Josipovici, Hollander, Cyril Connolly, Roman Jakobson, Mark Strand – it is a compounding of Pessoa's mystery that he has been anonymous for so long in Anglo-American culture. A 'canon' that includes Pessoa seems infinitely less claustrophobic and bossy.

There is, Pessoa writes in *The Book of Disquietude*, 'no better étude or melody for me than the lightly moonlit moment in which I don't know myself as knowable'. Though a source of dismay to him – self-knowledge is, after all, the traditional project – Pessoa's inability to recognize himself was his inspiration. His writing came out of what he was confounded by: an absence of biography, of any discernible or convincing continuity or pattern in his life. One consequence of being what he called 'a man for whom the outer world is an inner reality' was that his adult life was largely uneventful. Though he was active in Portuguese literary affairs, for thirty years he worked in Lisbon writing letters in French and English for commercial firms earning the modest living that would sustain his writing. He had friendships – though one doesn't often gather this from the writing – but he lived alone. He had apparently no love affairs, and published very little of the immense amount he wrote. He was not in circulation, except among his own moods. The only (recorded) time he fell in love – in 1920, to a girl in his office – he soon broke it off. Obviously quite at odds with the whole experience, i.e. terrified, he wrote to her, 'my destiny belongs to a different law, whose existence you do not even suspect'. Pessoa was never to be confident that anyone – and least of all him – had a clue about what was going on inside him. But by all accounts his was not a determined elusiveness; he was not on the run, or thrilled by being fascinating. It was as though he was almost not really there. 'Never, when I bade him goodbye,' Pierre Hourcade writes, who knew Pessoa at the end of his life, 'did I dare to turn back and look at him; I was afraid I would see him vanish, dissolved in air.' Always at the point of disappearing from himself, Pessoa clearly had to work quite hard, as a young man, to keep believing that what he was doing was writing great poetry and not merely going mad. There is an unusually frantic note written by him in English, when he was twenty: 'one of my mental complications – horrible beyond words – is a fear of insanity, which itself is insanity'.

As it happened, it was not beyond words. And the words he found in *The Keeper of Sheep* – his great breakthrough book, so lucidly translated by Edward Honig and Susan Brown – were a remarkable self-cure. What Pessoa seems to have realized was that it was the will to meaning that drove people mad; 'Because the only hidden meaning of things / Is that they have no hidden meaning at all. / That is stranger than all the strangeness' (poem XXXIX). *The Keeper of Sheep* – the opening lines of which are, aptly, 'I never kept sheep / But it's as if I'd done so' – is a book about how we destroy our experience, drive ourselves mad, by the ways we have of making it intelligible. 'Who ordered me to want to understand?', Pessoa asks; and his writing comes to life in abrogating the order, in affirming that his 'mysticism is not wanting to know', that 'What's past is nothing and remembering is not seeing'. For Pessoa, paradoxically, perception is not distorted by wish, but by our capacity for recognition. He implies that we have been tricked into various forms of transcendence: that Christianity, and our secular religion that's called history, have all been bolt-holes from the immediacy of nature. He, or rather his heteronym Caeiro, the putative author of the book, aspires to be 'Clear, useless and transient as Nature herself'. And of course, what rescues the poetry from being a kind of utopian paganism, from promoting some impossible immediacy of pure being, is that it is immediately answered back by another heteronym: 'the reaction', Pessoa writes, 'of Fernando Pessoa against his own non-existence as Alberto Caeiro'. If it is the need for meaning that drives one mad – 'I have no philosophy: I have senses', Caeiro writes – it is, by the same token, the meaning of this hostility to meaning, 'Of being only what I appear to be', that needs the address, and the redress of Pessoa's other heteronyms. If 'any real authentic unity / Is a sickness of all our ideas. / Nature is simply parts' then the poetic quest is always for the deeper disunity, the inspiration and comfort that accrues from the ways in which things don't fit together. For Pessoa it is disarray that is illuminating; if there is no system there is no need for the will. Nothing to try to conform to. 'Metaphysics', he writes in *The Book of Disquietude*, 'has always struck me as a prolonged form of latent insanity.'

The Book of Disquietude, Pessoa's *magnum opus* of poetic prose fragments that was never finished is, as it were, antimetaphysical by design; it has no design, could never have been finished, and is, in fact, a compilation made by others. It is, his excellent translator Richard Zenith writes, 'a depository ... various books (yet ultimately one book), with various authors (yet ultimately one author)'. The narrator of most of the book – a series of diary entries and reflections, but mostly undated and without context – sounds like the more 'emotional' heteronym Alvaro de Campos. But Pessoa suggested that the narrator was a 'semi-heteronym' ('because his personality, although not my own, doesn't differ from my own but is a mere mutilation of it') called Bernardo Soares who appeared around 1920. Pessoa only published a dozen of the *Disquietude* fragments during his lifetime, in literary magazines. Just before his death he placed about 350 fragments in an envelope marked 'Book of Disquietude'; but scholars have found an additional 150 fragments that seem of a piece with the projected book. Pessoa wrote of several ways of organizing the book, none of them chronological, so the book we have now – which has taken nearly fifty years to be published – is both his and not his. Zenith suggests that 'ideally' we would have a loose-leaf edition so the reader could order the fragments in his or her own way, but even this seems rather too programmatic, a bit too John Cage. It is certainly better to dip into the book rather than read it through – one of the many endearing things about Pessoa is that he makes conscientiousness seem silly – and the fragments should be read as a series of bulletins, without assuming one knows who or where they come from. By always implicitly or explicitly wondering what he's writing for, Pessoa has an uncanny ability to make the reader wonder what he's reading for.

If on the one hand, *The Book of Disquietude*, like all modern wisdom literature, is itself a spoof of the genre – 'better to write than to dare to live' – it is also a riveting account of what intense self-reflection sounds like when there is no self to reflect on. 'There's nothing in life', Pessoa writes, 'that gets less real from having been well described', including, of course, a so-called self. And yet he is 'a poor orphan abandoned on the streets of sensation' with no self there to organize it all, or be organized by it. 'It's all', as he wrote of his book that was neither his nor a book, 'fragments, fragments, fragments'. Quite what he was insisting on by reiterating the key word is ambiguous, poised as Pessoa often is, between exhilaration and despair. It is this implausible combination of the precious and the dead-pan that makes *The Book of Disquietude* such a relief. 'I'd woken up early,' he writes on the 25th of December 1929, 'and I took a long time to get ready to exist.'

Each of the 523 fragments, that range from single sentences to several paragraphs, are like false starts that have to be abandoned – aborted essays. Definitive statements – 'The human soul is a madhouse of caricatures' – and the portentous banalities of everyday life – 'Everything, finally is Destiny' – disssolve through a kind of psychic entropy, into states of bewilderment, what he calls 'absurd hollows of lost emotions'; or longings too suspicious of themselves to be fully believed, 'I had desires, but was denied any reason to have them'. There are reassuring orgies of self-pity and weariness – 'my life is entirely futile and entirely sad' – and wonderfully self-conscious brief literary essays on the big subjects: Christianity, the Classical inheritance, the ruins of Romanticism, the Soul's weather, Death and its drawbacks. The very real and often poignant anguish (and boredom) are tempered by a kind of fascinated horror at his own engagement. He goes on writing it down – 'Life pursues us like our shadows' – as though the writing itself was a lure, as though the book he is all the time writing is an obscure object of desire. The more he writes it the more there is of it. And yet if reading *The Book of Disquietude* is sometimes like overhearing someone trying to invent a religion, it is not a religion of art. The narrator, or rather, narrators, are rarely as boastful or supercilious as the average aesthete. All Pessoa's epigrams try to make of impossibility an ideal; he is always drawn to the elegance of the flawed:

Some have a great dream in life, and fall short of it. Others have no dream, and also fall short of it.

The perfect pagan man was the perfection of the man that exists; the perfect Christian man the perfection of the man that does not exist; and the perfect Buddhist man the perfection of no man existing.

Inviting us to imagine a non-cynical life without ideals, a visionary imperfectibility of man, Pessoa often sounds in this book as though he is on the verge of hysterical laughter.

And yet for all his self-estrangement, his delirious and melancholic sense of the self deceived by its notions of self-deception, Pessoa does, of course, have his themes. However decentred or evanescent, the self always has its circles, always homes in on its preoccupations that occupy so much time. It is perhaps not surprising that a writer so obsessed by the spurious cravings of and for identity, should be so interested in sleep and in work where, at least the story is, we lose and find our identities. And also in that transitional state of illness which is neither sleep nor work but a bit of both, the 'wish', as Pessoa writes, 'that life were a convalescence, obliging us to stay off our feet'. Sleeping and working we might wonder exactly what it is we are participating in. What all this joining in involves. It is always both a glib and a telling reversal to think that it is, 'As if sleeping, I wake up, and I don't belong to myself. Life, in itself, is a vast insomnia ...'. If, as Pessoa suggests in one entry, 'I wake up to make sure I exist'; or again, 'I sleep, and ... no person interrupts what I'm not thinking. I'm sleepy in the same way that I'm alive', the implication is that comparing sleeping and waking reveals our ignorance of both. And, indeed, the covert omniscience in all analogy (we must already know what something is in order to be able to compare it with something else). 'I feel permanently on the verge of waking up', Pessoa writes in the full knowledge that he wouldn't know what that was like.

Because sleep is factless – all we ever do in it is dream – it is exemplary for Pessoa; we don't know where we are when we sleep and we have nothing to show for it, except our waking selves. We are lifeless and completely alive. So his book is a record of somebody sleeping something off. 'In these random impressions, and with no desire to be other than random, I indifferently relate my factless autobiography, my lifeless history.' When he works, as he does every day, routinely, he is effectively subsidizing his sleep; the day-dreams and the night-dreams that are the only things that feel at all real to him because he knows that they aren't. The narrator prefers to live in his mind, prefers his loopy inattention to the so-called real world – 'my dreams are a stupid refuge, like an umbrella against lightning' – because his inner life is immediate, absurd, and utterly inexplicable. The narrator of the book, unlike Pessoa himself, so to speak, is, appropriately, a book-keeper. All he can do, as he says, is keep accounts. 'We sleep who we are'; there is no obvious waking, only dreaming. Work is a way of pretending not to be asleep.

Paz's description of Pessoa – his essay alone is worth the price of the book – is agreeably extravagant:

Anglomaniac, myopic, courteous, evasive, dressed darkly, reticent and agreeable, cosmopolitan who preaches nationalism, solemn investigator of futile things, humorist who never smiles but chills our blood, inventor of other poets and destroyer of himself, author of paradoxes clear as water and, as water, dizzying; to pretend is to know yourself, mysterious man who does not cultivate mystery ...

Pessoa, who has been blessed by his translators – Jonathan Griffin in the Penguin *Selected Poems*, and Keith Bosley, Richard Zenith, Edwin Honig and Susan Brown in the books under review – seems to prompt curiously unguarded responses in his readers. 'I'm the living stage', his narrator Soares writes, 'where various actors act out various plays.' Pessoa's work casts more than a spell.

On Translating a Person

> *... a translation issues from the original – not so much from its life as from its afterlife. For a translation comes later than the original ...*
>
> Walter Benjamin, 'The Task of the Translator'

1

In 1980 Raymond Williams published a book with the, to me, rather daunting title of *Problems in Materialism and Culture*. I had studied what was then still called English Literature at university but I had neither read, nor indeed been encouraged to read anything by Williams. I had, to put it briefly, no idea what the word 'materialism' meant; and that, indeed, was why I bought the book. And the first piece I read in the book, out of a kind of vague, idle curiosity, was entitled, 'The Welsh Industrial Novel'. I say that I read it out of idle curiosity because even though I had been born and had grown up in Cardiff – and from adolescence onwards had been very interested in what I thought of as Literature – I had no idea that there was such a thing as a Welsh industrial novel. In fact, I would have been hard pressed to name, and I had certainly not read, a Welsh novel of any kind. But what is of most interest to me now, looking back, is that I was not at all surprised by this. I read Williams's lecture rather as a tourist might read a guide book, with a mixture of genuine curiosity, duty and inattention. It was as though it had never occurred to

Gwyn Jones Memorial Lecture, Cardiff, 2000.

me that Welsh culture, as defined by Welsh people who lived it and struggled to make it, could be of any interest or use to me. That one could grow up in a place, and to all intents and purposes take so little interest in it; that, one's aspirations could so completely disavow, if not actually abolish a surrounding world; that one could live in one's ambitions, one's family's ambitions, and the ambitions sponsored by one's education, at the cost of living in a place. All these formative experiences, I imagine, have resonances in the history of Anglo-Welsh relations and the history of Jewish and other emigration and immigration. And they are all, whatever else they are, problems of materialism and culture. But they can also be seen, in a slightly different way, as failures of translation, and denials of reality. And so, from a psycho-analytic point of view, evidence of anxieties at work. Williams writing so forcefully of the difficult genesis of Welsh industrial novels is a useful parallel (if not a parable) of the predicament I am describing. 'From the beginning of the formation of the industrial working class novel', he writes, 'there were always individuals with the zeal and capacity to write, but their characteristic problem was the relation of their intentions and experience to the dominant literary forms, shaped primarily as these were by another and dominant class.'

In other words, the translation of their experience – their moving it across into the alien form of the English middle-class novel – could feel excessively alienating. As over-accommodation, or submission, or distraction. The form was foreign, and it was the form of a dominant, exploitative class. A welsh miner would not feel at home, as it were, in one of Jane Austen's drawing rooms. What Williams is alerting us to is that what he calls the emergence of 'structures of feeling' depend upon the cultural forms available for use. And each of those forms carries with it a history and a class consciousness. As a boy growing up in Cardiff, and one way or another living there until my early twenties, it was as though, my education told me, there were no Welsh cultural forms usefully available to me. I had never needed to find out what materialism meant. But after studying English Literature I became a child psychotherapist; that is, someone interested in how people grow up where they grow up; and in the senses in which people experience themselves as displaced persons within the immediacy of their surroundings. In short, in what people do with their histories; what they can make of what they are given. The finding, and the failure to find, good-enough forms for oneself, and the things one values. In other words, in the possibility of translation: of moving oneself within, and among, a variety of languages. From one's so-called mother-tongue, and beyond.

There was no conscious link in my mind, at the time, between where I grew up and my choice of profession. I seemed to think of myself as coming from a family, but not really from a place; and the more limited and limiting versions of psychoanalysis might have endorsed such a preposterous misconception. This active disowning of location and local culture – which I think of now as being about class and its emotional underpinning – is akin, in its own way, to some of the most extreme defences that Freud describes. And yet not to be interested in something or someone – to be apparently untouched by them – must be one of the commonest and most unacknowledged of defences. [Indifference can be more pernicious – and more insidously aggressive – than outright hostility] So I am very glad to be giving this lecture here today, both as some kind of redress or acknowledgement of all this, and also because, as I found out to my amazement – as though it was some uncanny kind of deferred action – Raymond Williams's 'The Welsh Industrial Novel' was, in fact, the inaugural Gwyn Jones Lecture, given in Cardiff in 1978. To be linked with such distinguished Welshmen is something of an honour; even though the psychoanalysis that I practise and value is, I think, something Williams would have had certain misgivings about, referring as he does, elsewhere, to Freudianism as 'a bourgeois version of society'. Which, of course, it is. And yet, in Williams's inaugural lecture he refers to the uses of pastoral in these Welsh industrial novels of the Thirties in a way that is germane to my subject. 'The pastoral life', he writes, 'which had been Welsh history, is still another Welsh present, and in its visible presence – not as an ideal contrast but as the slope, the skyline, to be seen immediately from the streets and from the pit-tops – it is a shape which manifests not only a consciousness of history but a consciousness of alternatives, and then, in a modern form, a consciousness of aspirations and possibilities.'

What Williams ascribes to the pastoral life I want to ascribe to psychoanalysis; indeed as a remarkable exact and exacting account of what psychoanalysis, at its most useful and interesting can be – a consciousness of history, a consciousness of alternatives, a consciousness of aspirations and possibilities: a wish for translation. But adding to this an acknowledgement of the unconsciousness of these things, and what that might involve. Without translation in its familiar sense of transferring from one language into another, and in its more metaphorical sense of moving across, or removing to another place, there can be no sense of history, of alternatives, of aspirations, or of possibilities. And contemporary so-called multi-cultural societies depend for their viability on their members' enthusiasm, however ambivalent, for translation. Our relationship to translation has become a virtual synonym for our relationship to ourselves.

2

Psychoanalysts don't tend to think of themselves as translating people. The analyst interprets, reconstructs, questions, redescribes, returns the signifier, as Lacanians say, but he rarely describes what he does as translating the patient's so-called material. Translation is what we do to texts, and we can't read people like books. Even though words are the thing in analysis, translation isn't often the word that comes to mind, at least for the analyst. And yet, of course, each of these techniques, or rather practices, both overlap with the work of the translator, or are just simply of a piece with what translation entails. To interpret, to reconstruct, to redescribe, to question – even to return the signifier, if only to the dictionary, or the author's other work – this is what the translator also does with his text. Such disparate practices share a likeness. So I want to consider what kind of analogy translation is for what goes on in psychoanalysis, how it is linked to a consciousness of history and possibility; and whether, by implication, this can tell us something about the act of translation, as well as about psychoanalysis itself. All the controversies about accurate or good-enough translations of Freud (and Lacan) are also – as well as self-evidently of some importance in their own right – some kind of parallel text for, or ironic commentary on, the anxieties involved both in the act of ongoing mutual translation that is the psychoanalytic relationship; and also of the ways in which psychoanalysis translates itself, and gets translated into the general culture (clearly the Freud 'everyone' knows about is in rather a gossipy translation). After an analysis, after a text has been translated, how do we know – who is in a position to decide – when the result is a good one? Whether, that is to say, we now have a reliable text to go on? The consequences of a translation

– as of an analysis – are unpredictable; even if we are capable of having good intentions.

After all, people come for psychoanalysis when their present language no longer works. Indeed, one could sensibly say that they are in need of translation; to move or be moved from one place to another, through language. As the *OED* has it in one of its several canonical definitions, they want to be removed 'from one place of interment or repose to another ... to carry or convey to heaven without death'. And yet when people come to see me I don't teach them French or German or Swedish, and not merely because I don't know these languages. People come for analysis when they have reached the limits of their language; and this means, going on using their own available descriptions of what's happening – of what they feel – has become too painful. So even though people do not come for analysis to learn another language, there is a sense in which this is exactly what they want. But they don't say, if I am unhappy in English, perhaps I would be better off in French. They say, in various ways, that they are suffering from something; and so are in need of something. If they are English, they want a different English: a better vocabulary.

I think it is worth wondering why analysts don't offer language courses, and what translators imagine they are doing for the authors they translate. Clearly there are writers who, one way or another, have felt better off writing in other languages; Beckett is perhaps the most obvious modern example, and he, of course, both had some psychoanalysis and partially renounced his mother tongue in order to find the words he needed. And there must be translators who, for whatever reasons, prefer facilitating both the words and the circulation of their chosen authors, rather than, in a literal sense, writing their own words. In each of these choices the other language becomes an object of desire. So I suppose one question here is, what is it for a language – say Welsh or English – to be, or to become an object of desire? And by the same token, as with the person who comes for analysis, what is it for a language to become a persecutory object, a hate-object, so painful that one needs to get away from it? The translator is both trying to stay close to the original language, and also quite literally, needing to get away from it. There could be no general answers to such questions, but the answers in any individual case, I think, couldn't help but be interesting.

I think the most useful general way of formulating what psychoanalysis is, is simply to say that it is an art of redescription. As Bion, the British analyst, once said, the analyst and the patient are trying to find stories for the inappropriate. A fresh account of the unacceptable is required. So I want to use this lecture today to consider two things. Firstly, in what sense is a redescription a translation? And I want to link this with what is simply a clinical impression (which I will come back to) – that when a patient feels translated by the analyst they don't feel transported, moved over to a better place, they feel radically misunderstood in a peculiarly disabling way. It is my impression that when my patients say that I have translated what they have been saying, they feel I have done them a kind of violence. No one has ever said to me about an interpretation, 'That's a great translation!' But people have said to me, 'Now you're translating what I'm saying to you.' And they are not pleased. Translating English into more English is obviously different from translating English into French; and yet clearly sometimes, for some people, they can feel akin. If we were to think of this spatially, in terms of distance, I could ask myself: how far do my words have to get from the patient's consciously intended meaning before they feel translated? And why would translation be a pejorative term, from the patient's point of view? And also to consider why, if at all psychoanalysis and translation might usefully need each other as analogies? To talk about analogy is not merely to talk in terms of the binary oppositions of sameness and difference; it is to talk, as in translation, about nuances of meaning. What the word translation gets used to do becomes part of the practice of what translators (and analysts) think of themselves as doing. And when it turns up, just as when it is disavowed as a good thing to be doing, it smuggles a good deal across with it.

3

In the second paragraph of the famous opening to *The Eighteenth Brumaire of Louis Bonaparte*, Marx writes:

Men make their own history, but not of their own free will; not under circumstances they themselves have chosen, but under the given and inherited circumstances with which they are directly confronted. The tradition of the dead generations weighs like a nightmare on the minds of the living. And, just when they appear to be engaged in the revolutionary transformation of themselves and their material surroundings, in the creation of something that does not yet exist, precisely in such epochs of revolutionary crisis they timidly conjure up the spirits of the past to help them; they borrow their names, slogans and costumes so as to stage the new world-historical scene in this venerable disguise and borrowed language. Luther put on the mask of the apostle Paul; the revolution of 1789–1814 draped itself alternately as the Roman republic and the Roman empire; and the revolution of 1848 knew no better than to parody at some points 1789 and at others the revolutionary traditions of 1793–5. In the same way the beginner who has learned a new language always retranslates it into his mother tongue: he can only be said to have appropriated the spirit of the new language and to express himself in it freely when he can manipulate it without reference to the old, and when he forgets his original language while using the new one'.

When Marx here wants an analogy – an instructive parallel – for revolution, it is interestingly to translation that he turns. What do people do when they are engaged in a 'revolutionary transformation' of themselves? They seek reassuring precedents; they make a costume drama of the past. And so fearful are they, they have recourse to magic, as though they can only become something by, at least at first, pretending to be it; and paradoxically, they can only become something new, by pretending to be something from the past. It is, as Marx describes it, a mixture of simple trickery, and a ritual of performative utterances: 'they timidly conjur up the spirits of the past to help them; they borrow their names, slogans and costumes so as to stage the new world-historical scene in this venerable disguise and borrowed language'. And for Marx this is most obviously like the process of learning a new language; you start by pretending to speak in this way – just like an actor, you try out the part, you try on the clothes, you use the words – and eventually, if the process is successful, *you forget that this is what you are doing*. You forget, as Marx puts it, your 'mother tongue'. You are successfully translated when you no longer need to do the translation; when you forget that it is translation that you have in fact done. To learn a new language means to forget the old one. It is a rhetorically powerful definition of a successful revolution: the forgetting of an old language. And yet how is this different from a conversion experience, from being initiated into a cult, or indeed from being brainwashed? It is, to some extent, self-chosen; but why wouldn't it be better to be always remembering, to be always doing the work of retranslation? And what happens in that gap that Marx wants to call forgetting, between translating and not needing to? In order to change dramatically why do we have to relinquish the old languages of the tradition of the dead generations which, as Marx says, 'weighs like a nightmare on the minds of the living'?

Clearly the dead are never quite dead enough, but a nightmare, of course, wakes the sleeper up. Freud would say, it wakes the dreamer up with something from the past, the representation of which – the language of which – the dreamer cannot bear. He needs to return to so-called reality in order not to be over-whelmed himself; in order not to die. For Freud, in a sense, as for Marx the past is both a nightmare from which we must awaken, but it is also our only resource. It is literally where we get our language from, where we learn it. To learn a language is to learn a history, and to acquire a medium from the past in which to reconstruct the past. But a language can also be like a nightmare from which we cannot awaken.

Psychoanalysts may be persuading their patients to forget their old languages, while at the same time reminding them of the histories, the always constructed narrative continuities between past and present. Just as a good translation doesn't exactly convince you that *Madame Bovary* wasn't originally written in French, but it tries to remove one obstacle, if you are not French, to reading a book nominally called *Madame Bovary*. If you read it in French and keep translating it into English you are 'reading' two books; if you don't need to bother to remember your English you are, so to speak, genuinely bi-lingual.

As a psychoanalyst one is, of course, glibly and not so glibly tempted by Marx's reference to the mother tongue. One has only appropriated what he calls 'the spirit of the new language', one can only express oneself 'freely' – a not incidental word in the context – when one can 'manipulate it without reference to the old' and 'forget the original language while using the new one'. From a psychoanalytic point of view one could substitute sexuality here for language; one can only be a sexual adult, in a Freudian sense, when one can be sexual 'without reference' – or without too much reference – to the mother (and father); once, that is, one can sufficiently forget them. Freud's work, if you like, domesticates the revolution Marx is talking about; for Freud the revolution is the transforming of infantile sexuality into so-called adult sexuality. Indeed isn't Marx's description of the revolutionaries also a marvellous description of post-war adolescents? 'They borrow their names, slogans and costumes so as to stage the new world-historical scene in this venerable disguise and borrowed language.' To be slightly more accurate perhaps one should say, adolescence is the time when one repudiates the more venerable disguises; but it is often a revolutionary costume-drama.

The irony that Marx is pointing to is that rupture is only possible by simulating continuity. In this sense his description exploits at least the English meaning of the word revolution; that it means both a recurrence, and a mutation, a return and a severance. And this, of course, is one of the paradoxes at the heart of the practice of Freudian analysis: that only by, in some way, returning to or recounting the past can one sufficiently detach oneself from it to make a viable future. Marx's comparison of revolution with both learning a new language and with translation is apt because only by returning to a supposedly original text (or language) can one make a translation. No mother tongue, no foreign language, no translation. But what is the patient's mother tongue? Is there an equivalence, does it make useful sense, to describe a person in analysis being or having an original text?

The original text, one might say, is the words the patient keeps bringing into the analysis; the stories – with all their gaps and slips and hesitations – that the patient keeps telling. Indeed one could say, the repetitions in the patient's life are something like original text; and to translate these repetitions, that Freud saw as integral to a life, would be to render them unnecessary. It is as though these repetitions keep coming back for more translation until there is nothing left to translate. The repetitions keep insisting, so to speak, that they are the original text of a person's life; and therefore that there is such a thing. And the analyst keeps talking in a way that might dispel them, and so persuade the patient that there is no such thing as an original text to a life. The analyst translates to diminish the power of the repetition – where compulsion was, something like choice might be – and so to make something disappear. And here translation means redescription: in the service of dissolution. The patient translates – in the sense of moves across, transfers – earlier loves into a love for the analyst: transference might be another word for translation. And then the analyst redescribes these translations, if not to dissipate them at least to diminish their grip. The patient translates everybody into his parents, and he needs to be able to translate his love for his parents into love for other people. This is the revolution Freud calls the Oedipus complex; the child cannot 'have' the original parents, so he must defer his desire until he can find a sufficiently good translation: close enough to the original to be desirable, but different enough to be acceptably desirable. He cannot – if I can extend this analogy a bridge too far – if he is French read *Madame Bovary* in the original, he will have to find the best available translation.

In other words, in Oedipal terms, the child, once he becomes an adult, will recognize a good translation when he sees one. A bad translation will be one that is too close to the original; apparently so accurate, so undisguised, so reminiscent that he simply won't be able to enjoy it. If the person he desires is too like the parents he will feel confounded, inhibited, thwarted. A satisfying translation must be discernibly different from the original; otherwise it will be inaccessible. It would be a kind of Borgesian fable to imagine a world in which all the famous translations of classic texts had achieved this status by

successfully disguising what texts they were actually translations of.

There is something akin to translation going on in the
individual's development, Freud implies, because there is
forbidden desire.[I only need to translate my desire, because
the original text is unacceptable, against the law.]So like the
poets of Eastern Europe writing under Communism, translation becomes the art, as it were, of disguising an original; of
finding a way of writing something that is sufficiently
acceptable, or sufficiently irrelevant to the censor. For Freud
all writing, all speaking is of this order. And so the analyst, in
Laplanche's term, 'detranslates' the patient's material; not in
the sense of merely translating it back to some putative original,
but rather in the sense of disrupting it. Not getting it back to
some original language, but moving it on – or over – to some
future language.[The patient's language is fixed in a syntax of
habitual association; the aim of the analysis is to undo the
patient's favourite chains.]

There may be some psychic relief (and Borgesian irony) for
the translator of a text that his translation can never be identical
to the original. But from a psychoanalytic point of view there
will always be a question about what the translator feels
internally permitted to make of what he is given, to make of his
chosen text. It could of course be silly to think of the text as a
mother; but it is nevertheless true – both for internal and
external reasons – that the translator can't just do what he
wants with it. So I want to say, in this context, not that the
translator's text, as an object of desire, is like a mother, but
rather, what does translation look like – what would the
consequences be – if we started believing that translation was
an Oedipal drama? That the text to be translated is akin to the
mother's body, when the translator gets to work? As a
translator, what can you legitimately do with a text and how

is it decided? The translator, the text and the reader make three: but who does the text belong to?

The text cannot answer back but the language – like patients' speech – can seem resistant to translation. It can seem to refuse to be turned into a different language. It is indeed integral to psychoanalysis that the analyst analyses the patient's resistances; that, for some people, is what analysis is. But clearly the translator can't assume – or can't afford to assume – that the language of the text is, as it were, deliberately or unconsciously thwarting him. Freud said that the resistance is in the patient; Lacan, interestingly, said that the resistance is always in the analyst. What kind of sense does it make for the translator to say that the resistance is in the language? Psychoanalysis, like translation, and as translation, deals in all the obstacles to transformation; and its aim is to promote the possibilities for circulation, for freer exchange, for what Williams called a consciousness of possibilities and alternatives. And yet if psychoanalysis as theory and practice in many ways can't do without the analogy of translation – whether it is describing transference, or interpretation, or the body's capacity for representation – there is something clinically, something personally offensive for the patient about feeling that they have been only translated; as though to translate were to impose a language rather than to negotiate the making of one. And this, I think, sheds some interesting light on the topic under discussion, about the range and the limits of analogy.

4

A sixteen-year-old-girl was referred to me partly because she was depressed about the fact that she would still occasionally wet the bed, and more generally because she was lonely. When the person who had assessed her had asked her what she hoped to get from therapy, she had replied, 'A boyfriend'. The girl who came into my room was obviously mopingly miserable. Her face barely flickered when she met me, and she sat on the chair leaning slightly forward, hidden by a dank curtain of hair which she twirled in her fingers. She was grimly silent, not so much resisting as shy and just obviously unhappy. I failed to engage her in any kind of conversation, and eventually gave up, hoping that my silence might produce something that my words couldn't. After a few minutes, still twirling her hair, she said to me, 'Boring, isn't it?', referring ostensibly to her hair. I asked if she found me boring and had been hoping for somebody a little more interesting. She said, 'No, my hair', and then rather proudly, 'Actually, I'm rather boring.' I said, 'Being an interesting person, being exciting, or clever, or funny can feel quite dangerous.' At this she perked up a bit – it was as though something in her sat up – and she started telling me about a boy who lived in her street who was 'very funny, and all the girls really liked him'. She talked with such rapture about this boy, such albeit timid fascination, that it sounded as if she was a bit in love with him. So I said, rather obviously, 'It sounds as if you really like this boy'; and she got huffy and said, 'No, no, it's not like that, I've just got a strong affuction for him', and she blushed. I said, 'I know these things can be a bit embarrassing, but perhaps you like him more than you think.' And she said very crossly, 'You're just translating what I'm saying to you now, like everyone does.' I asked her for another example and she said, 'I say to my mum, I'm going round the shops, and my mum says, you mean you're going to hang around with those boys again. She thinks she can read my mind better than I can.' If translation here meant, for her, having something about her sexuality or her sociability intrusively exposed, it also meant being second guessed by someone more powerful. Her sense – or her sense of herself as knowing what she was doing – was being stolen from her. Translation was daylight robbery. To redescribe someone without apparently requiring their confirmation, or caring about their response, is clearly a form of control, if not outright bullying (one redescribes someone without their confirmation, of course, when one translates a dead author, or one who only speaks his native language). But in the slip she makes – affuction for affection – she translates herself, one might say. The Freudian unconscious is always translating our words for us. Her original text was, 'No, no, it's not like that, I've just got a strong affection for him'; but something inside her translated a key word, and made her say something else. For something inside her – from one of her points of view – affection was not quite the right word. The original word was modified, not replaced, so she could have it both ways. And one could say – as she herself implied – that the way in which her slip (or self-translation) was received by me was every bit as significant as what she herself had done. I partly detranslated the slip by implying that the starker sexual desire was the original text. She and I at this moment are having an argument about which is the real, the original, the significant text (there is a whole rhetoric here of essentialism). And we both have the same problem: if a translation is assumed to have taken place, there must be an original text. I am in a more articulate position, because I am older, and the so-called professional she has been sent to; and because I at least speak as if I know, broadly speaking, what the original text is. It is forbidden sexuality. When she feels what she calls 'translated' it is as if powerful people are ascribing to her an original text, and then accusing her of abiding by it. Redescription, one could say, becomes translation when it implies that there is an original. And authority is conferred on to the original. If we were to turn this round, and look at it from the point of view of the translator of a real text, the question becomes, what kind of authority does the text have – what kind of authority has been conferred upon the original text – that will constrain the inevitable redescription that all translation involves?

It is perhaps more bracing – more morally and intellectually rigorous – to think of the authority of the original text as either tyrannical, or as simply conducive to the necessary probity of the translator. That the text itself – and the institutional and social contexts within which it lives and has its being – provides some kind of limit or constraint on the translator's particular art. But I think we should also talk – somewhat along these lines – of the comfort of the text; of there being some reassurance in the fact that there is a real text to translate. That in translation of a text – as opposed, perhaps, to a person – there is, as it were, something to be true to; there has to be some correspondence, without having to revive a dogmatic correspondence theory of truth. Clearly the whole notion of being in any sense faithful to an original is imbued with moral considerations. Robert Lowell warns us, in the Introduction to his *Imitations*, against translators of poetry turning out 'a sprawl of language, neither faithful nor distinguished', implying that the translator has something to be faithful to, which might also include distinguishing himself through the poem he translates, as well as showing the poem itself to be a distinguished thing. The translator also uses the text to reveal something about himself; but it depends upon there being something there to be faithful to. The comfort of the text is that it is there, and that it is as it is. The words themselves don't change around.

It is, of course, one of the pleasures and one of the irritations of going to see an analyst that the analyst – or at least, most analysts, most of the time – is always there at the appointed time. And this is a particularly vivid issue when adolescents come for analysis. In the war between safety and excitement, reliability is something of a mixed blessing. The adolescent who is hungry for new people and new satisfactions keeps coming back – if he is lucky – to the same old familiar people, his parents, and the person he has become in relation to them. He is at the same time translating himself and staying close to the original. He moves out but he keeps coming back. The question is, how far away can you go without feeling that you are beginning to disappear? Or beginning to turn into someone else? Someone perhaps unrecognizable to those people at home?

A fourteen-year-old Jamaican boy, who had come to this country to live with relatives when he was four, and had moved around between relatives and children's homes ever since, was referred to me by his school for what they called, 'violent, bullying, aggressive behaviour'. In our first meeting he stayed for about ten minutes, told me insistently that he hated his school, and made himself instantly likeable to me. It was obvious to me that he wasn't spiteful, but that there were things he needed to persuade people of. The only thing I managed to say was that I imagined there were things he was right to be very cross about. This was so obvious to him that he barely bothered to register it. But at the end, just as he was leaving, he said over his shoulder, 'Thanks for that, man', and I thought, or wished, that he was referring to my remark. Then he didn't come for several weeks. I pursued him with letters, and eventually he came back. He said that he had just forgotten to come. I asked him if he was worried about being forgotten, and he said, 'No one forgets me, I make sure'. I wondered if he had to work quite hard at this. And he said, curiously, 'By fighting, you mean?', and I agreed. And he said, 'Man, you're just translating my words, I don't need this every week', and he grinned, and then came every week. In Freudian style, he was affirming something by negating it. And the gist of this is

142

simple, even though the consequences are not. What I think was being confirmed at that moment, was that there was something there to be translated, and that it was worth translating. The comfort of the text is that there is something – or someone, in this case – that one might be faithful to. Though this requires secularizing the language of faith, and so another translation.

5

If we translate a text there is, in a certain sense, an original text that is there to translate. If and when we translate a person, is there anything akin to this original text? There are obvious candidates: the original text might be the version of myself I want others (and myself) to see, or the version of myself I work at concealing; or it could be the version of myself that my parents needed me to be; or some quasi-biologically based notion of an innate true self, my basic character, or temperament. If there is this quintessence of myself – that exists in representational form – to talk of translation or redescription would be utterly misleading. The project would be not redescription, but description; to get a more accurate, and therefore reliable sense of what I really am. The untranslated, and untranslatable self. The implication of this particular quest is that everything of value will follow from finding who one really is.

The alternative to this is the apparently more absurd and strangely plausible possibility that there is no original text, no essential self (or version of the self); that there are just an unknowable series of translations of translations; preferred versions of ourselves, but not true ones. So we need not aim to get closer to our true selves – or try to be better and better at being authentic – so much as be available for retranslation whenever we suffer and desire. And that we need not only suffer other people's redescriptions of us, but that we can also enjoy some of them, and be interested in the fact that this is what we are doing with each other. Instead of the culture of complaint in which we are forever aggrieved about being misunderstood, we would think of misunderstanding as the name of the game: except we would call misunderstanding translation (or dream-work). In this world we wouldn't bother to think, 'Why doesn't he/she understand me?', we would simply be endlessly fascinated by what people make of us. We would be as, if not more, interested in what people hear in what we say, than in what we think we are saying. And our conversation would then involve us working out, as far as we could, why we prefer some translations to others; and why we find some so offensive. But we would have to do this without believing that there is an original that we can compare the available translations with. The way people describe us, and the ways we describe ourselves, correspond to nothing except other descriptions (our mothers, our fathers, our analysts don't know who we are: they have their versions). There is no real, privileged, original me to refer back to; but you might ask me what I think of your descriptions of me. I don't, though, have the real, original text in front of me to check your (or my) descriptions against. I am like a country without a map; or a country that is being always impressionistically mapped. If racism, like sexism, is the militant refusal to allow people self-definition, the question then becomes, are people more or less vulnerable – and what exactly are they vulnerable to – without compelling essential definitions of themselves? What does not needing to believe that you have a true self, or a real identity, free you to do? If my own version of who I am (and what I want) is not a privileged one – is not taken into consideration – then I am less self-reliant than I thought.

144

The paradox I am proposing is the notion of translation without there being anything like an original text there to translate. So, in the notion of translating a person, what exactly is available for translation? Is the whole notion of translating a person simply a poor analogy? Or could it be part of what Raymond Williams called in his lecture, 'the will to a wider perspective' which, as he rightly says, 'is always more readily accessible to a fascinated observer than to the sons and daughters of the history who had its defeats ... in their bones'. In other words, it may be all very well for me to be promoting the wonders of translation – the fascinating freedoms of redescription – without taking seriously the very real constraints one comes up against in the quest for a wider perspective, a consciousness of possibilities. The defeats, over generations, that people have in their bones, could make the analogy of translation seem like part of the problem rather than the solution. Because one of the ingredients of the defeats Williams is talking about is of people being translated against their will, having translations imposed upon them by a dominant class or group. Not being permitted one's own version of oneself – as a person, or as a group – is a fundamental form of oppression. After all, if we are not the authority on who we are, who is? And if there is no authority now to confer identity upon us – if no original text of ourselves exists anywhere – how will we recognize an accurate version of ourselves? In other words, if oppression can be politely called imposed translation, what are the alternatives?

We don't tend to talk of a text collaborating with its translator, though the author of the text may do this. People often come for psychotherapy these days suffering from translations of themselves they don't feel that they have collaborated in. There is a difference between a parent saying to a child, 'You're a shy person', and their saying to a child, 'Are there situations that make you feel shy?' There is a difference between an analyst telling her so-called patient what his dream means, and telling her patient what his dream has made her think. In other words, at least in psychoanalysis – and perhaps not only there – the *only good translation is the one that invites retranslation; the one that doesn't want to be verified so much as altered*. When it comes to books we may want to be reading the definitive translation of *Madame Bovary*; when it comes to people there could be no comparable definitive version. The analyst aims to give the patient something he can use and not merely copy to make his own new translation – not with slogans, but with food for thought, not passwords but invitations.

And yet these admirable aims of the analyst as facilitator, or midwife, or provider of tools – the analyst as collaborative translator – is also a cover story, because the analyst himself has his own preferred versions of the patient. There is, that is to say, no good collaboration without antagonism. Psychotherapy produces competing accounts of the patient and of the therapist. But what are they deemed to be accounts of, and is the aim to produce a definitive or a provisionally satisfying version? Once again – or put like this – it seems like an absurd situation. Two people trying to make a sufficiently satisfying translation of a person that can't be located. Supposing there is agreement between the analyst and the patient about the patient's history, what is it going to be checked against? Instead of asking, as one might of a translated text, is it accurate, have we got it right, did these events that we have reconstructed really happen to create the present predicament, [we should be asking what kind of life would believing this make possible?] What could this translation lead you to do? One would be interested in the possible consequences of the translation; one would be referring forward, not referring back.

Nietzsche

" The falseness of an opinion is not for us any objection to it ... The question is how far it is life-furthering, life-preserving, species-preserving, perhaps species-creating". (Beyond Good &

In translating a person – if the analogy is to be of any use – we have to do something different. We have to translate while suspending our belief in an original; and in the full acknowledgement that we could never get it right. Indeed, to believe we had got it right would be to implicitly assume the existence of this original, this ur-text of ourselves. The quest might not be for the Grail, but for the quest itself. The aim of psychoanalysis would be to free people to translate and be translated, rather than to acquire a definitive, convincing version of themselves. In other words, when we set out to translate a person – to translate a text that doesn't exist – we have to make it up as we go along. But we have to make it up together.

Appreciating Pater

It is not portrayal that destabilizes, it is praise.
Dave Hickey, *The Invisible Dragon*

In a contemporary review of *The Renaissance* in the *Pall Mall Gazette*, the critic Sidney Colvin wrote that 'the book is not one for any beginner to turn to in search of "information"'. 'Information' was in inverted commas not because there were no facts or respectable opinions in the book, but because Pater did not seem to believe in information, as it was customarily understood in criticism of the arts. As most reviewers seemed to agree, he wasn't doing something new, he was doing something badly. 'In the matter of historical fact,' Denis Donoghue writes, joining in, as it were, 'Pater also took liberties, so many that it is a pity he did not derive more satisfaction from them.' But Pater was satisfied not by getting it wrong, but by not having to get it right[It was his style to affirm invention over accuracy and, indeed, satisfaction over argument]

Pater was neither scholarly nor overtly confessional; and he seemed unembarrassed by what a work of art could do to him, or how it tempted him to write about it. His approach tended to be, in Donoghue's arch but apt phrase, 'free of empirical duty'. Matthew Arnold and Modern Science could give you the object as in itself it really was; could give you the best, the most reliable, salutary truths. What Pater gave you were his impressions and his style. And his style unashamedly competed for

Review of Denis Donoghue, *Walter Pater: Lover of Strange Souls*, (Knopf, 1995), from the *London Review of Books*.

attention with what he was apparently writing about ('Pater's sentences,' Donoghue writes, 'ask to be read as if they wanted to be looked at, not merely to be understood'). The real interest for Pater was in what the art, and the life of the artist, could evoke in him; what he could use it to become. Or rather, to write; because it was only in sentences that Pater became himself. He was, in other words, at least as interested in himself as he was in the art or artists he wrote about. For those keen to humble themselves in front of Great Art – or, more important, Great Religion – this was something of an affront.

The 'chief question', Pater wrote in *The Renaissance*, that the critic must ask of the artist is: 'What is the peculiar sensation, what is the peculiar quality of pleasure, which his work has the property of exciting in us, and which we cannot get elsewhere?' The critic was not asked to describe the formal qualities of the work, nor its historical context: he was invited to describe his pleasure. This, of course, was a question, and an invitation, calculated to appeal to those young enough, or bold enough, to have confidence in their possibilities for pleasure. Pater assumed, at least in his writing, that pleasure and sensation – not to mention the peculiar – were morally good. So when *The Renaissance* was published in 1873 it was a scandal, at least in Oxford. Pater was a homosexual Oxford don who lived with his two sisters, and scandal was anathema to him. The subjects that he treated – Pico della Mirandola, Botticelli, Leonardo, Du Bellay, Winckelmann, among others – seemed harmless enough. But the book that Wilde would notoriously refer to as his 'golden book' was too timely to be the work of an innocent. 'The' was the misleading word in the title; Pater was proposing a renaissance of aesthetic values – the renaissance, during the Renaissance, of pre-Christian values – that was manifestly antithetical to the official versions of itself that Victorian England was promoting.

In flagrant disregard for the responsibilities of his academic position, Pater seemed to be encouraging the natural paganism of youth at a time in their lives when those privileged under-graduates – the 'beginners' Sidney Colvin covertly refers to – were supposed to be consolidating their faith in Christianity and the Empire. ('Pater's England,' Donoghue writes, 'is not the country as given; on that, he has little purchase.') Pater seemed to be suggesting in his infamous Conclusion that we have nothing to redeem but our moments of pleasure, and nothing to do beyond the having of special, pleasurable experiences. Life was about intensity and not achievement, about meaning and not profit; diligence was bad faith. His ideas, such as they were, were not original, nor did he claim that they were. An elegant confection of pre-Socratic philosophy, German Romanticism and French aestheticism, his writing mocked the grander ambitions of Late Victorian England as much by the oddity of its style as by the old beliefs it claimed were being recycled during the Renaissance. To the champions of moral and material progress – the scientists and the political idealists as much as the divines and the cultural critics – Pater had written a heretical text. 'Our failure is to form habits,' Pater had written. You couldn't make a society that was getting anywhere out of Pater's ideas.

The problem that every biographer of Pater has had is that Pater didn't make much of a life out of these ideas either. By all accounts he did not cut much of a dash in the world; there is more perplexity and distaste than affection or admiration in the reminiscences of him that Donoghue reports. And there was a dismal lack, at least from the spectator's point of view, of erotic or other adventures. He was physically unprepossessing, nice and rather remote: 'an ugly pig', as Arthur Symons put it, 'though learned and charming too'. Pater seems to have believed, perhaps like some of his biographers, that without looks you can't have a life. When Wilde was told that Pater had died, he replied that he did not know that he had lived. It was as though, even to his contemporaries, he was solely interesting for his writing. Unlike Flaubert, whom he admired, he had no Egypt. The style was the life, nothing else about him fascinated. Pater's peculiar sentences became his character; all that was left of him, it seems, even while he was alive. 'I think he has had – will have had – the most exquisite literary fortune,' Henry James wrote to Edmund Gosse when Pater died in 1894, 'i.e. to have taken it out all, wholly, exclusively, with the pen (the style, the genius) & absolutely not at all with the person. He is the mask without the face.' For James, Pater's biography *is* his style. But for many other people the ridiculous thing about Pater was that he had a biography without a life, a grand, unusual style uninformed by experience. As a person, Pater was often considered an unappealing mixture of the preposterous and the feeble; his writing has a talent for making people supercilious. But the derision itself – from his earliest reviewers to Eliot's influential essay of 1930, 'Arnold and Pater', and even sometimes to Donoghue – is telling. So much animus spells some complicity. And some doubt about how to make sense of Pater, when he kept himself to his sentences.

Modern biographers, thwarted by the fact that nobody knows anymore what is of significance in a life, solve the problem by trying to include everything, though the contemporary fantasy of what everything is is rather predictable. Biographies are so long now not merely because we have more information, but because lives no longer have plots, they only have detail. Biography gives shape to a life, but a life doesn't. When it comes to 'Lives' – as Pater clearly realized in his *Imaginary Portraits*, and his own autobiographical writing – less is more. But when it comes to Pater's life there has never been enough. Or no one has been sufficiently intrigued by the disparity that James, among others, remarked on.

For the critics of biography, Pater would seem to be an ideal case: there is no discernible or apparently useful connection between what Pater did each day and what he wrote. He seems, Donoghue writes, 'sentence by sentence, a textual self in the art of becoming'; and this makes him grist for the modern mill. There is nothing outside the text, certainly not a man who sits down to breakfast. And yet, paradoxically, all of Pater's writing attests to the necessity and the enigma of the connection. All of Pater's writing about art is an idiosyncratic mixture of the biographical and the autobiographical, as though for him they were always inextricable. There is no biography, he implies, without autobiography; but also, and more interestingly, there is no autobiography without biography. We make our lives, though often hermetically, out of the lives of others. None of Pater's biographers have taken up his ironic, implicit invitation to join him to his sentences.

When it comes to biography – the connections, if any, between the man who suffers and the mind which creates, in Eliot's lurid terms – Donoghue prefers a mystery to a possible oversimplification. 'There is a relation between them ...' he affirms, conceding nothing, 'but the relation is occult, it can't be specified. The best reason for evoking the creative imagination is that the phrase indicates our sense of this opacity.' As, one assumes, would the word 'God'. Pater, like all real artists, made things up, Donoghue asserts; that is what it is to have an imagination. But when people stand up for mystery you can never be sure which laws they are laying down. Indeed, one of the things that characterizes a genuine mystery, one might think, is its resilience. A 'mind' and its work would be virtually profaned, Donoghue intimates, if they were 'explained or explained away by reciting the personal, domestic, social, economic and political conditions of its production'. Creative imagination or wholesale reduction seem implausible alternatives, calculated to pre-empt the interesting complexity of the issue. The imagination can also, of course, speculate without specifying, make useful or intriguing links without merely fixing the material. The injunction not to enquire into such matters seems pointlessly prohibitive. Good literary biographies, though rare, have been written. This is not one; but partly because, by Donoghue's own admission, it is 'a critical biography, a Brief Life'. But why include any 'Life' at all if it merely gets in the way, if it is just an opportunity for false supposition?

As a biography of a person *Walter Pater* seems often cursory, and occasionally derisive of its subject. Pater, Donoghue writes, 'remained the don who got a poor second', lived in a 'bashful little house' with his 'spinster sisters'; and valued them 'for the civilized order they ensured while he entertained his undergraduates to hand-holding teas'. Donoghue makes as little as possible of Pater's homosexuality; and he reproves him, not infrequently, as though he were a boy, 'cheeky', 'insolent' and never bold enough. As an account of a style – though not quite a biography of a style – *Walter Pater* is often brilliant and always engaging, even when Donoghue's piety grates on one's own. Much like Pater himself, Donoghue uses his subject for his own purposes, not least of which is a spirited and eloquent contemporary defence of art for art's sake. Like all such defences it sometimes betrays the fastidious, precious enthusiasm that can make art sound like a monument to the most futile kind of moral superiority. At its best, though, Donoghue's eloquence shows us the good senses in which art might be better kept to itself; and what it loses when treated merely as a substitute or a symptom – viz. everything that makes it different from a substitute or a symptom.

For Donoghue, art represents the possibility of other (secular) worlds. But his misgivings about art as a substitute religion are as severe as his commitment to art as a haven. ('We should read literature in the spirit in which we enter a concert hall.') Pater is an important puzzle for Donoghue because he assumes the supreme value of art, but with a quasi-religious fervour; and his own art of aesthetic criticism seems often to level, and always to exploit, its subjects; to convert them, as it were, to his own style. Pater's writing celebrates idiosyncrasy, but avoids conflict – 'Difference, yes, but not opposition' is Donoghue's motto for him. Pater's 'appreciations' show an obtrusive disregard for everything other than Pater's style. Irreverent towards conformities, his style consumes everything in its path. What he is interested in becomes an opportunity to perform more Pater. For anyone concerned, as Donoghue is, about the ethics of a style – the imperiousness of certain kinds of writing – Pater is a provocation.

Like Swift, Yeats and Emily Dickinson – the other individual writers Donoghue has devoted books to – Pater unavoidably invites the questions that have always inspired Donoghue as a critic. Are writers people who, because they cannot bear the world, make it their own, in words; or are they people who so cherish the world that they want to show us the very different things it contains? Are they megalomaniacs or midwives? (The obvious answer is: usually both, like everybody else.) But this is the distinction – with its inevitable theological implications – that has been at the heart of Donoghue's remarkable critical project. What kind of god is the writer, an aesthetic narcissist or an aesthetic altruist? And what relationship, if any, does he have to God – competitive, complementary, humble etc? It is a question of 'the rivalry', as he put it in his Introduction to *The Ordinary Universe* nearly thirty years ago, 'between the persuasions of the natural world and the structure of one's own imagination, between Ordinary Things and Supreme Fictions'. In Pater the Supreme Fiction wins, but it is a style and not a myth.

Walter Pater becomes a remarkable book once Donoghue has got the determinedly Brief Life over with (it is a mere eighty pages in a book of over 300). What he calls 'Pater's quiet audacity' is like a foil for his own more abrasive refinement. Pater's shrewd refusals, his disavowal of the quotidian, confronts Donoghue with a new version of his own abiding aesthetic preoccupations. Though his writing has been impressively various, in successive books this conflict between the Ordinary Universe and the Supreme Fiction has been redescribed and theorized with a kind of stubborn eloquence. With Donoghue, unlike many other critics, passion has not shrunk to an obsession. His often brilliant close readings have been reassuringly unpredictable; but his surprises are always framed by an underlying contention. In *Yeats* (1971) he quoted Blackmur's distinction between the erotic poet and the sacramental poet. 'A sacramental poet,' Donoghue commented,

respects the object for itself, but even more for the spirit which, however mysteriously, it contains ... such a poet is always willing to 'let be', he is merely the spirit's celebrant. An erotic poet may respect the object in itself, but it is not characteristic of him to do so, and beyond the point of acknowledgment the only relevant spirit is his own and he is never willing to let be ... the object has helped him to define his power, and he is tender toward it for that reason.

In his wonderful T. S. Eliot Lectures, *Thieves of Fire*, Donoghue borrowed Adrian Stokes's similar distinction between carving and modelling in sculpture, as a way of talking about both different ways of writing and different kinds of writer: 'Carving is concerned with the release of significance deemed already to exist, imprisoned in the stone, and modelling is a more plastic process by which the sculptor imposes his meaning upon the stone.' These are useful descriptions because they imply that the artist's relationship to his or her medium is also analogous to a person's relationship with others, indeed with everything that is not himself. The aesthetic, that is to say, becomes unavoidably ethical. The writer's relationship to language – to what he seems to want to do with words – is a picture of a form of life.

The carver (Blackmur's sacramental poet) says: 'I'm not telling you, I'm showing you.' Carvers are akin to scientists in so far as they claim simply to disclose what is already there. What they discover, though, is often something we then have to submit to (or worship) like a natural law or an essence. The risk for the carver is that he may be merely complying with the way things are supposed to be; by realizing things as they are he leaves everything as it is. But then what could be more narcissistic, more grandiose, than the belief that one is in a position to recognize anything as it really is, the intrinsic essence of something (or someone)? The risk for the modeller (the erotic poet) is that he is an aesthetic entrepreneur: he can't leave anything alone because everything must be used for profit. Nothing is sufficiently real, or satisfying, until it is transfigured by his desire. The carver is always telling us, but sometimes under the guise of showing us. As a critic Donoghue has always been a carver trying not to be a modeller; and the critic as modeller is often one of Donoghue's targets (*Walter Pater* has a smack at Bloom). And yet it has been 'erotic poets' like Yeats and Stevens that Donoghue has been drawn to. Pater, the critic as artist, the modeller with the manners of a carver, is, therefore, a special case for him.

What exasperates Donoghue about Pater – and compels some of the finest criticism in this book – is that Pater tries to have it both ways; he has the shy modesty of the carver, and the arrogant obliviousness of the modeller. His modesty was a demand for submission. 'If a church, or any other object were completely itself,' Donoghue writes, 'it seemed stolid, impenetrable, opaque to the imagination. Pater liked to find its certitude a little ashamed of itself and willing to entertain at least an occasional doubt or misgiving. He wanted the imagination to have a chance of gaining access to any matter.' Donoghue is on the side of the imagination, but he is also mindful of what happens when nothing is acknowledged to resist the imagination. If it gains access to everything there will be nothing left. What Donoghue cares for is the imagination that can love whatever resists it; or can, at least, notice that there is resistance somewhere. In *Walter Pater*, though, you sometimes get the feeling that for Donoghue, Pater would have been better off if he had just believed in original sin; as though he needed to locate recalcitrance somewhere, needed something to make a mockery of his wishes. When Donoghue writes that 'Pater's chief concern was his pleasure in feeling alive,' you feel Pater is being mysteriously admonished.

Donoghue wants Pater to come clean and get his axes out ('His tone was consistently urbane, as if the grinding of an axe was the last thing he intended'). On the one hand, Pater is 'a witness to the charm of the intrinsic', but only of moods and feelings and the transitions between them. On the other hand, and less to Donoghue's taste, in Pater's writing 'the object doesn't matter; what matters is the mind's experience of pleasure in lavishing attention upon it.' The indulgence of Pater's determined disregard makes Donoghue droll with exasperation ('One of the limitations of Pater's essay on Vézelay is that he knew virtually nothing about the iconography of church architecture'). There is, it should be said, virtually nothing that Pater writes about that Donoghue knows virtually nothing about: indeed, judging by his corrections of

Pater, he often knows more. What Donoghue refers to as Pater's commitment to 'those visionary artists who refuse to transcribe the data before them and insist upon the privilege of their own vision' should have been a problem for him, as it is for Donoghue. It is clear that Donoghue wants Pater to be more troubled by his preferences and affinities, more bothered by his taken liberties ('Pater does not bother with meanings that may be established by scholarship'). He is continually dismayed by Pater's refusal of conflict, by the absence of drama in his writing. And yet when Donoghue's indignation about Pater's irresponsibility doesn't get the better of him – and there is some wonderful commentary in this book, particularly on *Diaphanéité, Plato and Platonism and Marius* – he defines better than anyone else the unique paradox of Pater's position: that he was antinomial without being oppositional. He found a way of being adversarial that wasn't merely a relish for conflict. Pater didn't go his own way because he was spoiling for a fight.

Donoghue's Pater is this 'antinomian'; he lived, Donoghue writes, 'by inflecting the official life offered him'. 'Inflecting' seems just right, as Donoghue often is in this puzzling and puzzled book; it catches the way Pater modifies rather than confronts, the way he can be radical without apparently having an argument. Pater's lack of reverence for antagonism – expressed in his almost total disregard for it – makes him, by definition as it were, difficult to place ('He claims for his refusals just as much respect as everyone gives to conflicts and causes'). Compared with the forthrightness of Carlyle, or Ruskin, or Arnold, or Wilde, Pater seems very hush-hush. But Donoghue is never quite sure in this book whether Pater is exemplary or just lazy. He is certainly an exemplary aesthete: 'An aesthete is an artist who considers what he can do by standing aside. What he does has its adversary merit in relation to the Victorian consensus on the moral value of work.' It is Donoghue's version of Pater as an asider – an insider as a middle-class Oxford don and an outsider as a uniquely bizarre writer, and a homosexual – that is the real interest of this book. 'He would prefer,' Donoghue writes, though he himself would not, 'to live without categories or definitions, or aside from them.' Pater is difficult to categorize as a writer because he was so uncategorical, so definitively vague.

It is almost as though Pater has allowed Donoghue to stand up for the virtues of aestheticism, while still being dismayed by its provenance, or even its necessity. He can only adopt Pater by resisting him, by making him out to be a slippery slope. 'Aestheticism,' he writes, 'was one expression of the premonition, sad indeed, that most of life, in the forms in which it presented itself, could not be understood and yet must be lived.' *Walter Pater*, among other things, is an irritated elegy for the contemporary death of aestheticism; and its severity is often as moving, and witty, as are its celebrations. Donoghue, though, does not tell us why it is quite so sad, nor why it should be otherwise.

For Pater, success in life was not to do with diligence or application: it was 'to burn always with this hard gem-like flame, to maintain this ecstasy' of secular epiphanies. No flame, of course, has ever been able to do this, let alone any person. But what Pater was repudiating with these bold assertions was, in a sense, as important as what he was affirming. Careerism and routine and transcendence were his targets, with objectivity as a necessary casualty (consensus, Pater implies, is just a way of making and enforcing new habits). The idea of genius was so crucial for Pater because geniuses are people who break our habits for us. If it is the distinctiveness, the achievement of a style that, as Donoghue asserts, 'is nearly all that literature from

Pater to Stevens claims to achieve', then Pater may, indeed, have given 'modern literature its first act'. That style should be the thing, that the erotic poets should triumph over the sacramental poets, is for Donoghue a mixed blessing. But it is because Donoghue won't let Pater be that he has written such an engaged, tetchy book.

Minding Out

If we picture the mind as an orifice then we cannot help but wonder what it should be open to and what it should be open for. And how it, or rather we, make such vital decisions. An open mind is not an open door: 'open-mindedness' merely describes what is, for some people, a preferred way of discriminating. This openness, once looked into, usually makes us seem rather more like connoisseurs than we might wish: more picky than free. After all, at its most minimal, the open-minded have to know what they must keep out of their minds to keep them open (sexual desire, religion and ideology are the traditional candidates). Religions and therapies help people to close out certain thoughts so they can be open to better ones. An open mind, as Northrop Frye remarked, has to be open at both ends. So when we think of ourselves as open-minded we think of ourselves as open to the right kinds of thing. We have doors in order to be able to close them. Our attention is not so much selective as exclusive.

People are radically perplexed and often go for therapy because they have been too open to something or other in their lives, too unprotected. Defensiveness is a reaction to violation. Freudians believe that we are inevitably violated both from within and from without: our egos are violated by our desires and by what happens to us. So the Freudian cannot imagine a life without defences, but only a life spent trying to find the best ways to protect himself from his life in order to be able to go on

Review of Jonathan Lear, *Open-Minded: Working Out the Logic of the Soul*, (Harvard University Press, 1998) from the *London Review of Books*.

living it, with sufficient pleasure. But if survival and pleasure have been the more or less common-sense purposes of a Freudian life, some of Freud's followers found this a rather drastic – not to say, secular – reduction of what a life might be. It was as though the aims of survival and pleasure needed the idea of progress in order to be taken seriously. So those who wanted more from life resorted to the ancient notion of a life having a telos, a purpose it is there to realize. We don't merely change over time, we (more grandly) grow. In this collection of essays Jonathan Lear, a philosopher and a psychoanalyst, wants to show us that it is what he calls the 'logic of the soul' to want open-mindedness; and this is because, in his view (and in the tradition of psychoanalysis that he values), the logic of the soul is a logic of development. Above all, we want to grow up, to become who we have it in ourselves to be. And this entails understanding and being understood. 'Each natural organism,' Lear wrote in his wonderful book *Aristotle: The Desire to Understand*, 'has within it a desire to do those things necessary to realizing and maintaining its form ... the strong desire to survive, to sustain life, to flourish and reproduce is, from another perspective, a striving to become intelligible.' If, at its best, living your life means feeling you are getting somewhere, then reading Aristotle will be more reassuring than reading Freud.

What makes *Open-Minded* so compelling is that it is born of an improbable and sometimes rather inspired marriage of Lear's two culture heroes, Aristotle and Freud. And even though his book has occasional longueurs of teacherly explanation – and very occasionally a distracting old-worldly donnishness ('most people have the unfortunate fate of having to live with a preconscious misconception of Aristotle's metaphysics') – it is more often than not vividly illuminating both about its chosen subject and about the way it goes about getting the odd couple together. Its thesis – or perhaps its faith – is that the suffering born of closure is worse than the suffering born of (at least relative) openness. And the route to openness, Lear believes, is understanding: a key word in his theoretical vocabulary, and a more controversial word in psychoanalysis than he acknowledges.

It has been one of the more interesting legacies of Freud's work to make analysts wonder whether there is such a thing as understanding between people, and if there is, how it works. Why we might want to believe that we are intelligible to ourselves and others was what interested Freud, not merely how we can get better and better at doing it. What is the wish for understanding a wish for? If understanding isn't the best currency we've got, then what is? 'Unconscious motivation,' Lear wrote in his previous book, *Love and Its Place in Nature*,

can be thought of as striving to be understood. Of course, in the most basic sense, unconscious wishes are striving to get themselves satisfied. But the fact that love is a basic force in the world means that these primitive mental forces also incline towards higher levels of organization ... in fact, the activity of understanding the wish ... is an expression of the wish itself at its highest level of development.

There are, perhaps, two facts too many here. It was that 'most basic sense' that Freud couldn't get round, and believed that we couldn't get round either, despite our talk of love and understanding; 'higher' levels of organization and development – all those old-fashioned progress myths that kept the primitives away – were like so much pulp fiction, irresistible (even to Freud) but suspect. From a psychoanalytic point of view sophistication is just another form of nostalgia.

For Lear, then, the enemy of understanding need not be unconscious desire – all those clamorous, striving primitive wishes – but knowingness. There is, he believes, 'a crisis of knowingness in the culture'. And it is knowingness as a fundamental form of self-deception that is the abiding pre-occupation of the twelve essays that make up this book[our minds as always already made up, rather than always in the making] We are suffering, in effect, from prejudice and dog-matism and not from our own nature. Desire is not intrinsically a problem so long as it is helped by others – a mother, an analyst, a culture – to evolve towards intelligibility. 'The point of a theory of drives,' he writes in an essay on the remarkable American analyst Hans Loewald, 'is to give us an account of the elements of mental life. We want to understand that from which mature mental life emerges.' The body, as it were, aspires to the condition of mature mental life. Those of us who aren't quite sure what mature mental life is may bristle at the terminology, but it brings with it a simple model of what the practice of psychoanalysis might entail if these are one's ambitions. 'The analyst,' Lear writes, endorsing Loewald, 'is more highly organized than the analysand. The psychoanalytic process facilitates a transmission of organization across this field.' I would guess that only a psychoanalyst would agree with this – or perhaps, someone in search of a philosopher-king. Of course the analyst must have, or rather be assumed to have, something of value that the analysand lacks. But to describe what mothers do for children and – by implication, given that this model is mother-child based – what analysts can do for their analysands as some form of organizing activity begs too many (psychoanalytic) questions. A life conceived of as progressively structured in the service of greater intelli-gibility is not to be scorned, but at its worst it is a tautology bordering on solipsism: if the analyst already knows what the more highly organized person is like, then he is only facilitating what he has previously invented. After all, how could the analysand even know what mature mental life was without being told by an analyst?

All this may just be a way of saying that the psychoanalyst – like Socrates, about whom Lear writes so well in this book – always runs the risk of being too knowing about knowingness. Inevitably, Lear's confidence in psychoanalysis and philosophy – and psychoanalysis is often presented here as the consummation of a philosophical tradition – is underwritten by the belief that one can know knowingness when one sees it, and not turn that recognition into a higher form of the thing one fears. To write about self-deception with any gusto or subtlety one has to be able to imagine the self undeceived. This is, needless to say, a more plausible project for Lear's Aristotle than for Lear's Freud. Because Man, as we used to be called, was for Freud the self-deceiving animal, through fear of his own nature. Freud didn't talk about 'human flourishing', he talked about compromise formations. 'Aristotle,' Lear has written, 'had great faith in the world: indeed, his philosophy is an attempt to give the world back to creatures who desire to understand it.' Freud, whose 'world' was rather different from Aristotle's, did not have this great faith.

If it is somehow reassuring to discover that Freud has such (uncontroversially) great, culturally prestigious precursors – that psychoanalysis is part of a respectable tradition, not a tacky one – it is at the same time interesting (and shocking) to see what links can be made between Freud's disputed 'science' and the abiding monuments of Western culture, Aristotle and his necessary precursor Plato. Lear wants Freud and Aristotle to get on, and this requires a certain artfulness. 'Philosophy, Aristotle said, begins in wonder,' he writes. 'Psychoanalysis begins in wonder that the unintelligibility of the events which surround one do not cause more wonder.' So is it more wonder that we should want, or more philosophy? Is psychoanalysis our best way of keeping the wonder going? Lear's questions in this book are so good that his answers don't matter that much: what he asserts never gets in the way of what he wonders about. So his fundamental point – the formulation that the book keeps circling round – is, deftly, an assertion about a question:

Plato, one might say, is working out *the very idea* of what it is to be minded as we are. And he does this in the light of Socrates' exemplification – a life spent showing – that one of the most important truths about us is that we have the capacity to be *open-minded*: the capacity to live non-defensively with the question of how to live.

Human life in general is a study of why this capacity is not exercised: why open-mindedness is, for the most part, evaded, diminished and attacked.

One way to live non-defensively with the question is to go on asking it, even though, in doing so, we are defending the belief that it is a good question. 'Non-defensively' might imply that we had nothing to protect, that we didn't need protection. And one form of protection we might crave is legitimation, being sanctioned by something or someone. The capacity that Lear is sponsoring, and that is so very difficult to be open-minded about, is something to do with not being bullied. Or not being bullyable. The paradox he hints at is that you can live non-defensively only if you feel sufficiently protected; and that the project of a human life is to question what the project of a human life is for. A life in this view – a life worth the name, so to speak – is essentially self-reflexive. I think about my life, therefore I am, therefore I have one. If this seems unduly restrictive, if self-reflexiveness often seems to be the problem rather than the solution, it is also, by the same token, a succinct statement of what has been held up as an exemplary form of life to us. Is the Socratic question, that Lear sees psychoanalysis as

166

keeping alive, a good question simply because Socrates asked it? What, in short, makes it a good question?

It is probably better not to assume that our reasons for living – our best self-justifications – are the real value of our lives. And Lear himself has a sober and lucid sense of the limits of our good reasons. 'What we work through,' he writes in an essay on Wittgenstein's later philosophy,

is a myth of legitimation: an illusion that giving reasons will provide an ultimate ground of our activity ... Having worked through the illusion, the philosopher in the kitchen may well still give reasons for his particular cooking activities ... but he no longer suffers a self-inflicted misunderstanding of what his explanation might do for him.

The philosopher no longer suffers from a 'self-inflicted misunderstanding' when he realizes that the only thing his explanation does is explain something. Socrates, Plato, Aristotle, Wittgenstein, Freud: they are all engaged, in Lear's view, in a high-level conversation about self-inflicted misunderstanding; and so about a self that keeps inflicting such things on itself, and is better off not doing so. Self-deception, they all agree (if for rather different reasons), is self-destructive. The truth is on our side; has our best interests in mind.

If Lear's approach risks smothering the differences between these figures – and he is as attentive to questions of context as space allows in these essays – it also alerts us to one of the more intriguing subplots of his book: the issue of cultural transmission. Just as the analyst/mother transmits more evolved forms of 'organization' to the child/analysand, so these figures seem, by implication, to transmit their preoccupations (and questions) to us: to organize our curiosity. But for Lear there is something equally, if not more important than this, which he refers to as 'legacy as task'. 'When we talk of a legacy,' he writes, our speech is often tinged with an ambiguity which suggests ambivalence. There is, of course, the straightforward sense of a bequest – as with Freud's passing on to us the idea of the repressed unconscious. But there is also a sense of legacy as that which a person did *not* hand down (but should have). Here the legacy is a task: it is the unfinished business which the child needs to complete in order to ... succeed the parent.

Whether he is writing of the apparent 'jumble' that is Plato's *Republic* or the apparent 'disparateness of Wittgenstein's *Philosophical Investigations*, it is Lear's inclination to see these works as not so much incoherent as inevitably unfinished: they leave the reader with something to do (next). Freud's legacy-as-task, or rather the task which Lear supposes he left us, and which he convincingly shows Loewald to have picked up on, was to develop a plausible theory of Eros. This was something of an oversight on Freud's part: he effectively tells us that there are two instincts ruling our lives, love and death, but he doesn't tell us what love is. 'It is a corollary of the Oedipus complex,' Lear writes, 'that creativity requires that one come to grips with the legacies of one's intellectual parents.' But there is a jump here where there should be a bridge. What is it the corollary of to think of oneself as having 'intellectual parents'? Or to put it more straightforwardly, what is the connection between the legacy-as-task of one's real parents and that of one's intellectual parents? It is noticeable, for example, that people are often rather more impressed by their intellectual parents than the other ones; the cultural re-parenting that goes on – the way children adopt new parents as they grow up – is a stranger process than Lear's reference to the Oedipus complex allows. It certainly tends to dignify one's affinities.

It is nevertheless more generous, and more truthful, to think of good writers not as somehow flawed, but as leaving their readers with unfinished business. As though these writers offer us irresistible invitations – to think, to write, to talk – and this is what keeps the story going. Another way of putting this would be to say that the dead are very demanding; and that we keep in touch with them, we keep them alive, by imagining they still want something from us (what we call a culture or a tradition becomes the way we go on running imaginary errands for the dead). But for Lear what the open-minded are open to, at their best, are the cultural and personal pasts they inherit. Unlike Harold Bloom's anxiety of influence, to which it is clearly linked, Lear's legacy-as-task speaks of the pleasurable challenge of influence. It is a less violent Oedipus complex he would wish on us.

It is perhaps inevitable that a book so haunted, and sometimes dogged, by affiliation and its attendant obligations, and so committed to understanding and development, would need to cut its teeth on tragedy and the idea of the unconscious – that is, a really unconscious unconscious, not one dying to be made sense of. It is the fact that terrifying and shocking and surprising things happen – that we *do* terrifying and shocking and surprising things – that is always tempering our hope for ourselves. A life that can be this daunting seems to need good stories about what might be going on. And Lear is surely right, in his brilliant essay 'On Killing Freud (Again)', when he says that,

there is something which would count as a global refutation of psychoanalysis: if people always and everywhere acted in rational and transparently explicable ways, one could easily dismiss psychoanalysis as unnecessary rubbish. It is because people often behave in bizarre ways, ways which cause pain to themselves and others, ways which puzzle even the actors themselves, that psychoanalysis commands our attention.

The fact that there is such a thing as motivated irrationality, the fact that we are not transparent to ourselves (and sometimes want to be) makes Freud at least a plausible contender in the explanation game. The onus, as Lear rightly says, is on Freud's critics to come up with a better story – if Freud was the loser in the so-called Freud wars, what have the winners left us with? But Lear's book also, almost inadvertently, makes us notice how strange our idea of rationality must be if it leaves out so much that matters to us. Freud clearly was not merely showing us how irrational we are: he was showing us how irrational rationality is; that we are at our maddest when we are at our most plausible (to ourselves). This is what tragedy reveals again and again. So in wanting a psychoanalysis that is of a piece with the Socratic or the Aristotelian projects Lear is encouraging us to be more rational, even if his version of rationality is ample and nuanced. It is as though the question Freud couldn't quite ask, and that Lear's book prompts us to wonder about, is: if we don't aspire to rationality what should we aspire to? For Lear Oedipus is too irrational: 'Oedipus's fundamental mistake lies in his assumption that meaning is transparent to human reason ... Oedipus assumes he understands his situation.' Oedipus would have been more rational, wouldn't have come to grief, Lear suggests, if he had taken his own irrationality into account. But this, I think, says less than it seems to be saying, and about as much as psychoanalysts too often say: real rationality fully acknowledges the significance of irrationality. 'He who humbles himself wills to be exalted,' Nietzsche said of Christ; and Christ here could be the enlightened ego, masterful to the end, rational even about his irrationality.

'Can mind comprehend its limits?', Lear begins the best essay in the book, 'Testing the Limits: The Place of Tragedy in Aristotle's *Ethics*'. And this is clearly a question both about whether it makes sense to imagine that there is an unconscious; and about whether we can say anything about tragedy that makes its catastrophe intelligible. One redescription of the question – can we comprehend more than we can comprehend – quickly turns it into nonsense; but the nonsense is instructive. There is a bind here that Lear lucidly expounds in his essay on Wittgenstein. 'Our problem is that being minded as we are,' he writes,

is not one possibility we can explore among others. We explore what it is to be minded as we are by moving around self-consciously and determining what makes more and less sense. There is no getting a glimpse of what it might be like to be 'other-minded', for as we move toward the outer bounds of our mindedness we verge on incoherence and nonsense.

This could hardly be better or more elegantly said. Our dreams and the poetry we write (and speak) verge on incoherence and nonsense; the moments when sense begins to turn, or fade, also define us. Going out of bounds might be as close as we can get to that recurrent fear of being other-minded which seems also to be a wish. The unconscious describes an apprehension that there are other minds – other, that is, than the one we easily recognize – going on inside us; that there is something inside us, and between ourselves and other people, that is forever verging on incoherence and nonsense. And whether we like it or not. But we only think something should be done about this when we suffer from it. Tragedy, at least in the first instance, is an irruption of incoherence. Lear's essay on 'Aristotle and Tragedy' is his most lucid account of the problem, of the animating conflict that makes this book of so much interest. And of interest because of, not despite, its undisguised pieties; Lear is often at his best when his allegiances are slightly ruffled.

If psychoanalysis 'hopes to chart how the individual emerges from less organized psychological states ... to understand how psychic organization, in particular the healthy developed personality, develops from less organised states', then tragedy might be just the thing to put a spanner in the works. Aristotle, 'trying to work out an embodied conception of human reason', and thereby becoming a kind of proto-Freudian, uses the example of tragedy as a laboratory to prove his hypotheses. 'The philosophical significance of tragedy, for Aristotle,' Lear writes, 'is that it shows that reason can give an account of even the most apparently "unnatural" alogon, irrational acts which truly human beings commit. The *Poetics*, then, is an attempted vindication of his ethical and political realism: it aims to show that the polis is adequate to capture all of human nature.'

For Lear, Aristotle's 'attempt to reclaim the opacity of human destructiveness' – 'to lend it intelligibility and thereby confer upon it some political value' – is unduly optimistic, doomed by its belief in the political power of reason. Aristotle wants everything that human beings do, all of human nature, to be reclaimable for the polis. If people are essentially creatures of the polis, then everything about them is a function of that fact. Like an over-zealous psychoanalyst, Aristotle believes that anything and everything we discover about people can be used, can be a contribution to the culture.

'Aristotle,' Lear writes, 'wants to secure the autonomy of human nature ... By contrast, Plato and Freud are less interested in human autonomy and more interested in pursuing the darker threads of human behaviour, even if doing so points beyond the bounds of intelligibility. They thus have a more inclusive conception of human nature.' That is, they acknowledge that there is something in human nature that wants, for no available reason, to destroy what we most value. A plausible version of human nature, then, has to include what our idea of human nature prevents us from making sense of. There is something beyond intelligibility that is causing all the trouble, and we are really up against it. So there are two kinds of people:

those who believe that it's just a matter of time before we work it all out (call them, say, technocrats); and those who believe that we never will because life isn't like that. What Lear refers to as the 'darker threads of human behaviour' is a way of naming all those things that make us unhappy, and that show no signs of letting up. We may live by trading with the enemy, but we can't force the enemy to trade. If there is meaningless destructiveness then we are all potentially inconsolable.

'People,' Lear writes, 'tend to be at their most parochial when they speculate about the human condition.' But Plato and Aristotle and Freud don't sound parochial to us, perhaps because they tend to legitimate their claims rhetorically by universalizing them, by speculating about the 'human condition' – or perhaps we do it on their behalf. Knowingness, that is to say, may be endemic to knowing. There is no reason to assume that the people Freud knew in Vienna were representative of anything other than themselves. Oedipus suffers as he does, Lear contends, because 'the claim to already know pervades his search to find out'. But everybody already knows something, even if what they know is that it is part of our intelligibility to ourselves – perhaps the essential part – to notice that we are unintelligible to ourselves; or, indeed, that open-mindedness is better than its alternatives, whatever those might be. But it is the virtue of *Open-Minded* to make us wonder whether knowing and understanding, however well done, should be the be-all and end-all. Madness is the need for everything to make sense, even if that sense is that everything is senseless. Perhaps good stories about our ignorance should not be too informative.

An Answer to Questions

He was all answer, with no question.
John Updike, 'Gertrude and Claudius'

'The traditional pursuits of philosophers are, for the most part, as unwarranted as they are unfruitful,' A. J. Ayer begins his infamous *Language, Truth and Logic* of 1936: 'The surest way to end them is to establish beyond question what should be the purpose and method of a philosophical enquiry.' Something has to be put beyond question so the real questions can start. And Ayer is perspicacious enough to know that to do this, to put an end to this superstitious metaphysical tradition, he has to know what a real question is. For Ayer, logic is a form of hyperbole that can show us the starkest of truths: a question is something that can be answered. If there is no way of answering then it is not a question that has been asked. 'We enquire in every case,' he writes,

what observations would lead us to answer the question, one way or the other; and, if none can be discovered, we must conclude that the sentence under consideration does not, as far as we are concerned, express a genuine question, however strongly its grammatical appearance may suggest that it does.

Ayer is offering us a new way to spot a genuine question; for this 'we' that Ayer gathers around him in his sentence, it is not to do with question marks or with wanting to know something. It is about what we can actually do to get answers – what observations can be made – so there can be no hallowing of curiosity. You will only know if what you had was a question afterwards; the answer won't merely answer the question, it will tell you whether it was a question.

It is, of course, traditional for philosophers to make a fuss about questions and about the traditional pursuits of philosophers. Ayer implies that questions hypnotize us to look for answers, when answers may not be possible. Only our answers reveal our questions to us (when it may be too late). 'Does God exist?' is not a question, in Ayer's view, because we only have observances and not observations to deal with it. If we took Ayer's method as a prescription for conversation, rather than for philosophical enquiry, the conversation would be halting, at best. At its worst it would be like someone trying to drive someone else mad. The Ayer-person would too often be saying, you can't ask for that because that's asking for nothing, you can't want that because it doesn't exist. If questions are ways of wanting, they are bound to be – as Ayer intimates, though this would not be his language, truth or logic – wishful. Ayer's word for wishful would be metaphysical, or nonsense.

One way of describing so-called growing up would be to say that it involves a transition from the imperative to the interrogative – from 'Food!' – through 'I want' – to 'Can I have?'. Questions are, among other things, the grammatical form we give to our desire. Once our wanting has become a question, we have acknowledged – started thinking about – the ways in which wanting in itself doesn't seem to guarantee satisfaction. There is something between us and what we want; and our wishes are leaps. If Ayer's concern about 'genuine questions' is redescribed as a preoccupation about genuine wants, it might lead us to ask: do we find out about wanting by seeing if what we want is actually there? And if it isn't actually, observably, there, what do we do? There is a logical sense in which you might decide a question is not a question, but there is no comparable way of making wants disappear. Who we are is what we can't be talked out of. In the world of wanting, the knowledge that my question has no answer can make it more of a question. My frustration may not be a satisfying answer to the question of my desire; but it doesn't – fortunately and unfortunately – abolish my desire.

If questioning is a way of desiring, answering must be akin to satisfying, a meeting of desire. Because we are often able to persuade children that 'I want' can be translated into 'Can I have?' there is something resembling socialization. To learn to question, and to learn not to, are the basic building blocks of development. To know just what can be questioned, and what must not be – and to learn, as Ayer wants us to learn, what constitutes a question – is what education educates us for. And questions about questions are worth asking because so many of the practices we value – so many of the practices we rely upon for our descriptions – depend upon them. How could we teach, litigate, cure, marry or talk at parties without asking? Without questions we wouldn't know how to torture people, or do consumer research. But if we believe that asking questions is the way, the route to the things that matter most to us – the truth, the facts, the answers, and so on – what kind of picture does this suggest we have of ourselves? If we are askers and answerers – or, indeed, as psychoanalysts are supposed to be, resisters of these rituals – what are we then like? Clearly we imagine that much of what we have inside us – much that is essential – can only be got at through a question. And yet language is the only medium for this double act of questions and answers; there are no questions in music, say, no answers in dance even though we may, as is our habit, ask questions about them. To conceive of a form of social relations in which there was no such thing as questions and answers seems virtually akin to imagining a world without language. So mesmerized are we by the question-and-answer format that it might seem silly to consider – even as a thought experiment – trying to discard it. What would we be able to do together – what would we be able to say – if interrogation was banned?

One of the notoriously annoying things about going to see a psychoanalyst, as it is euphemistically called, is that psycho-analysts often don't answer questions. Questions are encour-aged, but answers are not. And psychoanalysts, of course, have reasons for mostly not answering questions which they consider to be in the best interests of the so-called patient. It would seem simply human to at least try and answer a question if someone is obviously in need of an answer. So there would have to be good reasons for a group of people, bent on doing some kind of good, to quite candidly refuse to play the game, indeed, to make it integral to their specific therapeutic technique, essential to their notion of cure, to mostly not answer (of course, if they never answered there would be no meeting in the first place, and no telephone). It is as though psychoanalysts were people who had discovered something about answering that had both made them suspicious, and enlightened them.

It is in its scepticism about answers – or rather about answer-ing – that psychoanalysis comes into its own. But first the analyst has to persuade the patient of the value of the new game; because it requires the patient's co-operation it has to show him the benefit that might accrue from going on asking and being barely answered. The analyst wants the patient to ask without expecting an answer, without, in fact, expecting that there will be answers at all. There might be something else, but not an answer. Psychoanalysis, at least in some of its versions, says: it is human to ask questions, but it is misleading – somehow baffling or distracting – to be too interested in answers. The patient must learn to enjoy desiring, without needing satisfaction. He must travel hopefully, with no hope of arrival. 'You know what charm is?' the narrator of Camus's *The Fall* asks. 'A way of getting the answer yes without having asked any clear question.' Psychoanalysis is a way of getting the answer 'no' while being encouraged to clarify one's questions.

This not answering questions as one of the things a psychoanalyst does is a way of defining the situations that call for a psychoanalyst (rather than for a doctor, or a policeman or a florist). Psychoanalysis is best thought of as a temptation – among many other competing temptations – to see and describe one's life in a certain way. And this certain way is an enquiry, among other things, into the part questions and answers play in one's life; the part they have been forced to play, the part one allows them to play, and the part one wants them to play. When people want to know what the questions are that their lives seem to be answering, when they want to find out which questions about themselves can be answered, and which predicaments cannot usefully be formulated as questions, when people need a new question to ask of themselves – then it may be worth their while to go and see a psychoanalyst. If they are more interested in answers than in the trouble with answers, their time and money will probably be better spent elsewhere.

For Ayer, genuine questions have answers; for the psychoanalyst I describe, the problem with the question is its need for an answer. The philosopher and the psychoanalyst seek different satisfactions. The psychoanalyst wants to persuade us that there is a satisfaction in asking, and going on asking; the philosopher wants to get his asking right. The philosopher and the psychoanalyst agree that people ask, and ask for, what cannot be asked. For the psychoanalyst this is the point; for the philosopher this is the problem. What is not in question is the value of questions, and the value of asking questions about questions. The traditional pursuits of philosophers that Ayer was so dismissive of has been a quest of (and for) questions. What Freud did was to redescribe questions as part of the rhetoric of demand. To ask a question is simply a way of acknowledging to ourselves and other people that we are lacking something.

When the logical positivist meets the psychoanalyst perhaps the only thing they will have in common is an interest in asking. The psychoanalyst is likely to think that we are our ways of asking, or that our sense of who we are comes from knowing what we are asking for. For the philosopher, the question of who we are is nonsense – or rather, not a question – because there are no observations we could make that could possibly provide an answer. And yet their shared appetite for questions is itself complicit with a picture of ourselves as wanting something (truth, facts, satisfaction, and so on). People as the animals that question themselves – who doubt and judge and punish – has been one of our most spellbinding images and projects. As though questions signified the transition from nature to culture; as though culture turns appetite into a question; as though bringing up children is getting them to put some question marks in.

'Supposing no one asked a question. What would the answer be,' Gertrude Stein wrote in *Near East or Chicago*, tartly omitting the question mark. Much of what goes on between people goes on behind the scenes of this question and answer routine, this compulsive gift-giving and gift-withholding ritual. But the supposing that Stein proposes seems somehow beyond us. As though if we went along with her we'd be giving up something without quite knowing what it was. Is questioning the best way of wanting, and is wanting the best thing we can think of ourselves as doing? These are the pragmatic questions – as uncongenial to the analyst as to the positivist – that Stein pushes in our direction. Though it is not, of course, questions she is pushing. If the Old World was full of questions, she intimates, perhaps there is a New World that is full of something else.

Smile

Time is my own again.
I waste it for the waste.
J. V. Cunningham, 'Coffee'

'The aetiology of every neurotic disturbance', Freud writes in *Analysis Terminable and Interminable*, 'is, after all, a mixed one. It is a question either of the instincts being excessively strong – that is to say, recalcitrant to taming by the ego – or of the effects of early (i.e. premature) traumas which the immature ego was unable to master. As a rule there is a combination of both factors, the constitutional and the accidental.' Freud is distinguishing here between causes of neurotic disturbance and their relative susceptibility to psychoanalytic treatment. Either way – whether the disturbance comes from outside or from inside, or from a more plausible combination of the two – the patient has been overwhelmed by something. He is deemed to be reacting rather than acting; something happens to him that he then has to manage. But it is only in the treatment of what he calls the 'traumatic neuroses' that Freud allows himself to make strong claims for the value of psychoanalytic treatment. 'Only when a case is predominantly a traumatic one', he writes, 'will analysis succeed in doing what it is so superlatively able to do; only then will it, thanks to having strengthened the patient's ego, succeed in replacing by a correct solution the inadequate decision made in his early life.' There is the trauma of instinctual desire, and the trauma of contingent events; we have choice, Freud asserts, but only when it comes to the choosing of our defences.

The psychoanalytic concept of 'overdeterminism' had been at once a tribute to causality, and an acknowledgement of the individual's helplessness faced with his biological inheritance (the instincts) and the contingency of his personal history. By claiming that, at least with the traumatic neuroses, the patient was suffering from his 'inadequate decision', Freud was rescuing choice, and therefore the possibility of therapeutic efficacy – the revision of personal history – for his system. And so raising the question of what might constitute an inadequate decision, of what made a choice poor. It is as though the defences themselves were our automatic moral judgements, and needed to be morally assessed. We have to work out, Freud intimates, which ways of protecting ourselves from life make a good life.

When Freud tried to plot Leonardo's neurosis – his extraordinary life – in *Leonardo da Vinci and a Memory of his Childhood* (1910), it was exactly this indeterminate combination of the constitutional and the accidental that he found to be the source of Leonardo's fascination. And Freud's question, where does a person's history come from?, could only be answered by accounting for whatever it was that his subject found unavoidably interesting. As an art form and as a lived life, biography was a series of fascinations. Leonardo was both the object of Freud's fascination – and Freud is quite clear that from a psychoanalytic point of view the biographer's interest in his subject was initially (and perhaps primarily) *auto*biographical – and he was himself a man fascinated. Driven, indeed spellbound, as his paintings apparently showed, by 'the powerful fascination exerted by the smile ... at once fascinating and puzzling'. In his chapter on Leonardo in *The Renaissance*, which Freud quotes in his own essay, Walter Pater had suggested that,

'Fascination is always the word descriptive of him'. For Freud, Leonardo was the pretext for the psychoanalytic redescription of fascination as the key to a person's history; and of the ways in which a person's history was always also an attempt to stop his history, to make a travesty of time.

Freud's work is clearly of a piece with what Stephen Bann has described in *Romanticism and the Rise of History* (1995) as the Romantic (and post-Romantic) 'desire for history'. History redeems intelligibility. And psychoanalysis makes us believe in the narrative coherence of a life by showing us that what seems to undermine it – the unconscious, sexuality, language, contingency – is its ultimate guarantor. Once a person is defined by his history, made inextricable from it, we need to find ways of getting at the past. 'In the Romantic period', Bann writes, '... we can trace the emergence of this novel and irresistible capacity for multiplying and diversifying the representations of the past in such a way that a new code – or even a new language – was learned.' In Freud's *Leonardo*, to be fascinated by history is to be fascinated by fascination itself.

If fascination is the sign of loss, as Freud will say of Leonardo, then it is by the same token an opportunity (if not an invitation) to reconstruct a persuasive narrative history of Leonardo's life. We are only fascinated, Freud suggests, by something we have already lost. We are only fascinated, in other words, by what is missing – by the past. Fascination is the exhilaration of a mourning that never gives up hope. Leonardo's obsession with the woman's enigmatic smile – like the scene of a crime he keeps returning to – is the real enigma, sustained even by Freud's explanation of it. 'It was his mother', Freud writes, 'that possessed the mysterious smile – the smile he had lost, and that fascinated him so much when he found it again in the Florentine lady.' But Freud cannot explain his theory. What is this a fascination for, exactly? And what is fascination doing for Leonardo here, what is its function? After all, the Florentine lady could have just reminded Leonardo of his mother, he didn't have to make it so fascinating.

A common-sense Freudian interpretation might say that this woman's smile was 'fascinating' to Leonardo precisely because he didn't (consciously) know that she reminded him of his beloved mother. As though fascination takes over when forbidden memory fails. Or when the pain of loss has to be disavowed by the thrill of presence. Leonardo says to himself, 'I didn't lose my mother (and her smile) because I love this woman's smile'; his fascination ablates the past. In clinical terms this would make Leonardo's fascination – indeed, any kind of comparable obsession – a form of mania. If the past is always being lost, and we must avert a continual state of mourning, we must simulate our masteries. And yet the paradox that Freud and later analysts kept coming up against is that the individual is always enslaved by his mastery. When we are fascinated by someone or something we can acknowledge that it may have a cause, but it rarely feels like a choice. Fascination, Freud intimates in this essay, may not be so much a cure for loss, but rather the decision to abolish chance. When we are fascinated by someone we are refusing to take contingency seriously.

It is not accidental that in a psychoanalytic essay on fascination and biography Freud should pay his most eloquent and insistent tribute to chance, and not simply or solely, as he does everywhere else, insist on the daemonic power of instinct. 'If one considers chance to be unworthy of determining our fate,' he concludes his essay on Leonardo,

it is simply a relapse into the pious view of the universe which Leonardo himself was on the way to overcoming when he wrote that the sun does not move. We naturally feel hurt that a just God and a kindly providence do not protect us better from such influences during the most defenceless period of our lives. At the same time we are all too ready to forget that in fact everything to do with our life is chance, from our origin out of the meeting of spermatozoon and ovum onwards ... The apportioning of the determining factors of our life between the 'necessities' of our constitution and the 'chances' of our childhood may still be uncertain in detail; but in general it is no longer possible to doubt the importance precisely of the first years of our childhood.

If everything to do with our life is chance, how does psychoanalysis, as theory or practice, fit in? How can we then distinguish between a cause and a choice? There is constitution, there is chance, and there is fascination. Our constitution, in Freud's view, is instinctual and so everything, including our capacity for fascination, comes out of that. And yet, if Leonardo's fascination was in some sense an expression of his desire for his mother in the complicated configuration of his family, it was also, Freud implies, keeping chance at bay. As though Leonardo was unconsciously saying to himself, my desire for my mother, not chance, is determining my fate. There is a coherent and intelligible logic to my life which I am merely unconscious of. My life really comes from inside me, and it makes good sense. Freud shows, in other words, that by making Leonardo a psychoanalytic subject – by using the evidence of his life and work to validate psychoanalytic theory – he discloses the way in which Leonardo, and psychoanalysis itself, denies reality. By leaving out chance we may, absurdly, be leaving out everything. Freud's fascination with Leonardo reveals to him something essential about his own fascination with psychoanalysis. Fascination joins the ever-increasing repertoire of defences. The irony that Freud could never escape from – the tautology built into his system – is that, if you believe that everything is (his version of) instinct, you end up believing that everything is defence. The idea of compromise-formations soon seems like a loop-hole, where none is available.

This is illustrated by what is for Freud the primal scene of fascination, the difference between the sexes; Freud goes to great lengths to explain this in the Leonardo essay. If there are two sexes, what would a possible compromise be? It is the child's interest in his own and other people's genitals that is, Freud writes, the origin, as stimulus, of all our fascinations. Fascination is both the consequence of, and an attempted undoing of, the difference between the sexes. The male child is fascinated by female genitals because he cannot bear the thought of losing his own. To be spellbound by one's penis is to be spellbound by one's loss of it. The child's discovery that his mother doesn't have a penis is, in Freud's view, the formative event of his early and subsequent life. Fascination is part of the child's wishful attempt to restore difference to sameness; by looking so intently the child is looking to deny what he has perceived. If, from the boy's point of view, there are two sexes, then castration must be possible. There are either men, or there are castrated men, with women as some kind of unhappy compromise; or there are two sexes. Fascination, in Freud's version of the little boy's desperate logic, seems to be a way of keeping these fateful questions undecided, and thereby warding off the possibility of castration. This makes men's fascination with women a denial of their actual existence; a denial that there is such a thing as a woman. When a man is being fascinated by a woman he is being unconsciously relieved of the fact that there are two sexes. Once again, from a common-sense Freudian point of view – and no less plausible by being so – fascination is a defence against loss. But the secret irony here is that, at least from the male point of view, the existence of another sex is experienced as a loss; when it is, one might say, the ultimate contingency of life that there are two sexes. Loss, Freud implies, is easier to bear – indeed, vastly preferable to – an acknowledgement of the way things happen to be. Why, Freud makes us wonder by writing about fascination, is fate – or what I'm calling contingency – interpreted as loss?

'The thing that's between us', Marguerite Duras writes in *Practicalities* (1990), 'is fascination, and the fascination resides in our being alike. Whether you're a man or a woman the fascination resides in finding out that we're alike.' From Freud's point of view in the Leonardo essay, fascination resides in finding out that we could be alike, and that this alikeness, were it to occur, would be a punishment (the castration that would be a consequence of forbidden Oedipal desire). Either way, fascination is a refinding. It is like the woman's mysterious smile, at once secret elegy and forlorn hope. Like Leonardo we are only fascinated by what is most familiar.

We may be able to tell persuasive stories about how and why fascination begins, but how it ends is more obscure. What puts a stop to it is itself enigmatic, like all losing of interest or passion. But then, not being able to imagine its ending, its loss, is integral to fascination. And that, too, is the point. Leonardo, Freud reminds us, had difficulty finishing his paintings; a 'symptom' of this was the slowness with which he worked. This, Freud writes, 'determined the fate of the Last Supper – a fate that was not undeserved'.

Martin Amis
and the Female Policeman

For three words once, in 1987, Martin Amis sounded like D. H. Lawrence. 'Art celebrates life,' he wrote in his keenly anti-nuclear Introduction to *Einstein's Monsters*, and then he went back to being himself: 'and not the other thing, not the opposite of life.' Before nuclear weapons had dawned on him – 'I say I "became" interested, but really I was interested all along' – it was not always clear what life Amis's writing was on the side of. It had always seemed, reading the novels (though not, interestingly, his journalism), as if he wanted to find things to celebrate, but was hard-pressed to do so. Or that the reader had to work out what might matter to him, infer it from his exhilarated ridicule. The acute sense of people's vulnerability in his writing made him sound like someone embarrassed by his own seriousness rather than a natural satirist. He seemed unduly self-conscious about being committed to anything other than himself as a writer, and the studied recklessness of his remarkable style. There are novelists who want to interest the reader in their characters, and novelists who want to interest us in themselves. In the second case the style is always tantalizingly suggestive of the life the writer must be living, or the unusual person he is. One of the many remarkable things about Amis is that he's never been quite sure which kind of writer he wants to be; and at his best – in *Success*, in *Money*, in *Time's Arrow* – he has been able to be both. The moralist and the celebrity are awkward

Review of Martin Amis, *Night Train* (Jonathan Cape, 1997), from the *London Review of Books*.

bedfellows; they have to be as artful as Amis can be to pull it off.

The moralist in Amis has always insisted that not everything is literary; has done his best, that is to say, not to write campus novels – even though all his books are haunted by academics, either literally as characters, or as implied readers and critics. 'It doesn't look very literary out there, just now,' Amis wrote in 1985. But literariness is like the vanity of the Miss Bertrams in *Mansfield Park*, which 'was in such good order that they seemed to be quite free from it'. It doesn't look very anything out there, without our descriptions of it (and nothing could be more literary than that 'just now'). The idea of the literary has always been tricky for Amis – something both loathed and desired as a safe house – largely because he is a very literary writer obsessed by everything that is anti-literary in the culture (i.e. everyone and everything in the culture that doesn't like books). His way of showing us in his novels how supposedly unliterary it is out there has been to write about urban poverty, violence, the streets, people who don't read literature. And Amis then makes all this very literary indeed, which usually means, in his novels, frighteningly funny. So out there becomes in here very fast, and in here becomes very claustrophobic. Though he often writes about, indeed is fascinated by, the kind of people who would never read his books, or find them funny, it is not always obvious that there is an out there there. The longing in his books – and there is a lot, however muffled it often is by being too jokey or too explicit – is not merely for something more reassuring than contemporary life. It is for a way out of his vision of things. 'Novels,' he once wrote, 'are all about not going out of the house.' And his novels are most poignantly about style as solipsism.

Amis's fiction uniquely picks up on a curious paradox of contemporary life: that the more we are told – by modern science as much as by TV, two of Amis's obsessions – that there are other universes and other people, that there is more 'out there' than ever before, the more we feel trapped in our own lives. The more there is the more we feel excluded from. All Amis's characters seem to live in their own tunnels – and he has an uncanny ability to evoke the eerie isolation and isolationism of their lives – with a narrator always trying to find an alternative to tunnel-vision. Self-consciousness, as a threat and a promise (the furtive logic, the demonic secrecy people live by), has been his great preoccupation, which makes suicide, especially the suicide of the nominally happy – the theme of *Night Train* – an obvious subject for him. If the ur-title of Amis's work is *Other People: A Mystery Story*, the title of his least good novel, then we might have seen this one coming. *Money*, after all, for which *Night Train* is the darker sequel, was 'a suicide note'. Nothing makes people more other to us than their suicide. Nothing makes them seem both more and less the authors of their own lives. Every suicide, like every mid-life crisis, is a whodunnit. So after *The information*, in its wake as it were, comes the far more troubled and troubling *Night Train*: a mock-thriller about a subject profoundly unmocked by its author. And one of Amis's most interesting books.

In a sense *Night Train* is two books, one of which could be called 'A Reply to My Critics'. Writers, unlike politicians, should never listen to their critics. And on a first reading some of the least convincing parts of *Night Train* are those in which Amis tries to confront, if that's the right word, political correctness; or rather, his own much-vaunted lack of it. He is rarely good at 'doing' women and blacks, and often quick to satirize those who are eager to be virtuous. (He is also, it should be said, very good at doing the ways in which people are often not very good at 'doing' these things.) But the flaunting of men's idiocy about women, and their terror of other men, quickly became part of Amis's stock in trade. Since all good satire is complicit with what it exposes – and every prejudice is a boast – what Freud called 'the laughter of unease' cuts both ways. Amis's revelation about nuclear weapons was also a revelation about his own writing – nuclear weapons are the satirist's ultimate device. They make a mockery of everything. And if you can destroy everything it might make you wonder what, if anything, you might want to keep. Of course the guilt of the satirist – the sight of the compulsively facetious becoming importantly earnest – is itself ripe for satire. For post-nuclear Amis, derision has become a more complicated thing. 'Allow me to apologize in advance,' the policewoman Mike Hoolihan, the heroine and narrator of *Night Train*, says very early on in the book, 'for the bad language, the diseased sarcasm, and the bigotry.' *Night Train* tries to be partly about what there might be to apologize for.

In *Venus Envy*, the most riveting critique of Amis's style, Adam Mars-Jones mentions the pertinent fact that in his Introduction to *Einstein's Monsters* Amis 'makes no reference ... to the most single-minded demonstration of nuclear protest, the Peace Camp at Greenham Common, or the larger move-ment of which it is part'. Again, very early in *Night Train*, Mike Hoolihan, who seems unusually cultured (i.e. Oxbridge-cultured) for a middle-aged American cop, starts lecturing us, on her author's behalf, about murder:

in full consciousness and broad daylight men sat at desks drawing up contingency plans to murder EVERYBODY. I kept saying out loud: 'Where are the women?' Where WERE the women? I'll tell you: they were witnesses. Those straggly chicks in their tents on Greenham Common, England, making the military crazy with their presence and their stares – they were witnesses. Naturally, the nuclear arrangement, the nuclear machine, was strictly men only. Murder is a man thing.

191

The problem of writing from the virtuous point of view is that it comes out as cliché: virtue is mostly unoriginal. The writing only comes to life here with the 'straggly chicks' and the 'murder is a man thing': that is, where we want to take issue with the imaginative strength of the prejudices brought into play. 'Witnesses', a word made fashionable by the Holocaust Studies industry, is too portentous, too palpable in its designs on us. Amis often makes Hoolihan sound like a slangy, street-wise academic.

In *Money* there was a character called Martin Amis. In *Night Train* there is, in a sense, a character in drag called Martin Amis, who is the narrator of the book. Or, to put it another way, a character who is the opposite of the 'real' Martin Amis: 'I used to be something,' the female cop Mike Hoolihan writes, 'but now I'm just another big blonde old broad.' Hoolihan is so glaringly, so brashly literary that Amis makes us wonder what he's up to. Hoolihan is the writer of the book, a shrewd 'reader' of crime scenes, suicide notes and character; she solves crimes like a novelist writes a book ('I had to do this alone and in my own way. It's how I've always worked'); she makes umpteen literary allusions; she's even in a biography 'discuss-group'. Amis is so accomplished – so admiring of the word-perfect twentieth-century Flauberts: Pritchett, Bellow, Updike, Nabokov – that even though there may be notes we don't like in his writing, there are never false notes. And yet it is too obvious that Mike Hoolihan, however much (at long last) she 'represents' the female voice in Amis's boyish fiction – and she is, curiously, one of the most haunting narrators in Amis's work – does not sound like a female cop in Homicide in 'a second-echelon American city' (even though few of us have known any). A cop like Mike, who by her own account (the only one we ever get of her), has 'come in on the aftermath of maybe a thousand suspicious deaths', would not, one imagines, write a book like *Night Train*, or 'apologize . . . for any inconsistencies in the tenses (hard to avoid, when writing about the recently dead) and for the informalities in the dialogue presentation'. If there is a joke here who is it on? And why does the writer have so much to apologize for? An apology, as Amis knows, is also a justification and an excuse. Like a suicide note, *Night Train* asks to be read more than once.

In all Amis's fiction there has been a nostalgia – an odd mixture of yearning, excitement and dread – for a bit of amoral rough and tumble. For a tough and callous male world of the inarticulate and the sexually simple (like Keith in *London Fields*); for the streets as the extra-curricular, where violence doesn't seem to hurt. Mike Hoolihan, as a police-person would, has 'seen them all: jumpers, stumpers, dumpers, dunkers, bleeders, floaters, poppers, bursters. I have seen the bodies of bludgeoned one-year-olds. I have seen the bodies of gang-raped nonagenarians.' Amis is the master of the escalating list; of the grotesque or the bizarre hysterically whipping up into nightmare and nonsense (as in his description of John Lennon's decline: 'bed-ins, bag-ins, be-ins, in-ins'). But the effect of his often brilliant verbal delirium is to make things wordy and unreal, language warding off the experience it describes, whisking it away. So Hoolihan implausibly combines the thug and the poet. She has been through it – the contemporary civil war on the streets – has seen it all, and, in her own (that is Amis's) way, articulated it. And because she has been through it – has earned her words, something the novelist himself might worry about – and presumably because she is a woman, she is allowed to be a Sensitive Person. Or even a sentimental one. 'But the minute you really go into someone. You and I both know that there's always enough pain.' Hoolihan is talking here to the father of the girl who has just killed herself (he was once Hoolihan's boss). But in or out of context this is, by anyone's standards, an archly ambiguous construction. On the one hand, she is saying simply: everyone is more unhappy than they seem – this is what intimacy always reveals. On the other hand, she is saying something more unsettling about sex and violence: about what sex may be like (murder or suicide). And Amis is knowingly using her, his male-named female narrator, to say these things. In other words, Hoolihan as a device, as a shrewd and suspect invention, allows Amis a broader register of feeling than is usual in his narrators; some of it too deliberately assuaging of his critics, but some of it extremely puzzling. And not in a trivially self-conscious way; partly because the novel is more subtle than Amis's previous books about the terrifying mislogic of self-consciousness. Hoolihan doesn't sound like she ought to sound, if she is what she says she is. What she says, or rather writes – the way she represents herself – doesn't tally with what she is. Just like the faultlessly happy – 'a kind of embarrassment of perfection' – suicide, Jennifer Rockwell: at once the double and the nemesis of the narrator. If no one is out of character when they commit suicide, i.e. behaving eccentrically, what does that say about character or our capacity to make sense of it? This is not, in any simple sense, a literary question.

Amis may be trying to oblige his critics in this book – showing that he is taking them seriously as they get crosser and crosser with him – but he is also writing about one version of every parent's worst fear: the suicide of their child. That is, the death for which they would feel most responsible. The death they might feel to be their murder. Or, in the case of Jennifer Rockwell (the daughter of a cop), want to have investigated as a murder. So *Night Train* is at once a spoof of a detective novel – Hoolihan is investigating a crime that was solved when it was discovered, and for which the perpetrator cannot be punished, in which the punishment is the crime – and a metaphysical thriller about cause and effect: 'we all want a why for suicide,' as Hoolihan says. And the novel makes much gruesomely amusing play with the fact that when it comes to suicide it's easy to get the who and the how, but the why is a big problem. So the question that the novel investigates – the 'crime' that a novelist might be better equipped to solve than a detective – is: what is character without motive? 'Suicides generate false data,' Hoolihan informs us: 'As a subject for study, suicide is perhaps uniquely incoherent. And the act itself is without shape and form.' It makes a mockery, in other (more literary) words, of the expected satisfactions of narrative. Suicide violates our sense of an ending. And frantic to make sense of it, we are forced to go back to the beginning.

Whereas nothing could be more literary than murder (we say, 'it's a murder story', we never say: 'it's a suicide story'). It has an agent and an obstacle course; somebody does something to someone else: it's a conventional drama. 'With homicide now,' Hoolihan says, 'we don't care about motive.' Motives are easy to find, and they don't matter that much. Suicide, on the other hand, even makes us wonder what qualifies as a motive; and who, or what, all this motive-hunting is for, since it is so much after the fact. Seemingly academic. After a suicide, cause and blame become inextricable, and questions about personal agency become urgent and obscure. The first line of *Hamlet* – 'Who's there?' – made the question interesting. Amis suggests in *Night Train* that it may be impossible now to put the who back into the whodunnit. 'Stop, I said,' Hoolihan says during one of her 'interviews', 'the more you're telling me the less I understand. Give me the upshot.' The upshot of *Night Train* is that no amount of information is going to tell us who is there. And that this is no longer an Arts v. Science question, but an Arts and Sciences v. the Law question.

Trader Faulkner (you can tell how good a novel is by the

names of its characters), Jennifer's partner, can bear the enigma of his beloved girlfriend's death because he's a 'philosopher of science. He lives with unanswered questions.' Whereas Jennifer's father is a policeman (and a parent): he's 'going to want something neat'. It is only the law now that can make decisions, because it has to. Only the law that sticks to the old story of a beginning, a middle and an end. The law makes closure seem possible. It makes politics a form of correction. If someone is guilty there has to be someone there who can judge them. So it is not merely gratuitous that Amis's 'A Reply to My Critics' is about policing; or that a fictional investigation of a suicide is the setting for questions about the differences between the sexes and the correction in political correctness. Conclusions, Amis implies in this book, are too easily jumped to. Suicide is a revelation akin to the discoveries of modern science: 'At least 90 per cent of the universe consists of dark matter,' the 'TV famous' scientist who was Jennifer's boss tells Hoolihan, 'and we don't know what that dark matter is.' There is the 'naked-eye universe', but the naked eye 'isn't good enough and needs assistance'; and there is what Hoolihan calls mystically 'the seeing'. There is the world of character and motive and morals, and there is another world of dark matter in which time and space are deranged, at least by the standards of ordinary perception. Once a person might have been likened to a planet; now character seems more like a black hole. People are disappearances. Self-consciousness becomes cloud cover.

But Amis is not saying in a roundabout way that moral (or aesthetic) judgement assumes an omniscience we are not entitled to; that the 'dark matter' – with all its Shakespearian undertones – should temper the ferocity of our convictions. Or indeed that science is the ultimate satire on morality. Amis's materialism is not reductive. In trying to find something 'out there' that resists his own apprehension of it – that resists the fabulous voraciousness of his style – he has to look very hard (and *Night Train* is full of vivid descriptions of the ways in which, in both senses, people look, of the specific gravity of their eyes). In *Night Train* the moral quest of the book is to find bearable forms of self-consciousness. Political correctness heightens self-consciousness, and assumes this to be a good thing. In *Night Train* political correctness is part of a larger problem, of self-awareness experienced as an obscure punishment. 'I have no idea what I'm feeling,' Hoolihan says towards the end of the book, but she experiences 'random stabs of love and hate', as though she is being murdered by her feelings. As though she is committing suicide whether she likes it or not.

In the naked-eye world, morality is simply the avoidance of punishment: 'they had a guy come down from DC,' the only really repulsive character in *Night Train* says, 'to give a seminar on social etiquette. A seminar on how to avoid sexual harassment suits.' The police, Hoolihan implausibly insists several times in the book, never judge people, they are beyond political correctness:

We don't judge, we can't judge you because whatever you've done it isn't even close to the worst. You're great. You didn't fuck a baby and throw it over the wall. You don't chop up eight-year-olds for laughs. You're great. Whatever you've done, we know all the things you might have done, and haven't done. In other words, our standards for human behaviour are desperately low.

In a fallen world we aren't appalled by how bad people are: we are relieved to find how good they have been, considering. Amis is often particularly shrewd about the ways in which his characters can turn pleading into special pleading. Once you've seen the worst does it make you morally lax, or morally generous, and how can you tell the difference? *Night Train*, among many other things, asks us what the consequences might be if our standards of behaviour were desperately high.

After all, to be self-conscious, in the ordinary sense, is to fear that one is not being as good as one should be. If self-consciousness is a haunting intimation of failure, what would success – another of Amis's titles – be? 'Sir,' Hoolihan explains to the dead girl's father, 'your daughter didn't have motives. She just had standards. High ones. Which we didn't meet.' What is so horrifying about suicide – which is, as it were, nuclear war for one – is its implicit mockery of all the good reasons to live: its hatred of hope. The idea that life is not good enough for oneself suggests that there is something better. The suicide becomes the person with the highest standards of all. The person who, by celebrating 'the other thing . . . the opposite of life', offers the cruellest parody of ambition.

Hoolihan's investigation of this 'perfect crime' of suicide – and 'perfect' is perfect here – allows Amis a series of wonderful set-pieces; of combative dialogues between Hoolihan and the various colleagues, academics, scientists and suspects involved. Amis is a very traditional novelist in his (slightly guilty) relish for the educated in his novels confronting the uneducated. And Hoolihan herself, like the hero and heroine of many nineteenth-century novels, is an orphan, a 'state child', trying above all to educate herself, while at the same time educating the reader by her very lack of legitimate instruction. So the whole book is cunningly, not crassly, preachy in its literary affiliations. Amis often writes the film of the book in the book he is writing, but in *Night Train* he also partly makes a novel of a very interesting set of lectures: on cosmology, on TV, on the law, and above all on suicide. Robert Stoller suggested that the question the psychiatrist should ask of the transsexual is not, 'Why you?' but: 'Why not me?' *Night Train* is so accurately disturbing that it makes one ask the same question about suicide.

And yet the most remarkable writing in this book is of a piece, as it should be, with its abiding preoccupation. There are descriptions of the unselfconscious – of the grief-stricken, of the dead (after suicide, under autopsy), of people absorbed in their work – that are like illuminations. And, by the same token, descriptions of the drunk and the crazed that are irresistible. So, in what is a very dark and daunting novel about mortifying self-consciousness, about the need to come to an end, about just deserts, there is also always this: the prose-poetry that only Amis can write:

One night, near the end, a big case went down and the whole shift rolled out to dinner at Yeats's. During the last course I noticed everyone was staring my way. Why? Because I was blowing my dessert. To cool it. And my dessert was ice-cream.

Narcissism, For and Against

By decomposing groups of figures you compose
groups of movements.
May Sinclair, *The Tree of Heaven*

1

If much of the most interesting psychoanalytic theory today is sceptical of the whole notion of relationship (Freud, Lacan, Laplanche, Bersani), most of the best popular psychoanalytic theory takes relationship for granted (Klein, Winnicott, Bowlby). Either we are suffering from whatever it is that sabotages our intimacies, or we are suffering from the notions of intimacy that we have inherited. It is not clear whether better relationships are the solution to our suffering, or whether it is that very aspiration that we suffer from. Narcissism, unsurprisingly, has been a keyword in these debates, and what is loosely called morality is what has been at stake. What kind of regard we are able, and wanting, to have for other people, and how we might distinguish between the good and bad forms of so-called self-love have become abiding preoccupations.

It is not amazing that a Judaeo–Christian culture is un-impressed by, and suspicious of, states of self-absorption. Solitary contemplation of God (and his demands) and certain kinds of committed devotion to others (as one of his commands) have been for many people the prerequisites of a good life. Scrutiny of the self, but not celebration or adoration of the self and its less devout and considerate desires, has been integral to this project. What the secular narcissist – relatively untroubled by heresy – might be preoccupied by has become a contentious and disturbing issue. Whether narcissism gets a good press (in Freud and Kohut, say) or a bad press (in Klein and the post-Kleinians), it is always keenly moralized. Great claims, either positive or negative, are always made on narcissism's behalf; as though when people are talking about narcissism they are always talking about something else. Do 'creative artists' – the psychoanalyst's secular idols: all talk of creativity is quasi-religious in its allusion to a creator – need to be narcissistic, or is this what they suffer from, or both? Is masturbation bad for people because it doesn't involve other people? Are we primarily interested in other people, so that self-preoccupation is a symptom of thwarted involvements, or are we essentially self-involved creatures interrupted, every so often, by our unavoidable dependence on others? Or is it, as we are so keen to say, probably a bit of both? These are the old questions – with their oppressive historical baggage – that psychoanalysis has got bogged down in, and which are versions of a more interesting question: What should a good person – from a psychoanalytic point of view – be open to, and be closed to? When people write about narcissism, in other words, they are persuading us about what we should value, what forms of exchange we should aspire to. They are writing about, in other words, what, ideally, we should be giving our attention to. It is worth, therefore, considering the narcissism of psychoanalysis.

I want to start at one of the so-called beginnings – to which the more ambitious psychoanalytic theorists are always drawn – because it is one that I find particularly convincing; both evocative and instructive. It is Laplanche's notion of what he calls the enigmatic signifier. Despite the extremely complex and sophisticated theory Laplanche has woven around it, it is a mercifully simple and compelling idea. That every infant – and so every person – begins life being given what he calls 'messages' by the parents (at first by the mother) that are beyond comprehension. These messages are not exclusively, or even predominantly verbal; they may be gestural, olfactory, tonal and so on. And they are enigmatic in a double sense. The parents themselves don't understand them – or even know about them – because they are unconscious. And the child cannot understand them because his powers of so-called understanding are so undeveloped, and because they are puzzling. What the child is able to 'translate', in Laplanche's key word, he may be able to include, but the residue – which he intimates is always the larger share – constitutes an unconscious of 'foreign bodies'. 'The unconscious', he writes (in *Essays on Otherness*, 1999), 'is thus, in no sense, an other "myself" in me, possibly more authentic than me, a Mr Hyde alternating with a Dr Jekyll, the one with his hatred, the other with his love ... It is an other thing (das Andere) in me, the repressed residue of the other person (das Andere). It affects me as the other person affected me long ago.'

We are decentred in Laplanche's view because we have inside us the opaque messages transmitted by our parents, often in spite of themselves. 'To address someone with no shared interpretative system, in a mainly extra-verbal manner; such is the function of adult messages, of those signifiers which I claim,' he writes, 'are simultaneously and indissociably enigmatic and sexual, in so far as they are not transparent to themselves, but comprised by the adult's relation to their own unconscious, by unconscious sexual fantasies set in motion by his relation to the child.' And for Laplanche it is, as one might suspect, the child at the mother's breast that is the source, or exemplary scene for this tragi-comedy of mutual confounding that makes us who we are. The other's desire – in this case, the mother's – is both primary, and constitutive in its provocative enigma. As though the breast – as the precursor of all desirable cultural objects – is asking the infant a question. 'Can analytic theory afford to go on ignoring', he writes in his *New Foundations for Psychoanalysis*,

the extent to which women unconsciously and sexually cathect the breast, which appears to be a natural organ for lactation? It is inconceivable that the infant does not notice this sexual cathexis, which might be said to be perverse in the sense that the term is defined in the *Three Essays*. It is impossible to imagine that the infant does not suspect that this cathexis is the source of a nagging question: what does the breast want from me, apart from wanting to suckle me, why does it want to suckle me?

It is as though the mother's breast transmits an obscure sexual message that implants itself in the infant as a question he is ill-equipped to reply to. Whatever is being ascribed to the infant here in terms of proto-questioning, or a capacity for puzzlement, it does seem entirely plausible to imagine that parents convey far more than they intend, and that children take in, in whatever form, far more than the parents or the children suspect. In this view our lives become – and analysis becomes – the attempted translation and retranslation of these enigmatic messages our parents left us with; and our coming to terms with the limits of our capacity for retranslation. We can never pluck out the heart of the mystery. So what is inescapable in the genesis and development of every person is the presence inside them – the psychic force field, the aura, the atmosphere, the messages – of another person (at first the mother, Laplanche implies, then the father and so on). There is no escape from the uncanny influence of those primary others, the parents (and their parents, and so on) but there is the possibility of some translation. So what kind of sense does it make to say that we were trapped by having the parents we happened to have? As though we could have had other parents. By definition the ineluctable isn't something we can think of as being available to escape from. We can wish that it was – we can wish that we and the people we love won't die, we can wish we didn't have to eat – but with these things we have to do something different.

It is noticeable in Laplanche's account that it is as if the child is captured by, in thrall to these enigmatic signifiers, these radically perplexing decentring messages. Clearly there can be a way out of this, but there are no ways through, one of which, of course, is psychoanalysis itself. Indeed, it is the analyst's very attitude, how he positions himself in the project of analysis, that shows the patient that the only way out is through. Psychoanalysis, of whatever persuasion, always describes itself as anti-escapist; and it can only do this, in my view, by being unduly omniscient about what there is to escape from, and so about the nature of escapism. Narcissism, broadly speaking becomes one of the key-words in psychoanalysis for those forms of life that, in various ways, have tried to escape from all those things that are assumed, by the different psychoanalytic theorists, to make a life worth living. A good life is one in which one has been able to escape from the right things. It is in their theories of narcissism – in their uses of the word, rather – that psychoanalysts can often tell us what they want from life, and so what they want from their patients' lives.

Laplanche conceptualizes what he refers to as a kind of oscillation of the human soul, and he describes it, rather wonderfully, as analogous to the Ptolemaic and Copernican cosmologies: the sun going around the earth as akin to the narcissistic relation. 'One is entitled to claim', he writes, 'that the Ptolemaism of the human psyche, its narcissistic recentring, follows upon a Copernican stage as its presupposition, in which the nursling child is caught up in the orbit of the other and has a passive relation to its messages.' There is, he writes, an 'ineluctable narcissistic closure of the apparatus of the soul'. The infant, in narcissistic closure is, so to speak, in recovery from having been too open, too confoundingly receptive to the mother's messages. A familiar question returns; do we begin too open and need to find ways of closing, or are we born closed and need to be prised open? Laplanche's essence of the human soul is a traumatic but unavoidable – and therefore constitutive – receptivity to the other (the word relationship here would not be quite right). There is a systole and diastole of the soul; the picture is of an organ or an orifice that is too open and learns forms of closure (of course it isn't really *too* open because it couldn't be otherwise). It is as though the language is progressively or developmentally moralized; entrapment and escape get grafted on to open and closed.

But the correspondences are interestingly mobile. The infant is trapped by being open, but trapped in a different way by becoming closed. The way out, Laplanche intimates, is being able to bear reopenings. Indeed, his belief in psychoanalysis depends upon the possibility of reopening, and of what he calls 'a deconstruction of old constructions'. The aim of a psychoanalysis is to disturb the patient's inevitable narcissistic closure. And part of this closure has been effected by the patient constructing coherent narratives about himself. Coherence, the self-story hanging together is here a sign of closure. 'The aim here', Laplanche writes, 'is not to restore a more intact past (whatever would one do with that?) but to allow in turn a deconstruction of the old, insufficient, partial and erroneous construction, and hence to open the way to the new translation which the patient, in his compulsion to synthesize (or, as the German Romantics might have put it, in his 'drive to translate') will not fail to produce.' The analyst and the patient collaborate to open the way for the patient's retranslation of those constitutive enigmatic messages he received unknowingly from the parents. 'The development of the human individual', Laplanche writes, 'is to be understood as an attempt to master, to translate, these enigmatic traumatizing messages. Analysis is first and foremost a method of deconstruction (ana-lysis) with the aim of clearing the way for a new construction, which is the task of the analysand.'

It is in a sense the virtue of the message that it is enigmatic because this makes it subject to, indeed irresistible to, retranslation. And this, in itself, breaks the rigid determinism that too easily stifles much psychoanalytic theory. It makes the child and his future collaborators necessarily inventive. It leaves them with something to work on if not work out. 'With the concept of enigma', Laplanche writes, 'a break in determinism appears: to the extent that the originator of the enigmatic message is unaware of most of what he means, and to the extent that the child possesses only inadequate and imperfect ways to configure or theorize about what is communicated to him, there can be no linear causality between the parental unconscious and discourse on the one hand and what the child does with these on the other.' Meaning, fresh translation, is there to be constructed, and in Laplanche's view we are always translating a translation. Pathology is the conviction that there is a Standard Edition.

I have gone to such lengths here with Laplanche partly because, in my view, he offers us, in a psychoanalytic context, an exemplary myth of human origins; and for reasons I will explain. But also his myth is useful as a way into the broader question of the very real consequences of psychoanalytic myths of origin. What is inescapable for the infant and child in Laplanche's account is its proneness, its receptive openness to (in the first instance) the mother's messages; and it is unavoidable, beyond her conscious intent, that she should transmit such messages. And it is finally inevitable that the messages should be enigmatic, and so in need of translation (Laplanche simply reminds us that the parents have an unconscious, and the child has a relatively undeveloped comprehension). For Laplanche this is what might once have been called the given, the foundational experience, from which escape is not possible, of being the recipient of the mother's unconscious messages. Escape, one can say, is not an option here; it is not a question of how to get away, but of what can be done by way of continuing retranslation. So what distinguishes Laplanche's version of beginnings is the redundancy of escapism as a ploy. One can't escape from the opaque fact of one's parents' unconscious, any more than you can, in actuality, escape in Freud's and later Klein's versions, from the imperious urgencies of one's instinctual life. And so the simple point of my essay is that in psychoanalytic theory – and not only there, of course, do such tautologies exist – *that which the subject wishes to escape from but cannot is considered to be his essence.*

It is in describing the individual in his self-deluded, self-misleading project of escape that the analytic theorist unavoidably describes his sense of what matters most to her. Every time we show the patient, in whatever way, that he is avoiding something we are impressing upon him, however obliquely, our sense of what is essential, of what matters most. We have always already posited a reality and then defined a good life as the talent, or the capacity to abide by it. In other words, our accounts of the escapism of everyday life – our whole extensive vocabulary of defence and avoidance and flight – is the key to our most cherished essentialisms. If we want to find out what we take to be real – what we assume to be of the utmost value to acknowledge – then we must attend above all to what we think of ourselves as being on the run from. Our notions of escapism are entirely complicit with our fantasies of the real; and in this sense the real itself can be an escapist fantasy; in need of what Laplanche calls retranslation. Form a psychoanalytic point of view we are at our most absurd, at our most wishful – that is, at our most human – in our escapism; *because we only try to escape from that which is by definition inescapable*. We call this, of course, the now overly familiar divided subject; in our flight from sexuality, aggression, dependence, gender conflict, grandiosity, even conflict itself, we make a mockery of ourselves. Man's preposterous project is to escape from himself. And in the full knowledge that one's nature by definition cannot be left.

My hunch in this essay – which is a hint because I can't justify it – is that the kind of psychoanalysis I would prefer, if indeed it is conceivable, would be one in which the language of escapism had disappeared – no longer seemed useful, or relevant, or to the point of our newfound self-descriptions. I do realize, I hasten to add, just how silly this is. And I say this not by way of excuse, but by way of qualification.

All escapist theories need a concept of the real; that is to say, they are all, somewhere, essentialist theories. Though this makes them no less valuable – as belief-systems, or heuristic devices, or possible facts or regulative fictions – it does make them morally and epistemologically suspect. These theories – of which psychoanalytic theories are a kind of quintessence – are themselves also enigmatic signifiers, puzzling messages that invite retranslation. Whereas Laplanche's essentialism of the message, of the enigmatic signifier, is by definition – almost by design – provocative of redescription, his myth of origins so open in its consequences for any given individual – there are consequences more pronounced, more delimited in the myths of origin of Freud and Klein, as taken up by some of their followers. It is indeed paradoxical that determinism and escapism so often seem to go hand in hand; escapism as the wishful burlesque of determinism. That which I cannot escape I must find ways of seeming to escape: this would be the comedy-as-farce approach. That which I cannot escape I must ultimately and impressively submit to, at exorbitant cost: this would be the tragic view.

For Shakespeare and Kafka, Lionel Trilling once remarked, the world was a prison; but in Shakespeare the company is better. For Freud and Klein the prison is our instinctual endowment in its fraught meeting with culture. But the essentials of their theories – the instincts, and so the unconscious and the Oedipus complex – are not themselves seen as contingent historical inventions. It is often intimated that they are virtually ahistorical, acultural universals. This is the prison – the war between the life instincts and the death instincts – and even though the company doesn't make the feast, it makes a difference. Both Freud and Klein, in theory, dramatize a flight from, or attack by, something deemed to be life-denying; and a flight towards something assumed to be life-enhancing. Narcissism – the keeping oneself company at the cost of other company – has come to be seen, in its various denominations, as a peculiarly undesirable prison; as an always tempting, some would say, unavoidable solution to the problem of bearing one's instinctual life. For Laplanche, we might remember, it was as though there was narcissistic closure as a temporary resort from the desire, the terror, the disarray prompted by the mother's enigmatic sexual messages; the ego's attempt to seclude itself, to hive itself off from the other outside and the other inside.

But the viability of psychoanalysis as a treatment was predicated on the individual's wish to reopen; to reopen the endless question of those messages. To offer up his associations for redescription, deconstruction, retranslation. If narcissism has been the traditional enemy of psychoanalysis – its collaborative antagonist, more agreeable than psychosis –

then it must have some ideas about what the alternatives are to narcissism. If, as everyone more or less agrees, narcissism is a form of self-cure, then it might be better to describe the various narcissisms as the rivals of psychoanalysis. Its most difficult, recalcitrant siblings. If I can put this allegorically: the analyst and the narcissist – assuming that they are different – have alternative cures for a similar problem; but which is better and from what point of view are we going to arbitrate, or even discuss this? What does so-called narcissism offer the patient that the analyst wants to persuade the patient not to want? What are the good things worth seeking in life, and why would somebody want to devote their lives to more or less getting away from them? In the analytic descriptions of so-called narcissistic conditions, or narcissistic people, the patient and the analyst seem to be involved in some emotionally fraught debate about whether this is any kind of life for a person. Analysts who believe in something they call narcissism, I contend, have an especially strong sense of what a good life for a person is. If they did not have this largely unconscious sense they would have no way of recognizing what it was that the patient was supposedly in flight from. I don't mean by this that I think such analysts are more directive or even manipulative than others – though they may be – or indeed that their patients don't have comparably powerful beliefs about a better life for themselves. But rather that it is more interesting and useful analytic practice to have a glimmer of what it is one is promoting, and so be able to subject it to retranslation.

There can be nothing more narcissistic than believing in narcissism. So I want to take Narcissus – though there are, of course other candidates, Oedipus, Jonah, etc – as my exemplary escapist, for the sake of this essay to suggest two things. First, that theories of narcissism are peculiarly complicit with ideas about escapism. And that the theorist of narcissism always runs the risk of getting himself into a cul-de-sac analogous to the one he describes his narcissistic patient as suffering from. Both the so-called narcissistic patient and his analyst get their entrances and their exits confused. I want to take examples from the British psychoanalytic tradition to show how John Steiner's notion of psychic retreats and Neville Symington's notion of the narcissistic refuge are logical conclusions of aspects of the Kleinian and Independent groups, respectively.

2

*I do not like that presumptuous philosophy which
in its rage of explanation allows no XYZ, no symbol
representative of the vast Terra Incognita of Knowledge,
for the Facts and Agencies of Mind and Matter
reserved for future explorers...*
S. T. Coleridge, *Notebooks*

It is, above all, to psychoanalytic theories of narcissism that we should go if we want to find out what the various psycho-analytic visions of a good life are. We might go – and we would certainly once have gone in the days of radical anti-psychiatry – to psychosis, to schizophrenia, for the apparently deeper meaning-of-life stories, but that would be a different elabora-tion of my argument here. Theorists of narcissism always have a more drastic, a more absolute sense of what their nominated patient is escaping from, or attacking, and so, by implication, what it would be better for him to prefer. I think it is good, not to mention inevitable, that psychoanalytic theorists should each have their own good life stories, but not always good that we have to infer them from their theories of pathology. If the so-called narcissist is the negative ideal of the psychoanalyst (in my allegory), then he is also his double, his counterpart, his

211

alter ego; and at worst his scapegoat. As we shall see, in some versions of Kleinian theory the narcissistic parts of the personality are saboteurs, despoilers of life, liars, cheats and tricksters.

And it is part of the covert link, the elective affinity between the psychoanalyst and the narcissist, that her theories of narcissism, like narcissism itself, tend towards closure, towards strict definition. But of a subtle kind because their whole drift – what they explicitly proclaim and affirm – is in the direction of openness, of acknowledgement of the otherness within and the otherness without. In other words, in my caricature of this, both the analyst and the narcissist might endlessly accuse each other of being too knowing, at the most interesting of cross purposes. The analyst, of course, only gets to see the unhappy narcissist; the narcissist who, ironically, must be wanting something else, which is why he has come for analysis. But then, of course, this is the once-philosophical question of what it is we should want in order to make our lives good; and what the relationship is, if any, between what we want and what we should want. My question is: can a psychoanalytic theory of narcissism avoid being what Coleridge called 'a presumptuous philosophy' with a 'rage for explanation'? Indeed, 'presumptuous' should perhaps be a key word in any discussion of that great escapist, the narcissist. For 'presumption' the OED has: 'Seizure and occupation without right; usurpation; the taking upon oneself of more than is warranted; forward or over-confident opinion or conduct; arrogance, pride, effrontery, assurance … the taking of something for granted'. My discussion is about what the so-called narcissist and the so-called psychoanalyst take for granted.

If Oedipus is the family researcher in psychoanalytic mythology, the explorer of origins, the man who was dying to get home, then Narcissus is the master of isolation and ignorance (Tiresias, we might remember, told Narcissus's mother Leiriope, 'Narcissus will live to a ripe old age, provided that he never knows himself' (Robert Graves, *Greek Myths*)). Oedipus, like the classic neurotic, keeps arriving at the place he is running away from. The ironic escapist, Oedipus is in flight from the family he keeps getting closer to. Narcissus, in love with his own beauty, his own image, is in flight from his desirous admirers; his path, Robert Graves writes in a sprightly retelling of the myth, 'was strewn with heartlessly rejected lovers of both sexes; for he had a stubborn pride in his own beauty'. After one such lover, Ameinius, killed himself, the gods agreed to take vengeance. Through the ministries of Artemis, Narcissus is inveigled to fall madly in love, unknowingly, with his own image in the water; and he kills himself because Artemis, as Graves plainly puts it, 'made Narcissus fall in love, though denying him love's consummation'. This is a story, to put it equally plainly, about someone who would rather die than have a relationship with anyone; and who, we are persuaded to believe, had a self-destructive, indeed, presumptuous relationship with himself. Narcissus's pleasure, we infer, was in refusing people, including, of course, himself. If Oedipus was escaping from his family – from their welter of desires for each other – what, comparably, is Narcissus deemed to be on the run from? We are told nothing by Graves about Narcissus's suffering (or its absence); we are only told that, beyond a certain point, there was something the gods wouldn't let him get away with. We might say, commonsensically, that you just can't go round treating people, including yourself, like this.

Oedipus is an epistemologist, a quester; there are things he wants to find out. He is characterized by his curiosity. Narcissus is the antithesis of these things; indeed, Tiresias told his mother that his living to a ripe old age depended on his *not* knowing himself. That self-knowledge would not be good for him. This in itself makes Narcissus something of a problem for the psychoanalyst. And we could, of course, say that Narcissus was in flight from self-knowledge, and this makes Oedipus ultimately the success to Narcissus's failure. But there are, I suppose, two questions here: first, how do we think Narcissus's life would have been better if he had had – or been able to bear, against Tiresias's prophecy – self-knowledge? And was that, indeed, what he was trying to escape? Again commonsensically, we might imagine that he wanted to escape from the reproaches of his defeated lovers, and that he clearly couldn't escape from the wrath of the gods. These rather simple-minded suggestions are merely by way of pressing the question, what was Narcissus trying to escape from? Because this is the way the question has been posed by those psycho-analysts after Freud who have taken up the myth as a useful and provocative description of a contemporary predicament. In many ways I think the Oedipus myth has seemed less enigmatic than the story of Narcissus; it has sent us a more perplexing message, at the same time as it offers us a perfect amused emblem of the perils of interpretation. We gaze in fascination at something that is merely a reflection – a mirror not a window – and it does us no good at all.

I want to take as my psychoanalytic tag for this, Serge Viderman's formulation that the hell of the narcissist is the tyranny of his need for the other. All the quite various psychoanalytic theorists of narcissism agree, I think, that for the so-called narcissist, needing has become a specific kind of preoccupation; and that the narcissist, or the person in a narcissistic state of mind, is suffering from something to do with his apprehension of otherness, whether it is the other(s) within, designated as the unconscious, or the others outside. In ordinary language the narcissistic person is considered self-absorbed, and this self-absorption is experienced by the bystanders, onlookers and witnesses as both a shield and a weapon. Viderman's formulation interests me because it points us in several directions. On the one hand, it lets us wonder, what has to happen to needing, what has to be done to needing, to make it feel like a tyranny? What are the conditions in which needing is felt to be a tyranny. There are questions here about the nature of need, but also about the nature of tyranny. Need has become a tyranny, and tyranny, we would all agree, should be resisted. What we tend to do with tyrannies is conform, resist, use secret ruses to evade and avoid them, overthrow them – but not, generally negotiate with them. Because that is what makes something a tyranny, the impossibility of negotiation. And if there is also something intrinsically tyrannical about everyone's need for the other, is tyranny the right word here? We don't after all talk about the tyranny of breathing or of sleeping; with these, as it were, solitary pleasures, there may be a kind of tyranny in being unable to sleep or suffocating. But the narcissist's predicament is both terrible and paradoxical in Viderman's version, because he is tyrannized by what he cannot do without. Hell, of course, is a place from which one is unlikely to escape.

In finding his need for other people a tyranny, this narcissist is immoral and apolitical. Or to put it another way, the narcissist is at odds with democracy. The notion of collaboration is without meaning. For the narcissist in his unmisgiving project of self-sufficiency, there must be no outside. No others to ruffle his arrangements. He is not an object-relations theorist. And so he becomes, either as a diagnosed person, or as a figurative but prevalent part of everyone's self, the target, so to speak, of psychoanalysis. Addicted to his own propaganda, he is a fundamentalist of himself – or of one image or version of himself – and must be persuaded, convinced, seduced, encouraged, held, contained, loved, nurtured, 'appropriately

hated', confronted, understood, not colluded with, reconstructed, analysed: I'm not sure what the word is – he must
be shown the benefit of needing and being needed by others. I
think the dialogue between the analyst and the narcissist – and
calling it a dialogue already gives too many prisoners – is one of
the emblematic double acts of our time. It is one of our secular
redemption myths; from insulated impoverished isolation to
receptive, more generous free association. The conflict of need
made more than bearable. In my story of this it might be as
misleading to become card-carrying narcissists as to become
qualification-carrying psychoanalysts. The miseries of so-called
narcissism are often patent, and radically diminishing. The
narcissist, by trying to escape from the inescapable – his need
for others, whether it is described as a need for gratification, for
recogniton, or for relationship – has found a dispiriting self-
cure. But what does the analyst propose? Both agree, after all,
that something called otherness is both a problem, and the
problem. There is, apparently, something else that has to be
fully acknowledged – call it the unconscious, infantile sexuality, the life and death instincts, the object, people apart from
oneself, the non-human environment – and a good life quite
literally depends upon these things. The narcissist won't have
any of it (other than the death instinct). The psychoanalyst can't
imagine a morally and sensuously convincing world without
virtually all of them.

I think it isn't merely facetious to say that from the psychoanalyst's point of view the narcissist, or the narcissistic parts of
the personality, have got it wrong. But it is callous to put it quite
like this because the analyst, ideally perhaps, is also mindful of
the suffering both caused by narcissism, and the kind of
suffering, of trauma, that it is an attempted solution to. At its
most minimal and documentary, if external reality is unbearable, one needs at least the illusion of internal refuge. If

thoughts and feelings and wishes and desires and affections feel persecutory one might need the asylum of psychic anaesthesia, a retreat or a seclusion where one is apparently exempt from such terrors and perplexities. These exits are entrances; these flights are a kind of release.

I said earlier that our descriptions of escapism were the key, by inference, to our notions of the real, the given, 'that which it is impossible not to know', in Henry James's words: it is our chosen, or unchosen essentialisms that are our enigmatic signifiers, par excellence; the culture's apparently untranslatable messages. And in this issue which I am dramatizing, if not caricaturing, there is in theory, a conflict of essences. For the psychoanalyst the essence can be called otherness; for the narcissist the essence can be called the absence of otherness. There is something else there other than me as I want to be, or there is nothing else there other than me as I want to be. I think it is worth wondering – if it is possible to do this without portentousness – what kind of essence otherness is? Which in the context of my essay means looking at the ways psychoanalysts write and talk in sympathetic antagonism with the narcissism they find so debilitating in themselves and their patients.

I think I should perhaps add here that I don't think sufficient consideration has been given to the eagerness with which analysts want to, in Neville Symington's zealous phrase, 'flush out' the putative narcissism in their patients; which is merely morally high-minded scapegoating. Any conversation, external or internal, without a strong narcissistic voice joining in, tends towards dreariness; it is only when the narcissistic voice tyrannizes – which is, of course, its forte – that the conversation dies into monologue and hush. Any good conversation about the unconscious usually needs someone who doesn't believe in it. This, of course, is always the most problematic voice to deal with in any analysis.

3

*... even if a non-human authority tells you something,
the only way to figure out whether what you have been
told is true is to see whether it gets you the sort
of life you want.*

Richard Rorty, *Pragmatism as Romantic Polytheism*

Clearly the so-called narcissist has only turned up for analysis because what the analyst may call his narcissism has not got him the sort of life he wanted. He may be, in my shorthand sense, wishfully committed to the absence of otherness, but he must want something else. Of course, in actuality there could be no such thing as pure narcissism; even Viderman's formulation requires of the narcissist that he experiences a tyranny. So the narcissist, we can more realistically say, wants to keep otherness down to a minimum. He goes about diminishing difference, stripping the world of its opposition, its separateness. A personal religion of closure is actively and passively practised. But forms of closure are perhaps more hospitable to description than forms of openness.

In his meticulous descriptions of what he calls 'pathological organizations' within the self, the British Kleinian John Steiner invokes, perhaps inevitably, Narcissus. These pathological 'structures' as he calls them (in *Psychic Retreats*, 1993), have a 'central function: to contain and neutralize ... primitive destructive impulses'. Through projective identification – an active putting into another object the destructive impulses – states of mind are produced in the patient in which he feels 'stuck, cut off and out of reach'. 'A psychic retreat', Steiner writes, 'provides the patient with an area of relative peace and protection from strain when meaningful contact with the analyst is experienced as threatening.' But the effect of this avoidance of contact with reality – through the ejection of so much of the patient's internal reality – is stultifying. 'The relief provided by the retreat', Steiner writes, 'is achieved at the cost of isolation, stagnation and withdrawal ... Typically an equilibrium is reached in which the patient uses the retreat to remain relatively free from anxiety but at the cost of an almost complete standstill in development.' The function of this retreat then becomes 'an area of the mind where reality does not have to be faced, where fantasy and omnipotence can exist unchecked and where anything is permitted'. Any 'aspect of reality which is difficult to accept' – and Steiner offers, as one might expect, death, ageing, difference between the sexes and the generations – is apparently abolished in the retreat. The analyst, Steiner writes quite sensibly, 'must try to understand what it is that the patient fears would result if he emerged from the retreat'.

It is a retreat because it is a psychic and/or environmental space fabricated by the patient to free himself of psychic pain. It is a pathological organization, a structure, because it starkly arranges, through the subtlest mechanism of projective identi-fication, a certain relatively anxiety-free state of mind. And Steiner is characteristically lucid in his exposition of this, which leads him to Narcissus, and Freud's Leonardo. 'In the most straightforward type of projective identification', he writes,

a part of the self is split off and projected into an object, where it is attributed to the object and the fact that it belongs to the self is denied. The object relationship which results is then not with a person truly seen as separate, but with the self projected into another person and related to as if it were someone else. This is the position of the mythical Narcissus who fell in love with a strange youth he did not consciously connect with himself. It is also true of Leonardo, who projected his infantile self into his apprentices and looked after them in the way he wished his mother had looked after him.

Steiner does not describe his psychic retreats as specifically narcissistic; though narcissism, and Narcissus himself are clearly implicated. It is perhaps worth mentioning that in Steiner's brief account of the myth, Narcissus must have projected something rather enticing into his reflection, in order to fall in love with it. Whereas Graves's description of Narcissus's path 'strewn with heartlessly rejected lovers of both sexes' would fit with Steiner's account of a projection of both destructiveness and guilt into the forsaken lovers.

But what I want to focus on here is what Steiner believes is being escaped *from* in these psychic retreats. There is reality, the strain of meaningful contact, 'any aspect of reality which is difficult to accept', particularly ageing, death and gender and generational differences, and primarily primitive destructive impulses. But at a more fundamental level, subsuming all these other things, as it were, is the sabotaging of, the attack on, the escape from *development*. The Sadeian orgy in this retreat where 'reality does not have to be faced, where fantasy and omnipotence can exist unchecked and where anything is permitted' is an alternative to, a sanctuary from, emotional growth. Without this essential underlying principle of emotional development the whole project of psychic retreat, within this metapsychological system, loses its purpose, its telos (Narcissus as the great hater of time). What is to be escaped from – what is deemed to be too painful to bear – is development. And so all of Steiner's images of life within the retreat are an odd mixture of licence ('anything is permitted') and immobility, paralysis, isolation, stagnation, withdrawal, feeling stuck, cut off and out of reach. This escape – Steiner's bolt-hole – tells us that for Steiner time and emotional development are the reality. And the way in which his theory tends towards closure – itself a kind of retreat – is in its implicit claim to be able to recognize genuine emotional growth when it sees it. Is it not, after all, another kind of omniscience to consider oneself the arbiter of true development? Not to mention, of course, the assuredness of his conviction that there is such a thing as development. If, for example, we were to say that there is simply change, and thereby shrug off all the progressivist associations, we might say that different people prefer some kinds of change to others. Psychic retreats would then no longer look like retreats, but rather more like resorts and resources. By calling it a retreat one might have pre-emptively privileged the alternative. In other words, if we take up Rorty's quote, the point is not: certain ways of living sabotage something essential to your being called emotional growth, and that one must, if at all possible, be in contact with something called reality in order to foster this growth. The question would be rather: does doing this, living in this way, get you the sort of life you want? 'The way to solve the problem you see in life', Wittgenstein wrote, 'is to live in a way that makes the problem disappear.' It would, I think, be inaccurate to say that one can make the problem one sees in life disappear by trying to escape from it.

At their worst, both rhetorically and practically, the essences in psychoanalysis, like emotional development in Steiner's theory, function as a kind of implicit blackmail. If you don't do this – get in touch with what I call reality – then something terrible will happen to you. You will fail to do something I call 'develop'; you will stagnate. In other words, it's worth wondering how much otherness, or what kind of otherness, can be happily included in Steiner's system, before the patient or the patient and his analyst is assumed to be on the side of pathology. The analyst must be an expert at recognizing destructive, counter-developmental behaviour. He cannot afford, say, to think of every act as morally equivocal, or paradoxical, or intrinsically unpredictable in its consequences.

As Steiner's interesting account makes clear we cannot promote otherness – that which is beyond fantasies of omnipotence, that which the narcissist struggles to disavow – without to some extent defining it; and by describing what otherness might include we must, to some extent, appropriate it, bring it within the range of our descriptions. In theory it tends to become either each theorist's open category, filled with what it is assumed the patient needs to acknowledge for a good life; but at its worst, of course, it becomes merely another tyrannical super-ego demand. Worse even than the command 'Be happy, enjoy yourself' is the command 'Allow something other than yourself as you would like to be'. The double-bind of this is self-evident. It might be, within its own terms, the apotheosis of narcissism to be as unnarcissistic as possible; to risk living outside the retreat. 'We wish to have', Coleridge wrote in his lectures on Shakespeare, 'a sort of prophetic existence present to us, which tells us what we are not . . .' Only the omniscience of knowing what we are can produce the omniscience of knowing what we are not. The shock of the new, one might say, is the shock of just how knowing we have been about the apparently familiar.

So what is interesting about Neville Symington's *Narcissism: A New Theory* (1993) – which comes out of the British Independent or Middle Group tradition – is what Symington wants to add to the familiar theories of narcissism. Agreeing that narcissism is essentially destructive (of the individual and the group) and, as he puts it, 'deeply antagonistic to self-knowledge . . . projecting unwanted aspects of the self,' he also believes it – against the grain of much psychoanalytic determinism – to be essentially 'chosen'. What he calls the 'narcissistic option' becomes the patient's decision in the face of trauma. He usefully divides up previous theories of narcissism as trauma theories or phobia theories. Steiner's more Kleinian theory would be phobic in that the narcissist is deemed to be in flight from innate destructiveness that has been projected in and out. Fairbairn and Kohut would be trauma theorists because for them the narcissist is managing an environmental deprivation, or impingement or insult. Both kinds of theory are a kind of pernicious bad faith for Symington – though that is not a phrase he uses – because they both covertly shift responsibility from the patient. The phobia theory implicitly blames some putative death instinct (or innate aggression), the trauma theory blames parents (and this means usually mothers). For Symington, in his unembarrassedly essential language, 'the *core* of narcissism is hatred of the relational – a hatred of something that is *inherent* in our being'. In what he calls advertently, 'the narcissistic disposition, it goes profoundly against the grain to have to acknowledge that one is affected by another'. The narcissist is a kind of Satan, an anti-life figure attacking the putative *core* of our being, our relation with others. So the narcissist, or the person of a narcissistic disposition, is deemed both to know what is the core of our being, that is, he is himself a committed essentialist, and because he knows so exactly what nurtures the relational he can so accurately spoil it. The narcissist and his theorist (or therapist) have a kind of symmetrical or complementary knowledge. Both of them know – though quite how we are not told – what is life-enhancing. 'The therapist's task', Symington writes with a degree of assurance provided by his theory, 'is to protect the struggling life-enhancing side against the side that desperately wants to keep within that narcissistic refuge and remain anaesthetised'.

I am myself now taking up a knowing position in relation to Symington's theory; but this fact, I think, is illustrative of the predicament I want to illustrate. Just as Symington believes 'Narcissism always has to be flushed out', presumably in both senses of the word – something all theorists of narcissism must be committed to a version of – so I want to flush out the omniscience in myself and others that makes such theories plausible. Everyone in psychoanalysis is against omniscience, this is not news; it should be more interesting news that so-called otherness is so difficult to really write and talk about without fetishizing it as a concept. And obviously this has implications beyond the psychoanalytic consulting room. If it might be better to talk about preferred worlds rather than narcissism and its alternatives – different worlds inducing different kinds of pleasure and suffering – it is not clear whether psychoanalytic theory can accommodate such frank pluralism, or would even want to.

I, too, want to escape from the dangerous escapism that is omniscience, and that gets to be called in psychoanalytic theory 'narcissism'. Indeed, the ordinary image of the narcissist – in Symington's words, 'enclosed, shut off from the other ... not interested in communicating' – is, by seeming definition, a negative ideal. And yet, as I have suggested, there is a dispiriting tautology or double-bind. What could be more omniscient than knowing that I do not know myself? But I don't think we should get out of this dilemma, or find ways around it, so much as be in it in better ways. Perhaps, like many other people, I find Steiner and Symington's accounts both mean-ingful and clinically useful, and doing in their theory-making what theorists of otherness cannot help but do; but that is partly, I think, because they appear to solve a problem, when the problem itself might be more interesting than the solution. The question becomes obscured by its answers. How *do* we know what is good for ourselves and someone else? Or indeed, how do we know – by what criteria as it were – what is good about ourselves and others? Clearly they are not always the same. Psychoanalysis does not get around these moral questions with the language of pathology. If what we think

we want to escape from is a key to what we think of as real –
and the real in psychoanalytic theory is deemed to be of
essential value to a person – then perhaps we should always
treat our notions of the real as what Laplanche calls enigmatic
signifiers, confounding messages that we inherit and need to
retranslate. Anything, after all, can be used as a refuge; so we
should ask of each psychoanalytic theory what it might be a
refuge from? Not as a way of invalidating it, but as a way of
elaborating it, of retranslating it.

When Freud wrote in 'Group Psychology and the Analysis of
the Ego', 'Love for oneself knows only one barrier – love for
others, love for objects', he was retranslating, among other
things, the enigmatic signifier of a supposedly altruistic
Christianity. But he was also leaving a kind of riddle for the
profession he had invented. After all, what happens when the
patient becomes a barrier to the analyst's self-love?

Roaring Boy

In so far as there was a consensus about Hart Crane's poetry after his suicide in 1932, it took the form of invidious comparisons. 'Crane had the sensibility typical of Baudelaire,' R. P. Blackmur wrote in 1935, 'and so misunderstood himself that he attempted to write *The Bridge* as if he had the sensibility typical of Whitman.' Dylan Thomas's poems, Randall Jarrell wrote in 1940, 'often mean much less than Crane's – but when you consider Crane's meanings this is not altogether a disadvantage'. And whether he was thought to be confused and self-deceiving, or vacuous, or even crazy, Crane was such a troubling figure, both before and after his early death, that people were inclined to describe his poetry in a way that cast aspersions on his character; as though such unapproachable poems could only be approached biographically. Comparing Crane's 'epics' with Zukofsky's, Hugh Kenner wrote, in his once canonical *The Pound Era*: '*The Bridge* yields only to nutcrackers, "A" to reading.' There was certainly something that Crane's poems wouldn't let you do to them.

Crane produced two prodigious books of poetry, *White Building* (1926) and *The Bridge* (1930), and died at the age of thirty-three by jumping off a ship bound for New York. After such a brief life and dramatic death he seemed like the very stuff of poetic legend, a Chatterton-and-Rimbaud of his time.

Reviews of Paul Mariani, *The Broken Tower: A Life of Hart Crane*, (Norton, 1999) and Langdon Hammer and Brom Weber (eds), *O My Land, My Friends: The Selected Letters of Hart Crane*, (Four Walls Eight Windows, 1997) from the *London Review of Books*.

He was a famous drunk, he was homosexual (and occasionally heterosexual), and he was definitely either a fraud or a genius. There was also something about him that made people excessive in their reactions to him; and the people who knew him and the people who took against his poetry seem wittingly or unwittingly to have acknowledged this. So the kinds of point his early critics wanted to make (or score) were often at Crane's expense, as though his authenticity or his sanity were being assessed from some much more assured moral ground. If, as his friend and enemy Yvor Winters said, Crane was 'a saint of the wrong religion', he also confirmed other people in the rightness of their own devotions. What Mariani's useful and interesting new biography shows most clearly is the stir he created around him: the turbulence his poetry caused in the few people who were attentive to it, and the havoc wrought among his friends and lovers.

Critics trying to find the comparison, invidious or otherwise, that would illuminate Crane's often baffling poetic progress were only doing what he himself seems to have spent his life doing. The not knowing who (or what) he was like turned into a passionate, but mostly solitary quest for literary affinities. 'The *Aeneid* was not written in two years – nor in four,' Crane wrote to his patron Otto Kahn, 'and in more than one sense I feel justified in comparing the historical and cultural scope of *The Bridge* to that great work.' Whether he was used by poets and critics alike to represent the more disabling trends of what became known as Modernism – portentous ambition, impenetrable allusiveness, a programmatic resistance to being easily read – or the perils of styling oneself a poetic visionary, he always exerted a peculiar fascination. But it has never been quite clear whether his extraordinarily subtle and stagey poems are about something (let alone everything, as he sometimes claimed) or about anything other than his often expressed wish to be a great visionary poet, to join the 'visionary company'. Reading Crane – like reading Lowell, or Berryman, or Plath, among many others for whom Crane is crucial – one is never sure whether ambition is doing the work of the imagination, or whether ambition *is* the work of the imagination. This is the dilemma that makes American poetry of this century so exhilarating. Crane's need to be a great visionary American poet – which for him meant, essentially, to be the alternative to Eliot – is what the poetry is about. 'New thresholds, new anatomies!' he declaims in his poem 'Wine Menagerie', as though one might be able to go for both.

The brevity of Crane's life has made his biographers keen to be inclusive, if nothing else. His thirty-two years inspired an 800-page 'immensely researched life' (Mariani's words) from John Unterecker. But that was thirty years ago. Since then, Mariani tells us, 'new readings and new information have both become available, giving us further access to Crane's brilliant, multifoliate world'. Mariani has managed to keep Crane's world to just under 500 pages, and though his book is not dull as Unterecker's is, it nevertheless strains to find just what might be telling about Crane's enigmatic life. Most modern biographies are too long either because modern lives are uniquely well documented, or because there is now a pervasive uncertainty about the plotting of lives. Crane's biographers begin with the hermeticism of his poetry, and the necessary secrecy of his homosexuality. A lot of letters are now available – correspondence with his family and with Yvor Winters has been published, in addition to the present brilliant selection – but, unsurprisingly, they offer neither a straightforward commentary on the poems nor an unambiguous documentary of his day-to-day life.

'He did so much that was outrageous, but so much that was

unaffectedly kind or exuberant and so much that kept us entertained,' Malcolm Cowley wrote. 'Nobody yawned when Hart was about.' It was Crane's determination in virtually everything he wrote that there would be no yawning; his dread of the dull quotidian, of the ordinary as a form of corruption, fired his writing. It was a more fortunate Fall he was after in his idiosyncratic theology, to counter the smug pessimism of what he calls, as if for emphasis, Eliot's *The Waste Lands*. In his first great poem, 'For the Marriage of Faustus and Helen', it is clear that he knows what he wants – 'Brazen hypnotics glitter here' – which necessarily involves Faustianly not quite knowing what he is doing:

> Greet naively – yet intrepidly
> New soothings, new amazements
> That cornets introduce at every turn –
> And you may fall downstairs with me
> With perfect grace and equanimity.

Crane may be trying to tell us how we should read him, but the instructions are strewn with necessary impossibilities. To do anything with deliberate naivety already entails too much knowledge; a fall with grace that is a fall from grace is hard to conjure. 'You may' is poised between permission and good fortune. And yet the quest for 'New soothings, new amazements', linked to the drunk's wish to fall downstairs with equanimity, is magnificent visionary clowning. Crane, who met Chaplin, and wrote a good poem about him, saw more clearly than many of his contemporaries (and most of his critics) the burlesque in all grandiose ambition: 'We have (I cannot be too sure of this for my own satisfaction) in Chaplin a dramatic genius that truly approaches the fabulous sort ... I am moved to put Chaplin with the poets of today.' Grace, in its perfect and imperfect forms – as manners and divine election, as revelation and poise – was one of Crane's most urgent preoccupations. It was also, not incidentally, his mother's name. 'I'm not going to make it, dear ... I'm utterly disgraced' were virtually his last words, spoken to his lover, Peggy Cowley (Malcolm Cowley's about to be ex-wife).

Like most boys, Crane was a mother's boy, and Mariani's book is excellent on Crane's parents – informative and evocative about their disparate histories, and how they clashed – but less convincing, or less subtle, about what Crane made of them. Just how and why his project emerged from (out of?) the terrible scenes between the parents seems worth more thought than Mariani is prepared to give it. Biographers inevitably find it difficult to convey just how enigmatic parents are to children, with the result that we frequently assume the existence of some quite straightforward causal connection between what the parents were supposedly like, and how the boy turned out. But if biography tends to over-personalize the work by apparently providing it with a set of easy-to-use, ready-made referents, at its best it can show us how people went about finding, or not finding, what they needed to become who they thought they were, or wanted to be. Mariani provides a strong chronological narrative but he is wary of certain kinds of speculation about Crane's affinities and aversions. In Crane's life, which was so much a writing life, there is furtiveness everywhere, and not always for the obvious reason. The very real danger of being exposed as gay and the very real wish to be an entirely original poet were so essential to Crane's sense of himself that they can begin to seem too important, at the cost of so much else. After all, the wish for concealment has to look for its occasions, the need to hide needs opportunities to perform itself.

The opening lines of Crane's first poem in *White Buildings*, his first book, can be seen, in retrospect, to announce a project. The poem, aptly entitled 'Legend', begins with a two-line stanza:

> As silent as a mirror is believed
> Realities plunge in silence by . . .

In a mirror, as in a dream, things are seen without attendant explanation, without legend; we are shown something and told nothing. If 'plunge' captures in some uncanny way the shallow depths of the mirror, it is also the first of many fateful images of falling and jumping and dropping down that would be enacted at his death. It is a characteristically condensed version of a traditional poetic image, but it insists on the unspoken in what is so vividly seen. Crane's poetic legend of himself will be like a dumb-show in which things and people – 'realities' – will keep disappearing without being able to announce themselves. His poetry, for all its self-professed grandeur and self-confessing bathos, is always telling us that there are things he wants to hide, and that the hiding is as important as what is hidden. 'Frankly,' he writes to a friend, 'I admit to a taste for certain affectations and ornamental commissions.' He was as frank as he could be about his artful concealments.

His extensive correspondence with his family (just over 650 pages of letters to his mother, father and maternal grandmother), taken together with Mariani's gruelling account of the parents' marriage, makes it quite clear why he needed his sophisticated forms of privacy. And also why he might have felt a powerful affinity with the legacy of Emerson and Whitman that would counsel him not to be daunted or overimpressed by the past, or doomed by an inheritance. There was, Crane wrote, 'nothing but illness and mental disorder in my family', and these were things his poetry wanted neither to disown nor to be stifled by. Poetry would inevitably refer to the past – both personal and cultural – but it would not defer to it. 'Forgive me for an echo of these things,' he wrote in his poem 'Recitative', 'And let us walk through time with equal pride.' His poetry, which he seemed quite literally to live for, would restore him – 'In sapphire arenas of the hills/I was promised an improved infancy' – and renew America: *The Bridge* was to be his 'mystical synthesis of America'. But his pride had been plunged in his family's shame, and his country, sliding, as he saw it, towards a trivial and tawdry materialism, had failed to keep its promise. Indeed, family and country were complicit with each other and he felt he was drowning. 'Unless I isolate myself (and pretty soon) from the avalanche of bitterness and wailing that has flooded me ever since I was seven years old,' he wrote to a friend in 1926, 'there won't be enough left of me even to breathe, not to mention writing.' He was a victim, he believed, of a kind of cosmic catastrophe.

'Immaculate venom binds,' Crane wrote in an early poem. There are couples everywhere in his poetry, and most of them don't get on. 'For the moth/Bends no more than the still/ Imploring flame.' The unhappy wife and mother endlessly implored; the husband wouldn't bend to wife or son, and eventually left; and the son seems to have been both moth and flame (there had been suicide attempts before he finally succeeded; and the last five years of his life were like a slow suicide). Crane seems to have allied himself, in the traditional way, with his mother, while all the time furtively seeking out his father's regard. It is difficult to tell quite how the conspiracies worked. He tends to represent himself as persecuted by his mother's needs, and by his feelings for her; and abandoned by his father to be her life-support system. What makes the story at once intriguing and unsatisfying is that it tends towards allegory. Mother as hysterical muse,

encouraging the boy to be an 'artist' while the two of them
drowned in their feelings for each other; indeed, getting the boy
to change his name, once he becomes a poet, to Hart (her
maiden name) Crane, from Harold Hart Crane, giving him a
stage-name, so to speak, that is the starkest combination of his
parents. And father as capitalist – creator of 'the largest maple
syrup business of its kind in the world', inventor of the
Lifesaver, and a successful and then failed chocolate manu-
facturer – not duly impressed either by his son's poetic
ambitions or by his description of himself as 'the incarnation
of love's entrapment', encouraging the boy to get a real job.
'You don't seem to have enough of the earnest side of life,'
Crane's father writes to him after yet another request for cash.
'People may laugh at your jokes, they may regard you as a
prodigy; they may occasionally buy a book,' but 'sooner or later
your affections are expressed in beefsteaks.' Whatever else you
do, you have to eat and provide. There is wit in this, and in its
unglamorous truth-telling it gets a measure of his son. One of
the very real successes of Mariani's book is that it captures
something of the poignancy of Crane's defeated and devoted
relationship with his father. But by the same token very little is
seen – or seen sympathetically – from the mother's point of
view. Whether because the nature of the available material
dictates it, or because that is how Mariani frames the story,
Crane's mother comes across as at best an invalid. What was so
good about Mariani's biography of Berryman was that he let us
see what Berryman could also have loved and admired about
his mother. Biography should be a refuge from the scapegoating of parents.

The dumbing down of the mother sometimes makes Crane
seem too glibly the 'product' of his family; inevitably gay and
unavoidably the saboteur of his own professional prospects.
Mariani's account is not, it should be said, schematic in this

way; but because he so scrupulously underexplains how Crane became the man he did, he implicitly reinforces our most general assumptions. Biographies should theorize themselves (if they have to) to counter the taken-for-granted descriptions, the psychologizing, that make lives all sound more or less the same. 'Crane's life,' Mariani writes, 'reads like a great Greek tragedy, and I have tried to capture something of the meteoric rise and fall of this brilliant and tragic poet'; but what also needs to be shown is what Crane's choices looked like, and what actually looked like a choice to Crane. The biographer, in other words, needs to take advantage of the fact that he has more choices, when it comes to the telling of the life-story, than his subject did.

To write the life of someone who dreaded being caught (Crane himself spoke of his 'slippery scale-of-the-fish, continual escape attitude') but at the same time craved recognition – for his poetry, for the values his elusiveness embodied – is a project already ironized. In cruising the New York docks for sailors, as in his will to absolute originality, Crane was, by definition, trying to exempt himself from conventional definition. It was the same with his writing: 'If my work seems needlessly sophisticated,' he wrote to a friend, 'it is because I am only interested in adding what seems to me something really new to what has been written.' He demands a lot of his biographer because he wants to be seen hiding; because he suffers from and relishes what he calls 'the love of things irreconcilable'. 'I admit,' he writes in one of the many admissions he allows in his letters, 'to a slight leaning toward the esoteric, and am perhaps not to be taken seriously.' For 'taken seriously' read: 'taken in any of the usual ways'. When you read Crane's letters and poems, the phrase 'the erotics of style' makes a kind of sense.

In a way Crane's life is the familiar life of the modern poet: an attempt to transform childhood unhappiness into literary success. He was born in Garrettsville, Ohio, in 1899 to parents who were, as the editors of the letters put it, 'prosperous, ambitious and ill-matched'. The family moved to Cleveland, as his father's business became increasingly successful, and the couple divorced when Crane was seventeen, after a torrid and frustrating marriage. As a boy growing up Crane was the over-exposed witness, audience and accomplice of this terrible drama. Whether or not, as the editors say, 'the divorce ... wounded their only child and propelled him into poetry', it certainly seems to have propelled him into an eternal rest-lessness. At seventeen he left school and family for New York, and his brief life of homelessness and intense poetic ambition began. Mariani is very good on Crane's desire, rather than love, for New York; in the city, he could be anonymous and sexually alive. But what he couldn't do was hold down a job. He wrote advertising copy, but the economic depression of the times conspired with his loathing for the work. So he would sabotage jobs, in order to write, cadge jobs and money from his father and from his friends, and be forever moving around; from Cleveland to New York, to Upper New York State, to Cuba (where his mother's family had land), to Europe, to New York and eventually to Mexico, where his fraught and harassed life finally unravelled in alcohol and violence. He became obsessed with 'primitive' Mexican culture, and had his first sustained affair with a woman.

In this feverish escapade of a life Crane made and broke important literary friendships with, most significantly, the poet-critics Allen Tate and Yvor Winters. But despite his evident charm, there was something about him that people found impossible, and even towards the end, intimidating. Menace and amusement seemed to be coupled inside him ('The everlasting eyes of Pierrot/And, of Gargantua, the laughter'): a kind of demonic self-defeated trickiness that disturbed people. 'He did not even hate us,' Katherine Anne Porter wrote when Crane visited her and her husband and got resentfully drunk, 'for we were nothing to him. He hated and feared himself.' He found patrons to back and publish his strange poetry and, as Mariani shows, he could inspire extreme affection in people. But too soon they would feel, as William Carlos Williams wrote, 'uncomfortable' with his 'roaring boy, predatory reputation'. It seemed that nothing could contain him, except his poetry. So when the poetry stopped, in a very real sense he had nowhere to go.

Like the visionary company that he emulated (but also joined), Crane was determinedly self-educated, which is as close as one can get to being self-invented. He left school as soon as possible, and as Mariani points out with some relish, never went near a university. One of the fascinations of Mariani's book is the idiosyncrasy of Crane's reading life: Donne, Webster, Marlowe, Laforgue (Eliot's reading list); a passion for Vaughan, Traherne, Blake, Whitman; an immediate recognition of Stevens as the great contemporary poet. For all the frenzy and despondency of his life there was always the surety of his reading; and his sense that the reading was for the writing. The cogency of the personal aesthetic that he made up out of the vagaries of his erotic life and what he calls 'the whirlwind hysterics of Fate (if one may allude to one's family in that way)' comes across very strongly in the letters, as does his sense that there were obscure connections between what he and his family had been through, the boom-and-bust capitalism of America in the Twenties, and the cult of Eliot's wasteland sensibility. A break had to be made. 'The poetry of negation is beautiful,' Crane writes to his friend Gorham Munson in 1922, alas, too dangerously so for one of my mind. But I am trying to break away from it. Perhaps this is useless, perhaps it is silly – but one does have joys. The vocabulary of damnations and prostrations has been developed at the expense of these other moods, however, so that it is hard to dance in proper measure. Let us invent an idiom for the proper transposition of jazz into words! Something clean, sparkling, elusive.

As with most writers, the relationship between what Crane wanted and believed, and what he did was unstable. But he was quick to see the all too stable complacency (and complicity) of Eliot's glooms. Like most visionaries, he wanted to rhyme ecstasy with justice. It is perhaps a sign of the times that he has become more and more our contemporary as he is read less and less.

Frederick Seidel's New Poetry

In 1984 Frederick Seidel's first and, as it turned out, only book of poems was published in England, with the Browningesque title *Men and Woman*. Published in the Chatto Poetry series, it was in fact a selection of Seidel's poetry made by the poet himself; most of it came from a book published in America in 1980 called *Sunrise*, and there were new poems, some of which had been published in the *London Review of Books*. Seidel was, and has in fact remained, a relatively unknown poet in this country, and the book was soon, as it still is, out of print. The few reviews of it, as I remember them, were not notably either impressed or impressive. In a way, perhaps, this was to be expected because none of the many extraordinary contemporary American poets have ever really made their mark here since Robert Lowell; and even Lowell and his remarkable contemporaries – apart from Elizabeth Bishop – seemed to more or less disappear from (critical) view in the 1980s.

Seidel is clearly the heir of Crane and Lowell – and more obliquely of Whitman – and this in itself may have made his poetry difficult to hear, the 'visionary company' seeming to have rather lost its way in this country. Of course, one can never tell whether the resistance is merely to 'poetry', or to a particular individual voice; and a case is made for the poems in the pieces reprinted here. But there is something about Seidel's poetry that is unclubbable, and not for the obviously glamorous reasons. Seidel is rarely referred to in accounts of what modern poetry can and can't do, or why it might be worth reading.

These reviews wanted to say, among other things, why this is a shame.

1

There is a poem in Frederick Seidel's new book,* appropriately entitled 'Rackets', in which someone knowingly imitates someone else, but mockingly, to assert a difference. Or rather a double difference. She imitates someone making, or claiming, a distinction:

> She curled her pinky in smiling imitation
> Of the ancient crone she had known as a child
> Who seized every opportunity to say,
> Her fabulous diamonds winking away,
> 'I am Mrs. Reginald Fincke! Fincke with an "e"!'

If it is part of the modern poet's project to seize every opportunity to say that he or she is not anyone else, however similar, then he or she does this by finding a 'voice': a performance, a cadence, a signature they can in some sense repeat. At its most extreme, the function of the found, distinctive voice can be to stifle, or muffle, a multiplicity of other voices, whether they be the voices of tradition, the voices of circumstance, or the voices of a more private self. The journey from accomplished pastiche – being a new echo of old voices – to the finding of a distinctive private voice has become the modern poet's progress myth. But the risk is that poets begin by imitating other voices and end up imitating their own. Having found a way of continually quoting himself, the poet can do nothing else. In this brilliantly accomplished and disturbing book, full

---

*Review of Frederick Seidel, *My Tokyo* (Farrar, Straus and Giroux, 1996), from *Raritan*.

239

as it is of voices and voicings, of smiling imitations, Seidel both quotes himself – literally repeating lines and poems – and writes other poets into his poems. But he does so in a way that leaves you, as with Mrs Fincke, unsure of who the joke is on. It is as though self-assertion as self-definition, is somehow complicit with self-mockery.

Ending a poem about Leni Riefenstahl, for example, Seidel gives Sylvia Plath a walk-on part:

> Now in London Sylvia Plath
> Nailed one foot to the floor;
> And with the other walked
> And walked and walked through the terrible blood.

This is at once a deliberately kitsch piece of Plath, a horrified critique, and a grotesque cartoon – in a poem about the 'Aryan ideal' – of Rabbinic hermeneutics: walking round and round a problem. It features the kind of performed allusion that Seidel has made his own. In another poem, 'Glory', Ezra Pound is brought in on a perfect cadence from the *Cantos*, 'Pound reciting with his eyes closed filled the alcove with glory'. The line begins with his name and then formulates the project of his poem. The effect of these flawless, calculated imitations – Seidel's staging of other voices – is, of course, complicated. But one thing they do, among other things, is expose the sense in which a distinctive voice can be like a commodity. It can be reproduced in imitation (and parody) thereby becoming complicit with the Tokyo of Seidel's title poem ('Make more make more make more consumer goods,' the breathless voice in the poem repeats). In 1956 the critic R. P. Blackmur wrote that the modern poet 'has found himself seeking a private language and has grown proud of it'. The modern poet Blackmur refers to is someone supposedly exempting himself from the conversation in the market-place: privacy as purity.

'When he opens his mouth it is a choir,' Seidel once wrote of Eliot, the other poet from St Louis.

Seidel's ambitious and unsettling poetry has always been haunted by such willed exemptions; it has often been about what being or trying to be uninvolved involves you in (certainly nothing saintly). Much of the wit of his poetry, some of its terrible hilarity, comes from the poet's wish to be an aesthete, or even a dandy, in what often seems to be a revenge tragedy. 'Jacobean black and white', as he wrote in 'Erato' in his second book, *Sunrise*, 'The fantastic wrong and right, now dissolving / In Jamesian grey.' Dissolving is one kind of solution; it is not disappearing. In *My Tokyo*, again, these extremes of feeling, this Jacobean black and white, are countered by the work of trying not to feel:

Meanwhile the civil rights movement I completely missed.
I was so busy doing nothing.
I had no time. They lynched and burned.
I played squash drunk.

Reading this, drunk with the syntax, it seems for a moment to be the civil rights movement that lynched and burned; the pronouns make the civil rights movement disappear. But artful contempt for the evasive self is matched in Seidel's poetry by a pervasive sense of terror, of what Henry James called *the real* – that which it is impossible not to know. Obsessed, as his poetry has always been, by the insulation of art and wealth, by the fluencies of power and the anaesthetic of glamour, the poems in *My Tokyo* suggest that no degree of privilege, no sophistication, can protect the poet from the lurid brutality around him. He becomes, in fact, the virtuoso ventriloquist of this contemporary reality, and the book as a whole is a ferocious satire on the aestheticizing of politics (and poetry). He writes, for example, a sonnet, entitled 'Sonnet', about carnage, and concludes a poem punningly entitled 'From a High Floor', about the existential crises of the rich: 'The *homeless* homeless have / The center strip of Broadway. / To live where you should jump.' If *My Tokyo* wants an exit from High Art (and Tragic Flaws), it wants it in High Art. But it is the relationship – within individual poems and within the book – between sophisticated complicity and stark outrage that makes *My Tokyo* such a remarkable book. 'This century must end,' Seidel writes in one of its finest poems, and, 'To modern art I say – / It's been real.' 'TERROR' Seidel writes in his great long poem 'Sunrise', 'IS OUR PLEASURE.' In *My Tokyo* it's getting harder and harder, less and less tempting, to turn it into a pleasure.

It is difficult to recall any recent book of poetry – perhaps Frank Bidart's *Golden State* or *The Book of the Body* – that has so much terror in it. This is a book of poetry that is formally adept and ingenious about everything in contemporary life that makes poetry seem silly. And if some of Seidel's poems, or parts of them, can sound like, say, Lowell's poems as written by Don DeLillo, it is because they seem full of voices only just contained, poised somewhere between hysteria and cynicism, as though there were always too much of something that has to be managed, a nameless dread. ('Sympathized with,' he wrote in an early poem, 'Spring', 'it comes off on your hands.') Whether the 'too much' is of something present or something absent is usually left unclear, and this puzzle is often the focus of his most interesting poetry. 'Constant sunrise of feelings but no feeling,' as he phrases it in 'Sunrise'. That feeling too much might really be a way of feeling too little, or that one might not be able to tell the difference – it is this that gives his poetry a continual air of foreboding. Indeed, most of the poems in *My Tokyo* are organized around the prelude or the aftermath of a catastrophe, something from which there is no protection, unless it be, perhaps, the protection of a style, a horrified comedy, in some way commensurate with experience. 'I am a toupee walking toward me / With no one under it. / I put the gun to my head.' Seidel is perhaps the only contemporary poet who exploits the melodrama rather than the portentousness of surrealism.

If it is the pressure of James's *real* that creates the lure of a private language (and a private life) as both resistance and refuge, it is also exactly that pressure, as Seidel's work shows, that makes such privacy impossible. In his poetry the private, insulated self is continually being ruptured, or assaulted by reality. (Like a revenge tragedy, *My Tokyo* is full of dead bodies.) And he tries to represent and distance this reality by making his poetry into a kind of film; many of his poems are cinematic both in the way they sometimes cut abruptly from scene to scene, and in the smooth glide of their gaze. He also tries to tone down this reality by turning the sound off. This is both a recurrent phrase in the poems – Tokyo is described in this book as 'Elizabethan London with the sound off' – and also accounts for the eerie, slow-motion, dreamlike quality of the scenes he often sets. The voyeur, who figures conspicuously in Seidel's poetry, is of course the one who looks with the sound turned off, who doesn't want anyone else around distracting him. In his previous book, *These Days*, the poem 'Gethsemane' begins: 'My life. / I live with it. / I look at it. / My spied on, with malice.' The voyeur as mock-emperor of all he surveys – *my* Tokyo – is keeping his distance (in his extraordinary poem, 'The Trip in Sunrise', Seidel writes of the horizon, 'It I feel close to, it cannot come near'). But the poet keeping himself to himself, the poet as voyeur, never quite extricates himself.

In virtually every poem, Seidel enacts a curiously contemporary drama of distances and limits ('They can't get close enough – there's no such thing'). In *My Tokyo* relationships are defined, and terrorized, by their complicities: 'The bitch relieves the dog. The wound, the gun'; 'The famine's every-where there's UNICEF' (if you're part of the solution you're part of the problem). 'In New York the homeless / Reify the rich,' Seidel writes in the book's title poem, which wonders whose Tokyo it can be in the age of multinational corporations and the accumulating triumphs of capitalism; and in which the parasite and the voyeur become the representative figures. Sadomasochism is, for Seidel's poetry, what space travel was for Donne's: a way of finding the limits of his world.

This acute sense of complicities at work is reinforced by the way Seidel continually teases his lines with suggestive internal half-rhymes: 'He believed / The atonal was eternal' (of Anton Webern); 'Racially pure with no poor' (of Japan). The effect of this wordplay, deliberately arch, and often as not echoing nonsense verse and nursery rhymes, is to make the suggested connections enigmatic, even sinister. What's going on when words are almost the same? What is being repeated in a half-rhyme? Seidel plots his poems, and his book, in a way that makes us think about these differences – about, as it were, the politics of echoes. As the title poem insists, capitalism and fascism both brutally promote sameness: 'This spring our western eyes are starting to slant,' presumably under Conrad's 'Western Eyes'. Political ideologies, like poetic forms, can be terrifying imitation-games.

Seidel plays calculatedly intriguing and unsettling games in this book with repetition, and the (political and poetic) imitations and allusions that are forms of repetition. On the one hand he repeats lines and images from earlier poems, as he has always done. But in *My Tokyo* he both repeats a poem from a previous book, with one minimal change and a change of title, and also repeats a poem under different titles, within the book itself, again with one small, notable change – prompting the obvious question: what's the difference? And he follows the long poem repeated from *These Days* with a poem called 'The Second Coming', which is itself, of course, the second coming of a poem called 'The Second Coming'. Seidel's second coming, though, is no rough beast but a 'Half Japanese, half Jewish' girl; certainly not more of the same. Novelty is defined by what it fails to repeat. When is a repetition not a repetition? When it's more of something else. Seidel begins a remarkable poem, 'Hair in a Net':

> If you're a woman turning fifty,
> You're a woman who feels cheated.
> This message now will be repeated.

But not in the poem. In 'Glory', Seidel writes: 'Thanksgiving weekend 1953 I made my pilgrimage to Pound, / Who said, Kike-sucking Pusey will destroy Harvard unless you save it.' And after those two words the next line refers to another two words: 'I persuaded him two words in his translation of Confucious should change.' Two words repeated as displaced correction.

Seidel as the aspiring young poet wanted poetry to make a difference: 'My art will find and detonate your heart.' Not a change of heart but an explosion, one of many explosions in *My Tokyo*, which is full of deadpan apocalypses in which you can't tell the difference between the beginning and the end. 'It started to speak when it exploded,' he writes in a poem titled 'Untitled', 'I see I have described a confessional poet.' Did 'it' start to speak before or after it exploded, and how could you tell? Seidel, who could once have been described, mistakenly, as a confessional poet, is always trying to find a before and after ('I took for my own motto,' he wrote in *Sunrise*, 'I rot before I ripen'). The sophisticated eloquence of his poetry is always in the uneasy service of the many bizarre forms of chaos – both psychic and temporal – that it contains, and the poems often seem on the verge of breaking into several styles and voices. All his antic dispositions can only just about hold things together, and the repetitions can be like tricks for staving something off.

In *My Tokyo* Seidel often repeats a phrase or a line three times, making it sound somewhere between a litany and a taunt:

> It's that time of year.
> It's that time of year a thousand times a day.
>   A thousand times a day,
> A thousand times a day.

The insistence of the lines performs the relentless haunting of a memory that is being described. But repeating it three times keeps it just this side of sense, as though repetition both stops time and dissipates it. In Seidel's poems someone is often trying to put a stop to something, and every seeming repetition, every second or third coming of a word, or a phrase, or even a poem reveals the impossibility of this. So the poems often lurch between bafflement and dismay. The terror in these poems – that are so adept at endings – is the feeling that there's no end of something devastating, that 'The opposite of infinite / Is infinite.' The rituals and routines that his poems describe (and sometimes are), from the sadomasochistic to the mock-religious, are mostly parodic; not the rage for order but the rage of order.

It is striking how little Seidel figures in accounts of contemporary poetry, perhaps because there is something unassimilable about his poems; and this is particularly true of *My Tokyo*. It is as though the complex pitch of their intelligence, and their extraordinary formal accomplishment, are still in excess of a critical language that can make a sufficient case for their daunting precision. Every word works, and every false note seems calculated. Their public and private dread, their casual fluency and range of echo and allusion, are of a piece with their suspicions about art and its accomplishments.

2

When Wordsworth wrote his Preface to the *Lyrical Ballads* he was clearly thinking of Frederick Seidel.* 'For a multitude of causes, unknown to former times,' he wrote,

are now acting with a combined force to blunt the discriminating powers of the mind, and, unfitting it for all voluntary exertion, to reduce it to a state of almost savage torpor. The most effective of these causes are the great national events which are daily taking place, and the increasing accumulation of men in cities, where the uniformity of their occupations produces a craving for extra-ordinary incident, which the rapid communication of intelligence hourly gratifies ... When I think upon this degrading thirst after outrageous stimulation, I am almost ashamed to have spoken of the feeble endeavour ... to counteract it.

There may be escalating grounds for righteous indignation among the literate, but the most compelling voices in American poetry now have a kind of inspired complicity with much of what also dismays them. Wordsworth, unlike Byron, couldn't conceive of the poet as being morally strengthened by being morally compromised; that one could crave extraordinary incident and outrageous stimulation – as the poet of the archly entitled *Going Fast* has always claimed to do – and for that very reason sustain what Wordsworth called one's ordinary sympathies. It is the virtue of Seidel's poetry never to sell out on exhilaration – never to despise excitement – and yet to keep the discriminating powers of the mind going, even if they are also, in both senses, going fast. He avoids the smug

* Review of Frederick Seidel, *Going Fast* (Farrar, Straus and Giroux, 1998), from *Raritan*.

purities of the average jeremiad by being so flagrantly on both sides of Wordsworth's great divide. He can relish what he also wants to retreat from, so the moral thrills of his poetry can be as daunting as the moral spills, the cruel intelligence of glamour as alluring as the mystical stillness that is somewhere also at the heart of his poetry. In *Going Fast* people are always speeding to find out if they can stop, to find out what stops them: 'A man comes in from the whirl / To a room where he does yoga / High above the homeless. He runs smack / Into still space. / He sits in the air' ('Christmas'). It is the collision that grips Seidel in this enthralling new book; in which the whirl is almost the world, and the ordinary language of drugs ('high', 'smack') is the ordinary language for all this jarred experience.

What Wordsworth describes in the famous Preface is, if anything, truer now than it was then. But the values he wants to use his poetry to defend – a more meditative thoughtfulness, a more patient reverence for the natural world, and for other people however marginal – can be made to seem like an easy nostalgia for those affluent enough to afford such moral comfort. Still space is hard to find and harder to believe in. Combine Wordsworth and global capitalism and what do you get?

Combine a far-seeing industrialist.
With an Islamic fundamentalist.
With an Italian Premier who doesn't take bribes.
With a pharmaceuticals CEO who loves to spread disease.
Put them on a 916.

And you get Fred Seidel.
    ('Milan')

Here is the new kind of visionary, the person who really wants to change the world fast, the person who believes in something ('loving' to spread disease is clearly different from just spreading disease). Here is the growth of a poet's mind; but it is a combination, and of bafflingly disparate ambitions. And as usual in Seidel's poetry the literary allusions are all the more effective for being at once stark and luridly brash: 'The Ducati 916 is a nightingale.' Seidel's nightingale is non-stop and predatory, 'Sudden as a shark.'

Going Fast – with all its bikes and cars and planes and sharks and ostentatious wealth that have always been Seidel's paraphernalia of the contemporary sublime – is a book about torpor. Wordsworth's phrase 'savage torpor', which sounds oddly like Lowell, catches the violence in, and the violence that always surrounds, certain kinds of paralysis. The torpid are in suspended animation – high above the homeless, as it were – taking refuge from some unbearable excess (of grief, of shame, of ecstasy, of terror); hoping the freeze-frame holds. For Wordsworth the random energies of modern life dull people; but Wordsworth has to blind himself to the irony that it is these very energies – the daily assault of national events in the media, the crowds of people – that inspire the counter-action of his poetry. Far from blunting the discriminating powers of his own mind, this new multitude of causes feeds him his best lines. It was the social sublime of the cities, with their daunting excesses, that made the natural sublime such a necessary invention. Something as radically complicated and profane as living in a modern city had to find a more spiritually wholesome analogue. Unlike Wordsworth, Seidel loves going fast (there isn't much walking in his poetry); and modern cities are where he sets most of these new poems, relishing the '... stark / Deliciously expensive shops'. But like Wordsworth, he senses the moral entropy of it all. What Seidel calls 'reeking of allure' cuts both ways.

Seidel, who is virtually unique among contemporary poets in finding Lowell a plausible inspiration, shares Lowell's haunted appetite for the civic sublime, for the more that can never be enough – and in which the language of triumph is always threatened by the language of dejection (and abjection). 'First in his class at Cambridge till he received an inheritance' ('In Memoriam'); 'Even in First, there is only more' ('Victory'). The bare literary allusions in the titles of these poems suggest this atmosphere of terrified dismay – of the depletion gathering on the poems' horizon – about which they are so reckless and eloquent. But the visionary burlesque of these extraordinary poems – their gleeful, ferocious energy – is of a piece with Seidel's unreserved poetic ambition. 'Only more' is not merely a more or less interesting way of putting it; just as that other First nods at the poetic inheritances Seidel is so brilliant at exploiting.

Because these new poems are never solemn or sentimental – as poetic ambition usually is – they are always morally unsettling; at once playing upon the reader's complicity, and making him wonder what he's doing there, reading this poem:

> Your haven't come here only for the shark show.
> Their fixed smiles glide.
> Their blank eyes go along for the ride.
> They bury their faces in life explosively,
> And shake their heads back and forth to tear some off.
>   ('Anyone with the Wish')

Shaking their heads back and forth is the no that is yes, that is the emblematic gesture of Seidel's poetry. We haven't come here only for the shark show – *only*, again, is the word – but we have also come for the shark show; and our eyes go along for the pornographic ride, can't resist this love-of-life scene ('Sharks swim in the love'). What are we wishing for if we relish this? It is as though, Seidel intimates, there is some obscure, enthralling grandeur in the ruthless parasitism for which he has such an acute eye. And as though the poem itself can never be quite sure which side of the line it's on, whether it's ill or well:

> No civilized state will execute
> Someone who is ill
> Till it makes the someone well
> Enough to kill
> In a civilized state,
> As a poem does.
> ('Poem Does')

By the end of this perfectly morally perplexed sentence – in which the line-endings, as always in Seidel's poetry, do so much of the work – 'civilized practices', like the making (and reading) of poems seem rather a mixed blessing. 'Getting / Ready not to get deady, / Which is also what a poem does,' implies that if the poem enlivens us, what it can make us alive to may be unbearable. If the poem releases us from our 'savage torpor', we may begin to realize that we're better off dead. The awkward discomfort occasioned by the cutesy baby-talk of 'deady' also prompts us to undo it, and make another meaning equally integral to the poem: 'getting / Read not to get dead, / Which is also what a poem does.' For Seidel immortal longings are part of the trick of art, because 'nothing is next'. 'How to keep killing Hitler / Is the point. / How to be a work of art and win': but if we have to keep killing Hitler, there is no winning to be had. The how-to book title also reminds us that when being a work of art – as opposed to making one – is linked with winning, we get fascism. If Wilde also lurks in Seidel's poetry – 'I seek the most beautiful terror' – he is never, as is fashionable now, wholeheartedly embraced. For Seidel decadence is at once mortifying and a form of redress. We have to keep killing Hitler because we cannot resist the prestige of decadence, the glamour of appetite, the shark show. The ruthless knowingness of these poems is matched by a kind of horrified naiveté, as though the poems can't decide whether we have morality because we are so frightened, or whether it is our morality itself that terrorizes us.

So each of the poems in this book is a crisis poem, a drama of paralysis and anticipation, in which the uncertainties and self-doubts that the poems are riddled with – 'How can a boy renounce himself?' – are always ambiguous. The reader, and perhaps the poet, is never quite sure who the joke is on; or, indeed, whether it's heartbreaking or boastful. 'When I speak you hear / The exhaust note of a privateer.' You can hear the tear; but there is also the less familiar meaning of *privateer*. According to the *OED* the word, when applied to motor racing, can also mean 'a competitor who races as a private individual rather than as a member of a works team' – so it's not quite clear what the exhaust note of the private racer is. It may not be exhaustion that we're hearing about here, just a different note. Privateers, authorized but solo, legitimate but opportune, once again straddle the contradiction that Seidel, as moral immoralist, keeps racing through. The final pleasures can be hard ironies. 'The icing on the cake / Is stone. The Ten Commandments / Are incised in it' ('Israel'). It isn't really a cake, and there's no icing. There's nothing to eat; and there's only the Law to look forward to.

The first word of *Going Fast* is 'God', and the last word of the book is 'love'. But the portentousness implied by such calculation – the amused prophetic bookishness – is itself the subject of the book for Seidel. The imagination as apocalyptic, with all its grand and gothic anticipations, means we can't always tell the pathos from the bathos, the death wishes from the other kind of wishes:

The most underrated pleasure in the world is the takeoff
Of the Concorde and putting off the crash
Of the world's most beautiful old supersonic plane,
  with no survivors
In an explosion of champagne.
  ('A Gallop to Farewell')

Seidel can get the pain (and the sham) in the champagne, and he can also suggest in the uncanny density his poetry always has, that this is also a sexual fantasy (there is Concorde and *concorde*). But in this deliberately kitsch apocalypse, anticipation is all; every take-off puts off a crash, and this pleasure isn't only underrated because most people couldn't afford it, as it were; it is underrated because it is a pleasure that hasn't (yet) happened. And if there were no survivors how would we know it had been a pleasure? Champagne, Seidel wants us to realize, could explode in so many more ways than we have imagined. If prophecy, as Seidel intimates in this book, is our most disturbing form of hedonism, then poetry is complicit with all our moral equivocations. What Wordsworth called the 'discriminating powers of the mind' are always in the service of mixed blessings. Seidel's poetry is hauntingly tricky, rather than in any sense difficult, because it never has a palpable design on the reader. It never seems to know what it wants the reader to think or feel. So when Seidel begins a poem in this book pastorally entitled 'Spring' with the sentence, 'I want to date-rape life', what this does to the poetic conventions it recruits is comparable to its effect on the gentle reader. We may be hit by indignation, and we may be hit by wondering if that's what we're doing to life – or want to do to life – whether we like it or not. And we can't, though we are morally disposed to do so, ask life how it feels about this. Seidel, that is to say, is not writing about anything as consoling as moral muddles; he is writing about how life collapses the moral distinctions we make in order to live it. And this expresses itself in Seidel's poetry at the level of technique – *staging* would be perhaps more accurate given the drama of the poems – by the absence of similes. In *Going Fast* things are not compared with each other – they are not like each other – they are each other:

> A cat has caught a mouse and is playing
> At letting it go is the sun
> Over the desert letting the traveler reach the oasis.
> ('The Stars above the Empty Quarter')

If this cat-and-mouse game – in which the reader is also the mouse – was like that sun, its unlikeness could also come to mind. But by forcing such identities Seidel reinforces the no exit feeling of the poem. By the time we've got to the oasis we know it's not going to make any difference. And, as often in his poetry, the deft repetition of a word gives it (lets it have) a horrifying duplicity. These are permissions in which nothing is permitted but hope. A land of such likeness is eerily daunting because there aren't enough differences around. It's all the same in the empty quarter, as unchanging as the stars.

In Seidel's acute, simple sentences, that are like sound-bites of poetry, even the assertion of difference collapses when it's made. 'But we are someone else. We're born that way' – the poem 'Prayer' begins as though the poem began before it started. If we are someone else, we are also not. Everyone is forever saying now that we are strangers to ourselves, that we don't know who we are, and so on. But no one can compact the absurdity implicit in such intended meanings the way Seidel can. What could be more omniscient than knowing that we don't know ourselves? He elicits such odd meanings by making us wonder whether a word or two has been left out, or that the sentences may be somehow incomplete. So the poems can be like conversations we come into in the middle of and leave before they're finished, or riddles we can't quite get our minds around. 'God is everywhere you're not, / And you are everywhere'; 'The set itself is a subset of itself, / A jungle set in the jungle.' Using syntax to make the possibility of meaning fade, these vanishing acts of language are Seidel's touchstones, black holes the poems keep almost disappearing into. Everything is always about to go wrong, and it's all in the words. 'My penis is full of blood for you / Probably won't win her hand.' Romance and the hard facts of biology certainly don't fit; but it is the 'probably' in its horrible, ingenuous uncertainty that is the point. Seidel wants to gamble; and he gambles on the reader's uncertainty about what he is up to. The poems in *Going Fast* keep us guessing, in the full knowledge that there is nothing else we could be doing.

So it is not incidental that Seidel can do more in a poem by leaving a word out than most poets can by putting one in. He can, for example, creating a telling likeness, turn the subject into the object, by not having the last word. 'Hold the glass with both hands, / My darling, that way you won't spill' ('The Night Sky'). Or he can blur a distinction by making a patent omission. 'Your life is anything you want it to – / And loves you more than you can show or tell' ('Vermont'). The strange inversion 'your life loves you' leads the poet on to jumble up the kiss-and-tell of celebrity journalism, and the rather different distinctions of linguistic philosophy. Such calculated omissions and contaminations of language make curious commissions of reading irresistible. We are shown something by not being told it, and by being told too much.

And yet, as always in these poems it is the perplexity of hope – of what the future holds, of getting from one moment to the next, if only by going fast – that Seidel can't get away from; that taunts and haunts these remarkable poems that are always trying to avert the bad faith of elegy.

> Fall leaves inflame the woods.
> It is brilliant to live.
> The sorrow that is not sorrow.
> The mist of everything is over everything.
>   ('Lauda, Jerusalem')

Coming to Grief

Other people's mourning – like other people's sexuality and other people's religions – is something one has to have a special reason to be interested in. So to write a book, as Leon Wieseltier has done, about the mourning of his father is asking a lot (and to write a book of 585 pages is asking even more). One of the ironies of the so-called mourning process is that it tends to make people even more self-absorbed than they usually are; in need of accomplices, but baffled about what they want from them. In actuality what the mourner wants from other people is so obscure, so confounded that religions are usually still needed to formulate it. Even secular therapies – which are all, one way or another, forms of bereavement counselling – are keen to offer us guidelines about how to do it, and how to know if it isn't going well. Because mourning can make fundamentalists of us all; because grief (like sexuality) can seem like a cult that could kidnap us, there is always a great deal of social pressure on the grief-stricken to conform, to observe the protocols, to believe in the process (and that it is a process). And so recover sooner rather than later. But what would recovery be, what would have been recovered?

If grief doesn't have a shareable story, if there is no convincing account of what happens to people when someone they know dies, grief will always be singular and secluding: as close as we can get to a private experience without it sounding nonsensical. When someone dies something is communicated

Review of Leon Wieseltier, *Kaddish*, (Knopf 1998) from the
London Review of Books.

to us that we cannot communicate. Hence the urgency that goes into making death a communal experience. The fact that all cultures have been so determined to ritualize this experience reflects just how socially divisive, how maddening the experience of death is considered to be. The only taboo, where grief is concerned, is on not experiencing it: not feeling it and performing it appropriately. There are no grief scandals in the way that there are sex scandals; there are only scandalous absences of grieving.

'What death really says is: THINK,' Wieseltier writes in one of the many arresting sentences in this book. The problem, as he well knows, is that death says nothing to us except what we make it say. And 'we', in this context, are the people (in our various cultural traditions) who have gone before us in dealing with this unusually common experience. When his own father died Wieseltier found himself returning to the religion of his forefathers, which involved the observance of a year's mourning and a complementary enquiry into the provenance and meaning of the Jewish prayer known as the mourner's Kaddish. This book is at once a journal of that year and a kind of theological meditation on Judaism and grief. So it inevitably raises the question whether it is still possible to write an inspirational classic – a curiously nostalgic ambition in itself – without sounding like pastiche Kierkegaard, or indeed Woody Allen's *Death Notebooks*.

'One of the most dreaded eventualities in a man's life has overtaken me,' Wieseltier writes, 'and what do I do? I plunge into books! I can see that this is bizarre. It is also Jewish. Anyway, it's what I know how to do.' And what the books do, among other things, is tell you that this is the most dreaded eventuality in a man's life. The books tell you to open the books so that you can find out beforehand what will be the most significant events in your life. Above all, they confirm for

Wieseltier the value of the books; and the books he writes commentaries on, at some length, are mostly works of Biblical or Talmudic exegesis. So the exclamation mark here is either self-delightedly smug or genuinely puzzled by these old-fashioned reflexes. That he finds himself, at this most unsettling moment of his life, doing exactly what the books would want him to do is both reassuring and an inspiration. The problem is the pragmatic shrug: 'Anyway, it's what I know how to do.' He knows how to study these books, but he doesn't know how to miss his father. He doesn't know what to do with a death. And what he wants from the books becomes inextricable from what he wants out of the death. In the interesting twist that provides the drama of *Kaddish*, Wieseltier's natural naivety about the effect of his father's death gets displaced onto his religious tradition. He is suddenly confronted with his ignorance about the mourner's prayer. 'I was struck almost immediately by the poverty of my knowledge about the ritual that I was performing with such unexpected fidelity ... A season of sorrow became a season of soul renovation, for which I was not prepared.' His father's death makes him enact something that he then needs to know about. *Kaddish* is about the importance such knowledge came to have for Wieseltier. Not how or why it worked – his chosen texts are not treated as sophisticated self-help books – but the fact that his father's death made a certain kind of enquiry into the past imperative. It is not, of course, uncomplicated that such deaths are often renovations.

Kaddish is not the record of somebody's attempt to get over something. Wieseltier is not trying to find a way out, or even a way through, but a way into what has happened and is happening to him, through the tradition he was born into. Every death is a crisis of continuity; and Wieseltier's father's death is superimposed on family deaths in the Holocaust. So the people who are burying their dead are, at the same time, people who have been unable to bury their other dead. *Kaddish* is knowingly haunted by those who were deprived of their rightful death. In writing of these things, it is a notable difficulty to avoid the sanctimoniousness that is always a loophole for the soul; or the kitsch inner superiority of those who are deeply moved by the sensitivity of their own response. Atrocity doesn't bring out the best in people because, faced with it, people no longer know what the best in people is. One of the things our traditions are there to do is to remind us what the best things about us are.

In search of the history of the mourner's Kaddish – of ways the Jews have observed their deaths and the invocations and hopes buried in their prayers – Wieseltier kept a journal which, like many such 'journals', must have always half-wanted to be a real book. That is, to be read by people Wieseltier doesn't know. 'I recorded the ancient, medieval and modern sources that I found, and the speculations that they provoked. This volume is that journal. It is not exactly a work of scholarship.' But it is exacting partly because the scholar is so obviously Wieseltier's kind of hero. Not exactly a work of scholarship is certainly a nod to those scholars for whom nothing could be inexactly scholarly. *Kaddish* is straight-faced about scholarship – though not quite strait-laced: it sometimes sounds like a Jewish *Anatomy of Melancholy* but clearly dreads turning into a Jewish Rabelais – because it is essentially a tradition of scholarship that Wieseltier is after. But the unembarrassed ways in which he flaunts his piety, his being so staunchly undaunted by the antic disposition of his readers, sometimes makes *Kaddish*, with its devoted and devotional scholarship and its harsh critique of contemporary life, seem the blithest of provocations. It is a solemn book that asks to be read in exactly the spirit in which it is written. Or, to put it another way, Wieseltier is artful in creating the illusion that he would be the best reader of this book, which is best read, I think, as an occasionally remarkable philosophical meditation, often poignant in its belatedness; and as a letter to Philip Roth.

'The history of Jewish literacy: now there is a delicate subject!' Wieseltier exclaims. 'It turns out that rabbis have been complaining for centuries that the book has often been closed to the people of the book.' It might seem a bit offhand in this context to say that now books might just be for the people who like them (there will be no people of the video); or to speak up for the Golden Calf side of the tradition; or even to suggest that *Kaddish* would have been a better book – a more hospitable book, less proud of its restrictiveness – if Jewish literacy had been considered to be a more indelicate subject. Wieseltier is on the side of the rabbis and is not keen to countenance the ironies that attend the wholehearted promotion of virtue. To promote virtue, of whatever kind, forces people to be more of a piece, to be more consistent, than they can bear to be. For Wieseltier it is the great boon of the tradition that it effectively tells its members who they are. 'For ancient Jews and medieval Jews,' he writes, 'there was no escape from Jewishness, and this was their happiness. Can modern Jews understand such happiness?' Could those ancient and medieval Jews understand it? Did they understand it as happiness exactly? Was that always (often?) their word for it?

It is perhaps not entirely surprising that Wieseltier is unimpressed by revolutions. 'The voluntarism of modern Jewish identity,' he writes, 'was one of the great revolutions of Jewish history. Like all revolutions, however, it exaggerated. It made foolish Nietzschean demands of ordinary men and women. But most people do not invent themselves. Most of them choose to be what they already are. This is a kind of honour, too.' So-called ordinary people are always the fodder for these kinds of views, which can only be made to seem sensible, and even kind, by obfuscating the whole notion of choice. The fact that some things in life are unchosen doesn't mean that nothing can be chosen or that a lot of people aren't keen to make choices, and aren't happily enlivened by doing so. I can choose to go to bed, but not to go to sleep; I can't choose to fall in love but I can choose to make a pass; I can't choose not to be Jewish, but I can choose to go to synagogue, and so on. There is revolution when what is deemed to be ordinary is put into question, when what is considered to be beyond the realm of choice is discovered not to be. One may think, as one reads Wieseltier's book, that what people are capable of doing, or indeed should do, to improve their lives has already been decided. So *Kaddish* is often driven by an exhausted realism, a seeing-through modern life which is presented as the rediscovered wisdom of a tradition, rather than the sadness of a bereft son.

'The ideal of epiphany,' Wieseltier writes, 'the thirst for what Americans call "peak experiences": all this is a little cowardly, an attempt to escape the consequences of living in time ... The peak experience will peak. And there will occur, in the most quotidian way, an experience of eschatological disappointment.' These Americans, like those ordinary men and women, just don't know what's good for them. But what is it that Wieseltier is trying to secure for himself and his fellow Americans? Perhaps they should have eschatological disappointment counselling; after all, not being able to bear disappointment is hardly a good reason to avoid, or contemptuously dismiss, peak experiences. The unremitting fact of his father's death and the unthinkable fact of the Holocaust are then pretexts, licences for another contemporary jeremiad. And, like most jeremiads, this one has no misgivings about its own genre. 'In the company of death,' Wieseltier writes with that astringent clarity that is the best voice in the book, 'subjectivity is wild. So subjectivity must be tamed. The taming of subjectivity is the work of the Kaddish.' One sign that subjectivity is wild is when it starts speaking with too much conviction, on behalf of too many people.

'It is almost impossible,' Wieseltier writes, 'to think unsentimentally about continuity.' Sentimentality is one risk, but stridency is another. Imposing a pattern or form on experience over long stretches of time tends to make people very impatient because the material is always so recalcitrant. Continuity is always at war with circumstance, and the contingency of events. If a religion wants to be more than a refuge it has to develop, but if it adapts too eagerly it runs the risk of dissolving. At what point do you stop calling it Judaism and start calling it something else (literature, politics, obsessional neurosis)? It is the threats to continuity, the attempted redescriptions, that make people despondent or violent or write books like this one. The death of a parent is bound to leave one to wonder, one way or another, about parenting; about who, if anyone, one belongs to or wants to belong to; and where, if anywhere, one needs to imagine oneself coming from. For Wieseltier it is the notion of a Jewish tradition that holds it all together. That parents all the parents. And it is about the notion of tradition – and custom and ritual and observance – that he is at his most engaged, if not always at his most engaging. In so far as more and more people now believe in history but not in character – or at least find it easier to describe a person's history than who they are – *Kaddish* is very much of its time. As it is in its rather gleeful acceptance of its chosen determinism. What is more alarming is Wieseltier's wish that people should be, as it were, buried alive in their traditions.

'The right response to tradition is vertigo,' Wieseltier writes in knowing combat with the Existentialist's vertigo of freedom. For Wieseltier, it is the dizzying release from choice that engenders vertigo. Tradition is like the stern parent everyone needs to deal with the unbounded ecstasies of pain (and pleasure). 'Since death is final, grief is final. Since death will never end, mourning will never end. That is why the tradition must intervene to end it.' If tradition is the great punctuator that saves us from ourselves it also usefully cuts us down to size, reminding us that we're not that special, that our supposed uniqueness is trivial in the grand scheme of things. 'Tradition is the opposite of identity,' Wieseltier writes, relishing what he has been chosen to speak up for: 'Identity is an accident. There is no need to ready yourself for your identity, because it is your inheritance. And that is its scandal.' The portentousness of this final flourish could be exhilarating were it not for the snarl-ups along the way. Tradition must be the opposite of accident (whatever that might be: presumably design by God). But your identity, which is an accident, is in fact your inheritance (your tradition), which is not. Leaving aside what it might mean to ready oneself for one's identity – it's fortunate one doesn't need to do this because it isn't obvious how one would go about it – this does seem a misleading way of putting it all.

'Insofar as civilization is a communion with the past,' Wieseltier writes, 'and regards an absence as a presence, it is mysticism.' But it is rather important – as Burke, among too many others, unwittingly showed – to sort out the mysticism from the mystification. Real mysticism never seeks to convert others, real mystification always does. The trading in absences as presences is something to be vigilant about. And pragmatism, which has always been usefully attentive to such metaphysical conceits, is almost for this very reason anathema to Wieseltier. 'Pragmatism is such a puny theory,' he writes. 'There are so many questions for which the pragmatists have no answers. Human transformation is not a "practice". There are changes for which we have no rules and conventions. That is why we fear them and honour them; they are accomplishments for which experience cannot have been a guide.' Wieseltier's grief for his father is never proffered in this honourable book as a device for the abrogation of serious argument – rather the opposite, in fact. But, like many of Wieseltier's pronouncements about the even vaguely modern, his remarks about pragmatism are more prejudicial than anything else; righteous indignation that produces more righteous indignation. Human transformation may not always be a practice, but to assert that it never is, or can be, is to replace politics with mysticism.

Wieseltier is particularly alert to other people's failures of rigour. Mourning brings one up against the question of what it is to do things properly; and why doing things properly might matter. What, if anything, does one owe a dead parent, and how is it to be given? If one's life as a child is at least in part organised around what one imagines the parent wants of (and from) oneself, then the death of the parent might leave one stranded with unmet obligations. Wieseltier is averse to anything that smacks of modern psychological explanation – for him, not unreasonably perhaps, psychology is what happens when the tradition becomes decadent – but one of the book's consistent laments is that people, most often himself, are never doing enough. They are never sufficiently thorough, or penetrating or committed, unlike the Jewish theologians he prizes. ('Why,' he asks, 'is egalitarianism so often accompanied by a general slackening?') It is the sly evasions, the falling short that is so pernicious. And so, like the many Jewish prophets who turned their competition with God into a speaking on His behalf, this slack Golden Calf mentality, which seems to be everywhere, makes him want to lay down the law; or rather rule the roost. 'Whenever I read Kafka,' he writes, 'I wonder: what sort of dejection is this, that leaves one the strength to write, and write, and write? If you can write about the wreckage the wreckage is not complete. You are intact. Here is a rule: the despairing writer is never the most despairing person in the world.' Was Kafka lying, or even worse, boasting? Kafka may have lost the despair competition, may not have gone the whole way, but what is the game Wieseltier's rule lets us play? Given *Kaddish*'s Talmudic urgings, it would be churlish not to quibble.

It is a book in which doors keep slamming in the reader's face. 'When Nietzsche lost his faith, he concluded that God is dead. This is not critical thinking. This is narcissism.' This is not critical thinking either. And that in itself doesn't matter – a lot of so-called critical thinking is *Dunciad* material – if the sentences work (work something up), and the author doesn't humourlessly and endlessly advocate the necessary virtues of such thinking. 'The tradition,' Wieseltier writes, 'reveals an admirable indifference to psychology.' But the problem with 'the tradition' as presented (and represented) by him is that it seems self-admiringly indifferent to anything that might make it think otherwise. The mourning of his father that might have made him wonder about the tradition and his place in it told him what his mourning was: 'You do not mourn only because he died. You mourn also because you are commanded to mourn. There is your heart, and there is the Torah.' Psycho-analysis, for example, was a psychology that turned up as Central European cultures seemed to be detraditionalizing themselves. The rituals of traditional societies were being replaced by, or displaced onto, the repetitions in people's private lives. (Not everything of significance is merely a question of commands and observances.)

Kaddish makes one wonder whether it is as much the function of a 'tradition' to distract the mourner from his grief – by talking him into a specific version of it, or by not allowing for its absence – as to console him. It is possible that we have no idea what secular grief is; what grief unsanctioned by an apparently coherent symbolic system would feel like. It may, for example, be possible to miss people when they die without feeling that there is anything to be sad about. 'When you mourn for your father you serve things larger than him,' Wieseltier writes. The interesting question is why we think we need things larger than 'him'. It is a mystery why we should still be so daunted by our insignificance. Why we can't find the right size to be in the universe. In Wieseltier's tradition the will-to-meaning too often does the work of the imagination. If this is what Wieseltier calls the 'charisma of learning', we should forget it.

Editing Housman

'Passion and scholarship may enhance each other's effects,' E. M. Forster noted in his Commonplace Book with A. E. Housman in mind. Forster was always keen to reduce the incompatibles in life: Housman was less persuaded by such redemptive harmonies. He preferred the losing paradoxes to the winning ones: ' "Whoever shall save his life shall lose it, and whosoever will lose his life shall find it." That is the most important truth that has ever been uttered,' he said in his Leslie Stephen Lecture of 1933, published as *The Name and Nature of Poetry*. His poetry is always fascinated by what is irresolvable – 'Keep we must, if keep we can / These foreign laws of God and man' – and his scholarly prose concerned, above all, with such textual resolutions as are possible in a world of inevitably corrupt classical texts. Having lost his faith at thirteen – though never his interest in the Bible, as Archie Burnett's commentary on the poems in this wonderful edition makes very clear – he discovered a vocation for accuracy.

Housman didn't think of scholarship as merely a refuge from passion: on the rare occasions when he wrote or lectured about such things there is nothing to indicate that this was the argument he was having with himself. Indeed, the fact that he devoted most of his life to classical scholarship while also being the author of two popular books of terse, passionate lyric poetry – *A Shropshire Lad*, published in 1896, and *Last Poems*

Reviews of Archie Burnett (ed.), *The Poems of A. E. Housman*, (Oxford, 1997) and Tom Stoppard, *The Invention of Love* (Faber, 1997), from the *London Review of Books*.

(1922) – was not the problem for Housman that it was for others. Burnett could not have done a better job of convincing us that Housman was 'one of the true scholar-poets'; but one of the ways he has done this is by suggesting that the scholarship that went into the scholarship was similar to the scholarship that went into the poems, whereas Housman himself viewed the writing of poetry and the emending of texts as circumstantially different, as involving different skills and talents: 'the intellect is not the fount of poetry ... it may actually hinder its production, and it cannot be trusted even to recognize poetry when produced'. At the same time, 'literary' concerns, he insisted, could be a menace to scholarship. So when Burnett says in his Introduction that Housman had 'a mind trained to precision, amazingly retentive, and exquisitely sensitive to literary values ... as in his scholarship, such accuracy was a lifelong preoccupation', it seems both true and worth quibbling with – if only because the accuracy of textual conjecture is always a different matter from the accuracy of poetic allusion.

It is also worth asking what a life devoted to accuracy is a life devoted to. This, inevitably, is more the province of Tom Stoppard's often riveting play about Housman, *The Invention of Love*, than of Burnett's scholarly edition of the poems. While Wilde, whom Stoppard uses as a foil for Housman, warned against falling into careless habits of accuracy – as though accuracy (or rigour) were simply conformism, weak morality masquerading as strong epistemology – Housman with his own mordant wit worried that if the scholarship were not precise, we simply wouldn't be reading the right texts ('works of this sort', he wrote of one poorly edited classical text, 'are little better than interruptions to our studies'). But why isn't it better to be interesting than right? What's the big deal about precision as an end in itself? As Stoppard archly knows – and as Arnold and Ruskin and Pater and Wilde and Housman knew in rather different ways – so much hangs on the question of accuracy. Or what fantasies of accuracy are used to do.

' "To see the object as in itself it really is", has been justly said to be the aim of all true criticism whatever,' Matthew Arnold said in his inaugural lecture as Professor of Poetry at Oxford, *The Function of Criticism at the Present Time* (1857). The remark was more question-begging than he liked to think, and Housman, who knew all Arnold's poetry by heart, was pointedly to echo it in his first lecture as Professor of Latin at University College, London in 1892. 'It must in the long run be better,' he said, 'for a man to see things as they are.' ('I have spent most of my time', he remarked on another occasion, 'in finding faults because finding faults, if they are real and not imaginary, is the most useful sort of criticism.') Nothing has suffered more, in the transition from the nineteenth to the twentieth century, than the idea of the real. And the idea of how long the long run might be. Housman never lost his faith that there were real things – like suffering and love and knowledge and death – and that we are obliged to take them seriously. If, as he wrote, 'accuracy is a duty and not a virtue', it is not up for grabs; and it is part of Housman's finer rigour to make, as well as take on, such distinctions. 'Life', Stoppard's Housman remarks, 'is in the minding.' Caring about something is caring that it be as good as it can be. Housman took the kind of care of his chosen (dead) authors – often savaging those who could not do them justice – that he wasn't ultimately able to take of the man who was the love of his life, Moses Jackson. But the scholarship was not a substitute, or some kind of embittered retreat: it was another way of doing a similar thing. Accuracy was a form of love for Housman; and love always exposes one's incompetence.

The notion of producing an authoritative scholarly edition of Housman's published and unpublished poems, as Burnett's certainly is, could itself have been the subject, if not the pretext, for a Stoppard play. Burnett is neither coy nor unduly self-reflexive about the task of editing the most exacting of editors. He takes the pressure, and he takes the pressure off, by being at once thorough and painstaking with the required information, and by occasionally aping Housman's gleeful knockdown wit.

'Completing' the poems, whether by adding lines or by moving around other lines or phrases of AEH's, has no place in this edition. Those interested in creative writing may consult 'Two Housman Torsos' by Robert Conquest, *TLS*, 19 Oct. 1973. Those with a taste for highly creative writing should seek out A. E. Housman: *New Poems* [*sic*] ed. [*sic*] by John Edmunds, with a preface and notes by Hilary Bacon (San Francisco, 1985).

Every word, bracket and comma here is so entirely to the point that it is virtually a prose-poem in the genre that Housman made his own: the almost deadpan burlesque of poor scholarship.

Burnett ignores the more fashionable habits of accuracy in this edition, omitting 'mere slips of the pen'; and he is not above telling us that Bredon Hill is '961 ft high and commands extensive views', whether or not it improves our view of the poem, because Housman himself had a head for heights. 'AEH', he notes, 'paid particular attention to the height of the spire of St Mary's (220 ft): *Murray's Handbook for Shropshire and Cheshire* (1879) reported that it was "said to be the third highest in the kingdom". In his copy he underlined "said" and wrote in the margin "by liars".' Since for Housman, as he wrote to Gilbert Murray – in that British tradition of biting melancholy that runs at least from Johnson to Larkin – 'the state of mankind always had been and always would be a state of just tolerable discomfort', there was some comfort, and some justness, in that kind of truthfulness. Even if perfectionism was covert religion, trying to get things right was more reassuring than not being bothered. We should not be 'scamping our work', as Housman accused Shakespeare of doing too often. Short-cuts are no good in the long run if one cares about 'the truth of things'.

Housman's poetry, by the same token, is always more impressed by what actually happened than by what might have been ('An excellent topic for a poem,' Stoppard's Housman declares, 'false nostalgia'). And two of the things that actually happened, in Housman's experience, and that he didn't try and get round, were death (his mother, whom he nursed through a terrible illness, died when he was twelve) and the death that occurs when people lose someone they love (Moses Jackson, the love of his life from university days, was not gay and could not meet Housman's feeling for him):

> He would not stay for me; and who can wonder?
> He would not stay for me to stand and gaze.
> I shook his hand and tore my heart asunder
> And went with half my life about my ways.

There is necessarily something dazed about that 'who can wonder?' but there is also an unsentimental, straightforward loneliness in 'went about my ways'. This is what one does despite the endless wondering. So when Frank Harris says, in one of the many brilliant interludes in *The Invention of Love*, 'I think he stayed with the wrong people in Shropshire. I never read such a book for telling you you're better off dead,' he is right, but he's missing, as Stoppard never does, Housman's steeliness and the amused way he can also relish the grim. Housman can't cheer up, but he's not simply unhappy.

If he wanted to be able to die for someone he loved, as the speaker does in several Housman poems, it does rather imply that it was death he was really in love with:

It was not foes to conquer
Nor sweethearts to be kind,
But it was friends to die for
That I would seek and find.

Friends, it would almost seem, were the necessary pretext for something far better. If you want someone to die for, someone for whom you can sacrifice your life, then being alive with them must be something of a problem. And yet Housman's poems are preternaturally alert to what the idea of death can do for us in life. How we use it as a stop-gap: how it is always ironized, when longed for, because it is a self-defeating refuge. (Housman's wonderful, funny line, 'Oh who would not sleep with the brave,' acknowledges the fact that sleeping with the brave is likely to mean sleeping with the dead, and that's not sleeping with anyone.) He can convey with uncanny power the strange imaginative fact of death – not what it might be like exactly, but that it may not be like anything – yet he's never altogether seduced by death because he never finds solutions sufficiently convincing, let alone easy to come by:

I see the country far away
Where I shall never stand:
The heart goes where no footstep may
Into the Promised Land.

Whether the Promised Land is death or redemption hardly matters: it is so far away that to all intents and purposes it doesn't exist. Moses without monotheism, without any gods at all, is Housman's figure for the poet and the lover. His poems are accurate, above all, about longing, which we never get right, the longing for death especially:

Some can gaze and not be sick
But I could never learn the trick.

> There's this to say for blood and breath
> They give a man a taste for death

– the one thing you can't just have a taste of. The first line is Beckett-funny – and Beckett does seem the 'modern' writer with whom Housman has the greatest affinity and who would also know the outskirts of meaning of a word like 'trick': that the noun speaks of 'magic' as well as 'deception' and 'artifice', but the verb means also 'to trifle with', 'to dress up', 'to prepare food'. Without a few tricks life makes you ill; and you can't try a bit of death, even if you think you've got a taste for it. And that's true too.

So Housman is never fussily precise, in his poems or his prose, because he doesn't seem to believe in warding things off. That is to say, he doesn't believe in magic, or the more obvious forms of submission. Like hedonism, for example: the tyrannical demand that one enjoy oneself – the most punitive demand of all. This was something Housman was often more astute about than Wilde. 'Think no more, lad; laugh be jolly: / Why should men make haste to die?' It isn't clear here which is the most deathly: thinking or having what is pertly called a good time. Because the answers to the question are too obvious, the solution looks rather unpromising. The poem ends, appropriately, echoing its beginning: 'Think no more; tis only thinking / Lays lads underground.' One's own death never makes haste; and if thinking produces a kind of death in life – one may not be lost in thought, but buried in it – even thinking about not thinking won't stop you dying. Time also 'lays lads underground'; and as ever with Housman it is the oddly disturbing sexual connotation of the most ordinary words that has its way with the reader. There is no esoteric diction in his poetry, just the putting of ordinary, or the more traditional poetic words in unusual places. As in a joke, whatever is slightly incongruous is doing all the work. So when he writes in a poem published after his own death, 'For I was luckless aye / And shall not die for you', the poetic 'aye' is pointedly rueful in its acknowledgement that only the worst things seem to last for ever; that 'aye' is, as it were, a duplicitous pun.

'Even when poetry has a meaning,' Housman wrote, 'as it usually has, it may be inadvisable to draw it out.' Not because it may be disturbing but because it may be beside the point. For Housman the meaning of a poem too easily substitutes for what he calls the feeling in it. If poems had meanings they would not need to be poems. It is as though in his few prose writings about poetry he wants to dissuade people from having the wrong kinds of conversation about his poetry. So when critics write about his poems – and Randall Jarrell, John Bayley and Christopher Ricks have all written wonderfully about Housman – they have to struggle not to unpick them; not to treat them as metaphysical poems masquerading as ballads and traditional lyrics. Making the case for 'feeling', as Housman was so keen to do, has always been difficult – indeed, has often been best done in poems – and has perhaps never before been so difficult as it is now. At the dead-end of Romanticism, Housman's position on poetry can seem something of a bluff, given that his own poems are often powerfully moving and extremely shrewd. Nothing dates people like their manifestos, but in his own defences of poetry Housman is a caricature of the version of Romanticism represented most notably by Arnold's defence of Wordsworth as the poet of feeling – as though he struggled to be behind the times. And as though he didn't want his poems scrutinized in the way he might scrutinize a text: that is, for plausibility, for the coherence of its logic. But when one is being true to one's feelings it is not – or perhaps no longer – clear what one is being true to; whereas in editing a text there might be principles to abide by.

Housman's poems are all about what happens when one has nothing, or no one, to be true to.

So the decisions Burnett makes in editing Housman are an implicit commentary on the kinds of dilemma Housman himself faced. Housman described his four-volume edition of Manilius (published between 1903 and 1920) as 'the combination of a tedious author with an odious editor'. He clearly relished being so unenviable and so gruesomely clear-sighted about his project. Burnett is a generous and attentive editor, as principled in his intentions and as undazzled by ambiguity as Housman was. 'This edition has several aims,' he writes, introducing his Introduction, 'to print all of A. E. Housman's verse; to elucidate and correct the text of the verse published posthumously; to record textual variants from manuscript and printed sources; and to provide a commentary on each poem.' 'Commentary', possibly the only word in this sentence that invites interpretation, means mostly an incisive noting of the 'convincing' literary and Biblical allusions in Housman's now obviously rather allusive poetry. True to Housman's favoured distinction, Burnett writes: 'Passages are adduced for consideration with no indication of their status or significance: that is a matter for literary criticism and I have endeavoured only to provide a foundation for such criticism.' Editors of volumes like this may be the only people left who have such a clear sense of what literary criticism is. Or of what foundations are; referring briefly to three critical commentaries on one of the poems, Burnett concludes his note as Housman might have: 'All these interpretations lack is a foundation.'

There are 282 pages of verse in this edition, and 253 pages of commentary. Faced with a new theory, William James always wanted to ask: how would my life be better if I believed it? It should not now be irrelevant to ask how reading Housman is improved after reading the poems in this edition. Especially since, in the light of Housman's own strictures about poetry, a scholarly edition of his own poems might seem precisely to miss the point. He would certainly have wanted an accurate text, but a commentary? 'Poetry is either easy or impossible,' he wrote in a letter. He meant the composing of it, but much of what he wrote about poetry – his always unwilling excursions into literary criticism – suggest that he felt the same about the reading of it. 'Meaning is of the intellect,' he wrote in *The Name and Nature of Poetry*, 'poetry is not.' Whatever that means it meant something very important to Housman. Scholarship was about information and knowledge, poetry was about something else. This is not a fashionable view; nor one that could sustain a literary critical industry. And it would be usefully difficult now to take Housman on his own terms – or at least at his word. When poetry worked for Housman it had a kind of involuntary appeal; and when he tried to find analogies for its mysterious effect – like the hair that would stand up when he was shaving – they were not to do with high culture. Lines of real poetry 'find their way to something in man which is obscure and latent, something older than the present organisa-tion of his nature, like the patches of fen which still linger here and there in the drained lands of Cambridgeshire'.

What Housman is promoting here is neither the sublime nor the primitive, but what grows despite all kinds of cultivation elsewhere. He is not merely alluding to the rougher stuff out-side; nor is this the don's contempt for learning. It is praise for a certain kind of resilience. 'Life is not there to be understood, only endured and ameliorated,' the old Housman says to the young Housman in Stoppard's play – and it is both a good conceit and a brilliant dramatic device because the poetry gives the impression that the young Housman had always been in some kind of dialogue with an imagined older self, and often with a dead one; that he was always old before his time. So in the poems it is as though an older, more experienced voice is warning the young and innocent about life, in the full knowledge that they won't be able to hear – they wouldn't be young if they could. (Housman's description of Blake as 'the most poetical of poets' is slyly of a piece with the 'meaning' of his own poems.) And because Housman's disillusionment sometimes seems to be a subtle form of boasting, the poems often relish their sadnesses. It is not the virtues of youth that find an innocent echo in his poems.

In a sense, Housman was always the same age, even though he got older. So his poems don't seem to develop, but just to get more and more like his poems. Reading them in Burnett's edition shows how fiercely focused Housman's preoccupations always were. And not just thematically, but in their references and allusions. The great boon of this edition – apart from the previously unpublished notebook fragments that it contains, many as good as the best of Housman's previously published work – is that it shows the idiosyncratic range of literature that found an echo in his own words. It also makes evident the ways in which Housman knew what he was doing. 'No doubt,' he wrote in a letter in 1933, three years before he died, 'I have unconsciously been influenced by the Greeks and Latins, but I was surprised when critics spoke of my poetry as "classical". Its chief sources of which I am conscious are Shakespeare's songs, the Scottish border ballads, and Heine.' Burnett's edition confirms this, while also revealing how important Milton was for Housman, as well as the poets of the century he was born in: Arnold, as one would expect, given Housman's lifelong admiration for him, but Tennyson, Christina Rossetti and Swinburne all find their way into his always unostentatiously allusive lyrics. It is also interesting to discover, in a life devoted, as it were, to pagans, Housman's unbelieving devotion to the Bible. When John Sparrow sent him a copy of his paper, 'Echoes in the Poetry of A. E. Housman', he wrote back with some irritation: 'I see that you are not such a student of the Bible as I am.' It is worth wondering what a student of the Bible in the early part of the century who was also an unbeliever might be a student of. Whether there could be wisdom-literature – or wisdom in literature – was certainly an issue for Housman, but not one he was keen to be polemical about. He tended to sharpen his opinions about the value of literature by being relatively costive about them, at least in print. The brevity of his best poems is a testament to his implicit conviction that saying a lot was not necessarily saying very much. 'Swinburne,' Housman once remarked, 'has now said not only all he has to say about everything, but all he has to say about nothing.' For Housman, saying it all was not saying enough.

Housman's poetic output was comparatively small – two books published in his lifetime, and two published after his death – but his reading and his scholarship were prodigious. Burnett intimates that he was working on his poems for long periods of time even when he wasn't actually writing them. Entire poems and excerpts from poems were copied out into two notebooks from c. 1875–80, and again in the 1890s, and a great many passages in the books he read were marked out and annotated. 'The habit of mind cultivated in such ways', Burnett writes, 'meant that when he echoed or alluded to the words of others, he was often conscious of doing so.' This sounds plausible but it is, of course, impossible to verify. It's not obvious what makes one a good editor of oneself; and if one is conscious of echoing or alluding to something one is virtually quoting it, and Housman – unlike Eliot, whom Burnett mentions by way of comparison – doesn't sound like that kind of poet. (And if the allusions in his poetry are intentional does that mean Housman wants the reader to recognize them, and if so, why?) More like those of Hardy or Larkin, or the ballads he so much admired, his poems require a minimal literary and no serious classical education to be read and enjoyed. Unlike the scholarship, they are not intimidating. They are exacting in a very different sense: a sense not easily suited to the languages of contemporary criticism.

In a remarkable spat between Wilde and Housman towards the end of Stoppard's play, Wilde is made to sound flashy and dull, as though already dated by his own notoriety. 'You are right to be a scholar,' he says blithely to Housman. 'A scholar is all scruple, an artist is none. The artist must lie, cheat, deceive, be untrue to nature and contemptuous of history. I made my life into my art and it was an unqualified success.' But Housman, for whom there could be no such thing as an unqualified success, is made by Stoppard to seem by far the more impressive figure. This is not the usual way round, yet here Wilde's flaunting of his transgressions seems rather sad bravado next to Housman's more rueful histories: 'My life is marked by long silences ... Classics apart, my life was not short enough for me to not do the things I wanted to not do ... Your life,' he says to Wilde, 'is a terrible thing. A chronological error. The choice was not always between renunciation and folly.' The play is fascinating not least because Wilde seems to represent, among other things, Stoppard's own fluency and facility pitted against something, or someone, more reticent and cautious. And it is Housman's vulnerability rather than Wilde's that is made to seem the more inspired, the more resilient.

As *The Invention of Love* notices so well, Housman was never glum or solemn. And Burnett's Housman, like Stoppard's, is more interestingly deliberate than the more famous Housman of Auden's poem, with his defeated masochistic life. 'Deliberately he chose the dryasdust.' Housman wasn't fooled by his own diligence, in the way Wilde was fooled by his own determined lack of it. 'How the world is managed, and why it was created I cannot tell,' he wrote in the Preface to the edition of Manilius to which he devoted thirty years of his life, 'but it is no feather-bed for the repose of sluggards.' This was about as much amused vindication as there was for Housman, but it is a good thing to know. And as theology goes, it is mercifully brief.

On Eating, and Preferring Not To

A people who conceive life to be the pursuit of happiness
must be chronically unhappy.
Marshall Sahlins, 'Utilitarianism'

My title refers to Melville's remarkable story 'Bartleby, the Scrivener: A Story of Wall Street', that was published in 1853. It would be daft to say that Bartleby was a story about eating disorders; but even the most cursory reading of the story makes it more than clear that hungers and compulsions are somehow the metaphorical heart of the matter. It is set in the offices of a law firm, and is rife with the language of appetite. The narrator describes himself as an 'eminently safe man' who, oddly like an analyst, says that he 'seldom loses his temper', 'and much more seldom indulges in dangerous indignations at wrongs and outrages'. When he describes his employees, he gives them telling nicknames: Turkey, Nippers and Ginger Nut. Nippers, whose name is not as overtly foody as the others, is described as the 'victim of two evil powers – ambition and indigestion' (though I will come back to this I want to think of eating disorders as a form of ambition). When the narrator first hires Bartleby to join the office, he did, we are told, 'an extraordinary quantity of writing. As if long famishing for something to copy, he seemed to gorge himself on my documents'. Bartleby, like a starving man, is hungry for work.

But very soon there are problems; problems that are, I think, akin to the kind of difficulties therapists often have in working with people who are called anorexics. The person who refuses to eat can do something so devastating to the environment – the parents, the therapists, the hospital staff – that they often need to dissociate parts of themselves to manage it. The food refuser, often unconsciously, engineers the possibility of a dissociation in the people who try and help. At first the boss takes it for granted, in a commonsensical way, that Bartleby will do the work demanded of him; just as, in a commonsensical way, one might assume that people will eat, simply in order to live, or feel well; as though food only has a use-value, and not an exchange value as well. The boss assumes, in other words, that there is a kind of natural (or contractual) order in the office, that people are there because they have agreed to play the game:

I abruptly called to Bartleby. In my haste and natural expectancy, I sat with my head bent over the original on my desk, and my right hand sideways, and somewhat nervously extended with the copy, so that, immediately on emerging from his retreat, Bartleby might snatch it and proceed to business without the least delay. In this very attitude did I sit when I called to him, rapidly stating what it was that I wanted him to do. Imagine my surprise, nay, my consternation, when, without moving from his privacy, Bartleby, in a singularly mild, firm voice, replied, 'I would prefer not to'.

I sat awhile in perfect silence, rallying my stunned faculties. Immediately it occurred to me that my words had deceived me, or Bartleby had entirely misunderstood my meaning. I repeated my request in the clearest tone I could assume; but in quite as clear a tone came the previous reply, 'I would prefer not to'. ... This is very strange, thought I. What had one best do?

Bartleby's refusal, 'without moving from his privacy', reminds us that the refusal itself is a way of not moving from a privacy, and indeed might constitute that privacy; and that conclusion, 'This is very strange, thought I. What had one best do?' is the refrain, albeit calmly put, of every parent whose child won't eat, and every therapist who works with people who would prefer not to eat. What Melville is fascinating about, and fascinated by, is what Winnicott would have called 'the effect on the environment', the world Bartleby creates around him, by his phrase, the performative utterance, 'I would prefer not to.' Winnicott's sense of what he calls 'the nuisance value of the symptom' seems pertinent here. 'Nothing so aggravates an earnest person as a passive resistance', Melville's narrator remarks (on behalf of all parents and therapists).

The second confrontation between the Bartleby and the boss-narrator cannot help, I think, remind the earnest therapist of her forlorn endeavours:

'Why do you refuse?'
I would prefer not to.'
With any other man I should have flown outright into a dreadful passion, scorned all further words, and thrust him ignominiously from my presence. But there was something about Bartleby that not only strangely disarmed me, but, in a wonderful manner, touched and disconcerted me. I began to reason with him...

'I prefer not to,' he replied in a flute-like tone. It seemed to me that, while I had been addressing him, he carefully revolved every statement that I made; fully comprehended the meaning; could not gainsay the irresistible conclusion; but, at the same time, some PARAMOUNT CONSIDERATION PREVAILED with him to reply as he did.

The narrator concludes, like the exhausted therapist faced with this well-named 'PARAMOUNT CONSIDERATION':

It is not seldom the case that, when a man is browbeaten in some unprecedented and violently unreasonable way, he begins to stagger in his own plainest faith. He begins, as it were, vaguely to surmise that, wonderful as it may be, all the justice and all the reason is on the other side. Accordingly, if any disinterested persons are present, he turns to them for some reinforcement for his own faltering mind.

In this essay, it is the parents and/or the therapist being browbeaten in some unprecedented and violently unreasonable way that I want to consider; just what this preferring-not-to does to the people addressed. Do they, we, begin to stagger in our own plainest faith (in our therapeutic beliefs)? Are we able to experience, to find useful words for, what I want to call the aesthetics of defiance, and Melville calls the vague surmise that all the justice and all the reason is on the other side? That the person who refuses to eat is acting honourably, that the person who prefers not to is doing the right thing, the beautiful thing in the light of their own paramount consideration? It is Bartleby who, the narrator observes, 'never went to dinner', who is quite literally the hero of the story; in a way in which people who refuse to eat are rarely the heroes and heroines of the case histories written about them.

In the story we find the narrator (who is Bartleby's boss) struggling to, as we say, contain himself; to remain, kind, patient and pragmatic. Bartleby's 'perverseness', he writes, 'seemed ungrateful, considering the undeniable good usage and indulgence he had received from me'. In short, the narrator goes through the rigmaroles, the contorted ordeals of the dismayed therapist. After a fascinating meditation on the kinds of suffering in others that kills what he calls pity, he has recourse – again like many a desperate therapist – to something called common-sense. 'To a sensitive being pity is not seldom pain. And when at last it is perceived that such pity cannot lead to effectual succour, common sense bids the soul be rid of it.' Common-sense equals, get rid of what you cannot effectually succour. It becomes, as it sometimes must, a situation in which the sufferer might seem to be driving the helper mad. 'I thought to myself,' the narrator writes, 'surely I must get rid of a demented man, who has already in some degree, turned the tongues, if not the heads of myself and the clerks.' There are, of course, as psychoanalysis shows us, many ways of getting rid of someone (or something), one of which is dissociation. And in certain versions of psychoanalysis the therapeutic guideline is: what the patient wants to get rid of, the therapist must tolerate, hold, contain, consider, redescribe. I want to emphasize here – though I will come back to this – that I think the patient is often somewhere puzzled about why the therapist is prepared to do this for him. Why, that is, the therapist wants to suffer so starkly, and, supposedly, for someone else's well-being.

Anyway, the narrator tries what family therapists call a bit of positive reframing: 'I strove to drown my exasperated feelings towards (Bartleby) by benevolently construing his conduct.' But exasperation is the term that recurs; the narrator refers to his 'exasperated connection with ... this intolerable incubus'.

Ultimately Bartleby defies his boss's wish to get rid of him, and so the boss leaves instead; he moves into new offices. Refusing to move even with the arrival of the new tenants, Bartleby is carted off to prison. In one of the last scenes of the story the narrator goes to visit Bartleby in prison, and finds himself talking to the prison cook, referred to as the 'Grub-Man', whose abiding grievance is that Bartleby won't eat, that he 'lives without dining'. 'Ah, Bartleby! Ah, humanity!' are the famous last words of this great story. Bartleby, the narrator wants us to remember, is one of us, we are one of him. He has needed to live out, at whatever cost, his own personal aesthetic of defiance.

I would prefer not to, one might say, is a sophisticated version of Freud's paradigm for aesthetic/emotional judgement in 'On Negation'; it is a spitting out of something. Bartleby dies, the narrator implies, from an obscure form of heroism, from an intransigent commitment to a personal preference. Preferring not to is both the means and the end of his personal ideal. If we are, as it were, therapeutically minded

– or even relationally-minded – we might wonder whether, or to what extent, the responses to Bartleby by the people around him were complicit with his predicament. One of the more intriguing things about the story is that Melville keeps distinctly unclear the question of what it would mean to help or hinder Bartleby. Should he have been persuaded, one way or another, to prefer to, should he have been accommodated, or should he have been, as he was, got rid of? In what sense, from which points of view, was Bartleby's life a failure or a success? What would a persuasive account be of why it is a good thing not to eat; of why preferring not to eat would be a good thing to dedicate one's life to? We are probably more or less familiar with the religious stories about this, and the more contemporary fashion stories, which are all stories about people trying to live what are, in their view, the best lives available to them in their time.

I want to suggest that what are called symptoms – of which refusing to eat and being unable to stop eating are often stark and frightening examples – are experiments in living. Children put out probes to their parents, samples of their internal worlds, as rudimentary forms of such experiments. What kind of mother or father will I have, or create, if I say I'm not going to bed, or say I love my teacher more than my mother, or indeed, if I refuse to eat, or eat too much? What we think of as eating disorders are elaborated versions of these common childhood scenarios, whatever else they are. Most children, in my experience, experiment with not eating and tend to get a rather vivid message back from their parents which, in its turn, modifies the experiment. Preferring not to creates a certain kind of relationship, a certain kind of atmosphere, it calls up something powerful, and sometimes almost daemonic in the people to whom it is addressed. So one kind of paramount consideration is, what kind of people will I have on my hands if

I prefer not to eat? And one straightforward answer is, you will be faced with people you would prefer not to talk to, people who are frantic, bossy, manipulative, defeated, enraged, concerned and so on. People, in other words, obsessed by food, who might feel so intensely about you that they might have to dissociate some of these feelings in order to psychically survive. So what kind of experiment in living, what kind of ambition, from a psychoanalytic point of view, is refusing to eat? What constitutes a paramount consideration such that someone might die for it, rather like they might die for their country or for their religion, or for their child? As Melville's narrator found, like many a therapist has found, starting to reason with people who prefer not to, has an ironic effect. Because, of course, the other thing they prefer not to do is what is called reason. Indeed, nothing exposes our fantasies of reasonableness more than the refusal to eat. It explodes the categories of good sense, and even of good taste.

When Freud described sexuality in the *Three Essays* as leaning on nutrition, he provided us with useful analogies and disanalogies between nourishment and sexuality; each can and can't be used to redescribe the other. Just as it became apparent to Freud that sexuality was sexual disorder, we might say something similar about eating. What would it be not to have an eating disorder? Who do we think of as being a normal eater, and what do our criteria, on reflection, seem to be for this reassuring assessment? The reason these kinds of questions seem particularly pertinent in relation to eating is that hunger as an appetite tends to make us essentialists, tends to make us revert, so to speak, to biology. A person has to have a certain amount and quality of food in order to survive; the same thing could not be said, in the same way, about sexuality. At the more extreme end of the so-called sexual perversions, we call the police; at the more extreme end of the so-called eating disorders we put people in hospital. In the case of sexuality we are forcing people to behave themselves; in the case of self-starvation we are forcing people to survive themselves. Long-term work with people who starve themselves, of which I have not done much, is, among many other things, an opportunity to think about what makes life worth living, and what might be worth dying for. It is for the therapist, and occasionally for the so-called patient, a particularly grueling kind of moral education. It makes one wonder, in short, what a paramount consideration is, and why it might be worth having. Working with, as it were, card-carrying anorexics is a graveyard for the more zealous forms of psychoanalytic optimism. And therefore, it would seem to me, rather promising ground; if one can be bothered to bear it.

I have a temperamental aversion to diagnostic categories. I prefer not to; partly for old sixties-style ideological reasons, which I still believe in, but also, and more pressingly, I never seem to have acquired what people call clinical experience, if by that they mean a kind of accumulating inner archive of types of people which one recognizes and treats accordingly. And this particular issue is, I think, pertinent to the whole question of eating disorders. The adolescents I have seen with this as their designated symptom, are exceptionally wary of the therapist's knowingness. After all, nothing could be more omniscient than the claim to know about someone else's appetite. I only want to say this as a preamble to the brief case-history and vignette I am about to present, just to make it clear that these are impressions, and not theories, and only representative if seen to be so. I have no convincing general-ization about eating disorders, nor have I in any sense specialized in them. But after many years of child psychother-apy, all sorts of so-called eating disorders, as peripheral or prominent symptoms, have been prevalent in the children I have seen. This may be no more than saying that everyone is faddy when it comes to food (and sex), and that our fads are akin to our dreams in that they link us to our histories and our physiologies. They are redolent with meaning, or useful to make meaning with. Perhaps unsurprisingly, it is my impression that most children have some kind of eating difficulty as they grow up. And that this itself is pertinent to the more extreme predicaments we are discussing. It is that continuum, at least, that I have in mind when I see people who are diagnosed as having eating disorders. Diagnosis is the way analysts cure themselves of anxiety, when their anxiety can be the most valuable thing they have.

Chloe was referred to me because her parents, who had been divorced since she was ten, were concerned about her weight loss. She was fifteen, obviously worryingly thin, and not worried about herself at all. She told me that people eat far too much in the West, that she liked being 'lithe and boyish', and she didn't want to come and see people like me who just 'force feed people with their own weird ideas'. 'Lithe?', I said. She said, 'you know ... thin ... you're lying if you don't know what that means'. I said, 'What's lying got to do with eating', full, as usual, of good intentions. And then there was my first experience of the leaden silence that was to be the climate of many gruelling sessions. She simply sat there practising the great adolescent art of making the so-called adults feel stupefyingly redundant. After this brief interchange in the first session – which set the pattern – we settled into that most unpromising venture, enforced psychotherapy; the truly impossible profession. Her parents had given her a choice; me or hospital. I had told them, and indeed her, my misgivings about this, but I suggested that we would see what, if anything, was possible. We, Chloe and I, would meet for six sessions and then review it. One detail in her history, that the parents recounted, had struck me as both interesting and hopeful. That she had first, as her mother put it, 'got difficult with eating and moody' – when demands lose their self-confidence they turn into moods – when her brother was born, when she was six; and she had started eating again normally a year and a half later, after having an operation to have her tonsils out. She came out of the anaesthetic, her mother told me, and she asked for strawberry ice-cream, and 'I knew she was alright again.' And she had been more or less alright about eating until soon after she started menstruating at thirteen. It was then that she had become 'super-picky' about food, unable to eat what parents always call 'proper meals'.

Of course, as a middle-class modern adolescent she knew, as she put it, 'everything about anorexia ... there's nothing you can tell me'. I said, 'So I have got nothing you want either.' 'Correct,' she said, and the silence descended. Of course, if she would rather not eat she would rather not talk about not eating. Like Bartleby's boss I went through my repertoire of silence, ingenuity, exasperation, patient kindness, impatient kindness, unkind patience and so on. I reflected out loud, as one does, about the links, if any, between what I was thinking and feeling and what might be important to her. She was really very patient with me as I did my best, that sometimes terrible thing one is prone to do. But in this sparse and mostly unpromising encounter there were a few minutes in one session when we had a good conversation – when we wanted something from each other in a way that made us forget that that was what we were doing. There was, in other words, some mutual appetite that dissolved self-consciousness. I had been musing aloud, in a slightly fraught way, about what her mother had told me about the operation for tonsils; I was giving her a lecture that went something like this: 'I've been wondering whether you started eating again after that operation because the operation felt like a punishment you deserved'. Usual silence, but she shuffled in the chair and rubbed her eye. So I carried on. 'I imagine it something like this: when your brother turned up you were so upset you started hating your parents by not eating ... or maybe it was a competitive thing, the baby was the best eater so you'd be the best non-eater ... anyway there was something that made you feel really bad, so you felt like a criminal who deserved a punishment, who went looking for one. And that's what the operation was like, you'd had your punishment and now you could go back to ordinary life, to eating. It's something to do with punishment.' There was brief, but lighter silence, and she said, 'Why do you put up with this?' I said, 'With what?' 'With me sitting in silence'. I said, 'That's a very good question, why *would* anyone put up with this, what's the point? It's punishment.' She said, 'Why don't you think about that for a change?' And that was the end of the session. She had made me think in a way that was quite unlike the dissociated, therapeutically intent so-called thinking I had been doing in and between the sessions.

The next day her mother telephoned to tell me that she and her ex-husband had decided that they were withdrawing her from treatment because the therapy wasn't making any differ-ence. They were undissuadable, and I never saw her again. Of course, this may or may not have been linked to what seemed to me to be a minor breakthrough; and as everyone knows, families are acutely sensitive and responsive systems. But in actuality, I could not, and do not know the reasons why that moment was chosen to stop whatever was or wasn't happening in the therapy. What I do know, as I say, is that Chloe had left me what it is not glib to call food for thought.

As always in psychotherapy, as in so-called ordinary conversation, the links between what one person says to another and what that other person then says, are obscure. It is possible, though, that something in what I had said in my musing had called up a thought in her about her punishing me, and others, her seeking punishment, and, most interesting to me, my seeking or accepting punishment from her. That taking a certain, but I think common, therapeutic position *vis-à-vis* the so-called patient – that is, accepting projections, containing them and, as it were, feeding them back – shows a strange willingness to suffer. What is being modelled – to use the old family therapy term – is a form of self-sacrifice. And this sacrifice, that therapists routinely go through, and are trained for, requires, I suggest, a dissociation to make it possible. And if one wanted to describe in shorthand what has to be dissociated – what I was unwittingly dissociating with Chloe – it is, paradoxically, appetite. As Chloe's therapist I had a problem with my appetite; I couldn't, as it were, bring it into play. To put it at its most extreme, one humiliates the patient if one allows the patient to humiliate oneself.

At two developmental crises in her life – the birth of her brother, and adolescence – Chloe had come up with the solution of not eating as an experiment in living; this evoked in the people around her a kind of exasperated collusion. They had to dissociate to manage their rage, and this meant that Chloe was, as it were, abandoned by real people and left with ghosts. So the people around her, including me, became cross and helpful, but never really hungry enough. Just as with Bartleby, everyone's appetite failed him, including his own.

It is perhaps an interesting and obvious question to ask about clinical work; which versions or parts of oneself does one feel under pressure to disown in the presence of any particular patient? Which parts of oneself need to be sacrificed – or at its most extreme, dissociated – in order, apparently, to sustain a relationship with this particular person? With Chloe I had to struggle to be neither a person obsessed with appetite, nor a person oblivious to my own appetite as a way of fostering hers. 'The anorexic', the Lacanian analyst Nasio writes (1998), seems to be saying, ' "No, I do not want to eat, because I do not want to be satisfied, and I do not want to be satisfied because I want my desire to remain intact – and not only my desire but that, as well, of my mother.' Anorexia is a cry against all satisfaction and an obstinate maintenance of the general state of unsatisfaction.' In this version the anorexic is so in love with her hunger that she must not violate it by eating. What Nasio points out is that it is part of the idealization of appetite to refuse appetite; as though the anorexic is asking a profound and paradoxical question, how does one keep appetite pure? What interferes with hunger is eating. My guess here is that the wish to purify appetite is reactive to, or a consequence of, something already having been done to a person's appetite; that the refusal of appetite is a belated attempt to restore the viability of appetite.

There must be as many, as it were, distortions of appetite as there are individual people; indeed, the word distortion is misleading because it implies some kind of basic norm. But I want to propose, by way of a conclusion, that something can be done to one's hunger that is akin to what we call sexualization. In some kinds of sexualization it is as though something traumatic is evoked by an object, and that this is unconsciously transformed into sexual fantasy and desire, as a form of self-cure. Perhaps something comparable, or similar is sometimes done by the person with an eating disorder; but they have not sexualized the occasion or the relationship; instead they have, for want of a better word, appetized it. It has been translated into a question about eating and being eaten, about digesting and being digested. The need then to appetize trauma becomes, as in Bartleby's case, voracious. A world is created in which nothing can be eaten, nothing must be taken in.

In sexualization the person turns the trauma occasioned by

the object – and desire for the object – into a scenario of sexual excitement, or sexual nullity. The person with an eating disorder – all of us, to some extent – appetizes the trauma occasioned by the object, and the desire, into a scenario of bingeing or refusal. Anyone, in other words, who prefers not to, once, very definitely, preferred to – and it got them into trouble. And it is this trouble that we always end up talking about, and they often don't.

The Pragmatics of Passion

... a final eccentric solitariness.
Annabel Patterson, *Andrew Marvell*

1

What does the analyst want for the patient that the patient can at least hope for from the analyst? One of the striking things about André Green's writing has been his willingness to formulate answers to this question. Green has never been shy about making claims for analysis; about what psychoanalysis really is – both what it entails and where it cannot suspend its judgement – and so what its aims might be. The idea of psychoanalysis having an aim – the relative freedom to love and work, the achievement of the depressive position, the capacity to play, the flourishing of one's true self – is one of the ways psychoanalysis makes sense of itself. An aim, after all, gives direction to our wishes, it gives hope a target. We think of the patient's purposes, his sense of direction, changing during an analysis, but not of the whole notion of a sense of direction being put into question. In psychoanalysis – both as theory and practice – the teleology of a life is recomposed but never disappears as a guiding principle. It gives the idea of the unconscious its necessary minimum of intelligibility: we may not know *what* we want, but we know *that* we want. We are always going somewhere for something.

Despite, or perhaps because of the rigour of his theorizing –

his always acute and incisive Freudian inductions – Green's stated aims of analysis have always been poignantly simple, with none of the covert moralism of the more esoteric versions of psychoanalysis. In 'Has sexuality anything to do with psychoanalysis?' (1996), Green writes, 'My hope at the end of the analysis will be, according to Freud's guidelines, that my analysand will be able to enjoy life a little more than he used to do before coming into treatment or, as Winnicott says, that he will be more alive, even if his symptoms do not all disappear.' And after going from Freud to Winnicott he can, as ever, make good his return to Freud: 'Is our psychoanalytic puritanism', he continues, 'responsible for the fact that we would consider sexuality as negligible in such enjoyment?'

'What I think we are doing in analysis', Green says in an interview (*New Formations*, 1995),

is to enable the people who come to us to increase their feeling of freedom. In what way? In order to liberate the forces which are present in themselves to enjoy life, not as scared people looking for all sorts of safety, nor as repenting sinners, but as human beings who are inhibited by something which makes them move on in quest of something they value. Analysis should improve their capacity to cathect something. We don't have to say what, they will find out ... In other words, analysis should improve what the patient already has, or give him the possibility of finding that life is worth living.

Enjoyment, aliveness, love of life, the feeling of freedom, cathexis as the quest for something of personal value, the possibility of what Green calls 'sexual ecstasy'; these, quite explicitly, are Green's values, the demands, one might say, he makes on analysis.

And yet inextricable from these particular aims and inspirations is always another aim that functions ambiguously in Green's writing as both a means and an end. 'Just as the instincts "seek representation" ', he writes in 'Instinct in the late works of Freud' (1991), 'psychoanalysis can have no other aim than the working out of the activity of representation in the widest possible sense.' 'So what should the aim of psycho-analytic work be?', Green asks elsewhere, 'To help the patient go as far as possible in the representation of his internal world and of his relationship to the external world as well, but mainly of the internal.' In practical terms it is 'for the analyst to devote himself to the task of elaboration ... to give effect, albeit provisionally, to symbolization which is always begun and never finished' (*On Private Madness*, 1986). So for Green the 'only aim, in varying the elasticity of the analytic setting' – that is, in any way modifying the prescriptions of so-called classical analysis – is 'in searching for and preserving the minimum conditions for symbolization'. And because it is representation – the apparently fundamental capacity for symbolization – that is the aim and the object of analytic practice, then what is the connection, if any, between what Green calls 'maximal symbolization' and love of life? If, as Green suggests in a resonant sentence in his book on tragedy, *The Tragic Effect* (1979), 'The confusion between the unrepresentable and the non-represented seems to be the source of errors of interpreta-tion', then how would clarifying this confusion, if such a thing were possible, enable us to enjoy life a little more? Does maximal symbolization – the hitherto unrepresented that is available for representation – lead to love of life, guarantee it, as it were? It is an act of faith – an act of Eros perhaps? – to believe that what is there to be represented, what can be represented, is necessarily on the side of a person's life. Green's work circles around a question that seems almost quaint now: what kind of good can it do us to make the unconscious conscious? In what sense is loving (and therefore fostering) representation loving life? The belief that symbolization is good for us – as a general principle, not, say, true for some people but not for others – is one of the foundational assumptions of psychoanalytic practice.

It is as difficult to define representation as it is to imagine an alternative to it. If, as Freud says in the phrase quoted by Green, that the instincts 'seek representation' it seems as if there is at least something – call it instinctual life, or even affect – to set against representation; something that is not yet in representational form. Words like instincts, drives, urges, affects, are, paradoxically, our representations for whatever both seeks and resists representation. There is a story here about how something that is not language is turned into language, how the infant or the body articulates itself, engages in what Green calls, 'the work of inner transformation'. Dreams, and affect, and states of emptiness or absence have been the essential perplexities of Green's work because they are the areas of experience (or anti-experience) in which the nature of representation itself is put at risk: its very possibility is put in question. Representation is the individual's acknowledgement of insufficiency, his attempt to make more life rather than more death-in-life out of the inevitable (if temporary) absence of what he depends on. It is as though absence can only be borne if it is recognized as such; the question for the individual becomes symbolization, or the abolition of need. 'The dream remains a paradigm', Green remarks,

because it is the model for the whole of our work ... the importance of the dream is closely linked to the importance of the concept of representation because, once again, what I think is most important is the dream representation, the thing which repeats itself in the absence of the object ... the mind has the capacity to bring something back again which has been related to an object, without the object being there. (*New Formations*, 1995)

It is worth noticing here that Green does not say the *object* has been brought back but something which has been related to an object; feeling for the object, desire for the object, has been restored, via representation, in its absence. As though representation prevents our becoming oblivious of our affective life (despair is a form of inattention). 'In the end', he writes, 'what I maintain in that affect is representation' – meaning that it can take no other form, or that affect in some way constitutes representation? – 'Signifier of the flesh is what I proposed in *Le Discours Vivant*. Today I would rather say the representative of passion'. Analysis becomes a way of keeping our passions in play, 'the extension of the field of passion'. The capacity for representation is deemed necessary – though not instrumental – to this project.

Our passionate selves are our best selves; and a passionate life is only possible, by definition, if we can make our passions known; to ourselves, by the absence of the object stimulating desire and its correlative representations; and to the object through the articulation of love as demand (what we are moved and enlivened by is our medium of contact with others and ourselves). There can be no passion – or rather, no recognizable passion – without representation. But this compelling psychoanalytic picture leaves us with a logical, and therefore an emotional conundrum; can there be passion without recognition? Is a private passion akin to the impossibility of a private language? Passion entails circulation and exchange; it is, in Green's felicitious phrase, a field. But why, after Green's uniquely interesting Freudian detour – after his own elaborations of Winnicott and Bion, and his agonistic relation to Lacan – does he end up with the traditional value of passion? What does his work add, or indeed does the relatively new work of psychoanalysis add to the old idea of passion; what further justifications does it offer?

'The object', Green writes, 'is the revealing agent of the instincts'. More impressed by the immeasurable solitude of the baby than its moments of contact – committed, that is to say, to primary narcissism rather than the consoling sociability of the newly over-observed infant – Green has steered subtly between the Scylla and Charybdis of contemporary psychoanalytic theory. If, in psychoanalysis, we are endlessly offered either sexuality as the denial of the other (with its apotheosis in perversion), or concern for the other as denial of sexuality (with its apotheosis in reparation) Green has been able, nevertheless, to go on asking the Freudian question: what, if anything, has our passion got to do with so-called other people? 'Again', Green writes in his Sigmund Freud's Birthday Lecture (1996),

... we are confronted with our ideology of what psychoanalysis is for. What is its aim? Overcoming our primitive anxieties, to repair our objects damaged by our sinful evil? To ensure the need for security? To pursue the norms of adaptation? Or to be able to feel alive and to cathect the many possibilities offered by the diversity of life, in spite of its inevitable disappointments, sources of unhappiness and loads of pain?

Passion, or our anxious concern for the other which is always, whatever else it may be, an idealization of safety? Without a sophisticated capacity for symbolization we can achieve none of the aims listed above, however ironically, by Green. There is nothing intrinsic to our capacities for symbolization, that will make us more reckless; feeling alive is not bound up with our capacity for symbolization, but with our use of that capacity. Green's critique of psychoanalysis is only plausible because it implicitly acknowledges how representation can be the enemy of passion, and not merely when it is in the service of the death instinct. Kleinians promoting reparation or ego-psychologists promoting adaptation both think of themselves as the guardians of Eros.

And yet, of course, to talk of the uses of representation – to talk pragmatically – in a psychoanalytic context, can only beg the question. In what sense, at least in psychoanalytic language, can we describe a person as choosing the use he will put his representations to? No one in the psychoanalytic community would claim to be speaking on behalf of the death instinct. And yet clearly one person's psychoanalytic aim (or ideal) can be another person's problem. It is curious how devoted one can be to the picture of a struggle – or indeed a war – between the life instinct and the death instinct – without there being any kind of consensus about how to recognize the workings of Eros. Reparation, adaptation, safety, aliveness, passion; Green, like anyone else, can assert his preference, but does it need backing from a god?

There is clearly a question here about how we go about legitimating our psychoanalytic aims, bound up as they are with fantasies about the kind of world we would prefer to live in. And this may not be a matter of providing foundations where none can be found, but rather of producing persuasive descriptions of why certain things, like aliveness or passion, might matter. How, if we take these things seriously, good things follow (if we start preferring aliveness, to adaptation, say, how will our lives be different?). If psychoanalysis saw itself as rhetoric rather than metaphysics – as persuading people to prefer certain ways of living to others, rather than revealing the truths about, and causes of themselves – we might have better descriptions not only of the aims of analysis, but of why we should value such aims. Slogans like 'Love and Work', for example, would be less likely to catch on so easily; and we might be wondering then why so much of what Freud calls love sounds like work.

So by way of conclusion I want to deduce, through a brief reading of Green's great paper, 'Passions and their Vicissitudes', why he thinks it might be a good idea to value passion, and what Green adds to our commonsense view of passion that makes it even more attractive. It is one of the great virtues of Green's writing that it always performs what it claims to value: the work of transformation. One of the vicissitudes that the passions undergo in this paper is the imaginative work Green does on them.

2

For Green the question is not, is a passionate life a good life?, but rather, given the passions, what life can we make that feels worth living? Passion, reduced to its scientific signifier, instinct, grounds the intelligibility, however vagrant, of both sanity and madness: 'instinctual life which is, after all, life itself', as Green writes in *On Private Madness* (1986), is – whatever kind of mythological status we give it – the ultimate psychoanalytic referent. Without the life and death instincts, and their historical precursor, the passions, the human subject would seem disembodied. Now that the soul has fallen out of our vocabulary we are left with the passions as the heart of the mystery. It can only sound crass to talk of the pragmatics of passion – to ask why we might choose or value a passionate life over any other kind of life – because passion itself is *the* secular essentialism. The death of God can be proclaimed, but no one is going to celebrate the death of passion (though we should: when people are described as passionate, it usually means they are impressively sensitive and extremely bossy). As Green states quite explicitly: 'We know enough now to understand that passion, be it mad or psychotic, calls the tune', but 'let us say to begin with that we (psychoanalysts) have taken care to recognize it only where it already exists. We have not introduced it. It is where it has always been. And if it was necessary to recognize it, it is because we undermined its importance.' The paradox that Green begins with is that passion has always been there, but that psychoanalysis began with Freud trying to push it out of the picture; undermining it, as Green says (at least in translation), as though passion needed to be sabotaged. And now it needs to be reinstated, where it's always been. The return of passion as the repressed of psychoanalysis is the gist of Green's intent. This brings with it, of course, the assumption that something essential has been lost, and needs to be refound.

For Green there is an 'original madness', not a psychotic core that defines the human subject, and in his view Freud 'minimized ... the intrinsically mad essence' of the instincts. Original madness is no more and no less than the individual's inborn instinctual life. So to understand neurotic conflict, for example, as merely a question of super-ego prohibitions of the normal functions of nourishment, sexuality and work is consolingly bland. 'Should one not rather think', Green writes, 'that it is the risk of the appearance of this potential madness in the execution of these functions that makes it so dangerous to carry them out, and so implicitly disorganizing for the ego' (1986). In other words, there is an excess here, an intensity of something, that psychoanalytic theory itself conspires to conceal. Freud failed with Dora, Green suggests, because he focused too much on her dreams, 'in other words, on her unconscious representations – while minimizing her affects'; and because he was 'obliged to keep the transference outside the analysis, because with it the primacy of affects over representations appeared'.

Representations, Green remarks, sustained a 'mediating distance' for Freud, ensuring he was 'well guarded against dangerous false connections'. There is something immediate – too present, too urgent, too invasive – called affect for which representation provides a boundary; both a barrier and a channel. But in the first act of the drama that is Green's paper there is a natural antagonism between passion or affect, and representation. And the 'dramatic' emblem of this antagonism is the sheer physicality of the hysterical fit, 'the element of passionate frenzy, linked to an instinctual upsurge'. There is an intensity of affect that representation cannot bind; the ordinary madness of love articulates, above all, the insufficiency of language. Passion without representation – in autistic states or Green's blank psychosis – is death-in-life, suicide by insulation, but the representation of passion ruptures language, reveals a daunting lack in representation itself. 'Fantasy binds libido to representations,' Green writes, and yet,

To concern oneself in preference to these representations is to analyse, but perhaps it is only to half analyse, if the suffering caused by this impossible love is not taken into account. It is to fix one's attention to the sexual theories of children while failing to recognize that the solution they present is only partial compared with the quantity of libido which they do not manage to bind by this means, and which remains a burden for the child.

Despite the technologies of technique – the elaborate sophistications of theory, the racket of profundity of competing analytic schools – psychoanalysis becomes simply and starkly: the emotional impact two people have on each other, whether they like it or not. 'It is a question', Green writes, spelling out the necessary impossibility of the venture, 'of binding an unquenchable libidinal tension through meaning.'

Green's paper hurtles towards passion as catastrophe – 'Is passion the best or the worst of things? One is bound to admit that it is more often the worst than the best' – and the therapeutic pessimism that always follows in the wake of relinquishing all the versions of instrumental reason. Burdened by the burden of the child Green refers to, what is to be done? Is meaning up to the task we have set it, or more often than not a betrayal masquerading as an affirmation, of the passionate life

inside us? Having got himself into a familiar corner – and
passion, after all, is what always corners us – Green makes
some useful distinctions in his defence of the very thing that
leaves us defenceless. 'It seems to me essential', he writes, 'to
re-establish madness in the place where it has been recognized
for all time: at the heart of human desire.' And re-establishing it
can only mean, given its rather obvious resilience, redescribing
it in more promising form. If, as Green writes, 'Freud's logic is a
logic of hope because it counts on wish', then passion is
primordial hope.

Having shown the daunting incompatibility of representation and passion – and, of course, their necessary complicity;
there can be no communicable, no hopeful passion without
representation – Green describes how the mother is the one
who gives the infant's passion a chance, as it were. His lucid
distinction between madness and psychosis, and his account of
the origin of psychosis – 'Psychosis emerges when the subject is
forced to mobilize his destructive instincts as a means to
putting an end to a fusional relationship with a primordial
object' – are committed to the necessary value of binding
the unbindable. 'Without representation instinct has become
blind,' he writes; but with representation what does it become?
'Tolerable' is Green's word. Without representation the ego is
overwhelmed, 'subject to the anxiety of separation and
intrusion'. And yet there is an equivocation here – an ambivalence about representation – that echoes throughout Green's
work; that the very thing that makes the individual's passion
viable – representation – also gives it the lie. That representation is never good enough, and by the same token it is the only
thing that is good enough.

Green leaves us with a contradiction that we should prefer to
see as a paradox. On the one hand, he writes, 'I do not believe
that affect escapes from symbolization, or from metaphor'; in

other words, there is a sense in which affect can only reside in, be recognized through, its representations. On the other hand, implying as he has done throughout that we may be bewitched (defensively over-impressed) by representations, he suggests in another personal confession: 'It seems to me that the attention given to representation comes from the concern for scientific demonstrability'. And what then, we might wonder, is that a concern for? Cultural prestige, legitimation, reassuring forms of consensus? When Green, who has written with such illumination and consistency about negation goes on to say, by way of internal debate, 'I am not saying that the work (in psychoanalysis) on representation is of little value ...', he gives us pause for thought. What else could we write about – or with – but representation? What would psychoanalytic practice be like – what would we do differently – if, to reverse Green's earlier formula, we gave primacy to affect over representation?

What Green's extraordinary Freudian meditation on passion leaves us with, then, is not the virtually nonsensical question – is keeping faith with representation keeping faith with passion? But the more pragmatic question, apparently incompatible with what we might think of as a psychoanalytic ethos – what kind of representations sustain our love of life, or foster that form of hopeful passion that Winnicott called aliveness, and that Green himself promotes? If we take seriously Green's preference for the Freudian language of pleasure and un-pleasure, as opposed to the Kleinian language of good and bad, we would talk about a person's capacity, or appetite for pleasurable forms of representation.

We need to distinguish between what Green calls in this paper 'Freud's double equation, Eros = binding, destructive instincts = unbinding'. This, of course, is the distinction that grounds all of Green's formulations; and that makes Bion's work integral to his own perspective. So it is instructive when, under the guise of being rather fussily punctilious, Green appears to underemphasize a crucial point. 'For binding and unbinding', he writes,

are always at work in madness as in psychosis. It is the resultant that counts, making transformations of the products of creation, or debris, products of disintegration. One must also insist, if one wishes to dot one's i's, on the positive role of unbinding, which produces discontinuity without which the mechanisms of recombination could not take place ... (1986)

If there is a 'positive role' of unbinding what are the criteria by which we recognize it? If unbinding makes possible a more fruitful binding then Eros and the destructive instincts are collaborators and not exclusively antagonists. The individual's destructiveness may be integral, indeed essential to his passionate life, even if the consequent work of transformation seems to work against him. The logic of a life may be in excess of the distinctions we can make about it. Or to put it another way, how does one know when someone is being self-destructive? To think of oneself as one's own best enemy implies an omniscient knowledge of what is good for one. Passion, as Green eloquently reiterates, leads people to apparently ruin their lives – 'acts which can compromise an entire life' – and yet from which of the many points of view in oneself is it ruin? 'Beyond the wish to recover, Freud says, the analysand clings to his illness,' Green writes, 'and I say that he prefers the object of his passion.' A good life may entail the destruction of all that one apparently values; this is what Green intimates, this is the loophole he adds to our story of the passions. Passion always makes action morally equivocal. The passionate life is a good life because its goodness is always in question.

Passion, Green stresses, is the object of analysis and sets the limit to analysability. It both tests and constitutes our capacity for representation; because it is a threat to this capacity, it is the source of its renovation. The lifeline that is a death-line.

If *The Dead Mother*, whatever else it is, is Green's history of the psychoanalytic movement – a history of analysts brought up by, trained by, analysts mourning the death of the analytic parents – then 'Passion and its Vicissitudes' is Green's genealogy of morals. Green's psychoanalytic aims, after all, cannot help but echo Nietzsche's paradoxical moral aim of 'more life'. And the dead mother, in Green's description, turns the infant's passions to persecutions. It is the fate of the analyst's passions – in the practice of analysis, bound and unbound by the analytic setting – that provides the sub-plot, the uncomic relief, of these remarkable twinned papers. How does the analyst keep his love for analysis, his aliveness to the work? The passion for analysis, one might say, is in Green's terms, the struggle against the dead mother. But if the passion for analysis is merely the analysis of passion, then what is the analyst consigning himself to?

Farber's Quibble

Or, to put it another way, the analyst is able to hear only what he, potentially at least, is able to say.
Leslie Farber, *Martin Buber and Psychoanalysis*

In the symposium (published in *Salmagundi*) on Lionel Trilling's *Sincerity and Authenticity* it was the authenticity that Leslie Farber had a problem with. 'I don't use the words "sincerity" and "authenticity" very often in my speech', Farber remarks at one point, 'yet I'm so taken by Professor Trilling's descriptions that I've wanted to make up words for them myself. For example, I've thought about "sincere" for a while and decided that a word I'm more apt to use is "serious". I don't know just what to use for "authenticity".'

To be thus taken by someone else's terms was a prompt for redescription (which is what happens in a psychoanalysis). But his chosen word for sincerity is as revealing, in the circumstances, as where he draws a blank. The distinctively unmodish 'serious' is not obviously compatible with doubts about authenticity. So when Trilling himself presses Farber, later in the discussion, to own up to a kind of authenticity test amidst the affluent ease of contemporary life – 'And, if one has confronted a period of danger in one's life – any kind of danger – one knows that some things are real and that one is real in confronting them' – Farber is notably unimpressed by such rhetorical heroism. 'I would like to quibble just a little bit about that,' Farber replies with characteristic wit – a quibble is always a little bit, and like most so-called quibbles this one is undaunted – 'It seems to me entirely within human possibility to confront danger and still succumb to sentimentalities about bravery and the ability to face death and so on. Don't you? I don't think that danger itself confers any kind of authenticity.' Once you have the word you then, supposedly, have something (or someone) that confers it. If Farber performs here the thing he distrusts – it is, I think, a remarkably 'authentic' answer to Trilling's eloquent point – he also states plainly what all his unique writing is an unfailing testament to: to succumb to sentimentalities, of whatever provenance, was to cheat ourselves of our best human possibilities. This entailed, among other things, not conferring significance where significance wasn't due. Our very need for meaning can usurp our capacity to recognize it. 'It is clear by now, I suspect, that I have come to consider the revelatory mode to be a form of lying,' Farber writes in one of his many canny summations. What makes Farber's writing so timely, now perhaps more than ever before, is the generosity of his suspicions. His unsadistic, unvengeful commitment to the telling of truth; his wariness of the rhetoric of conviction. So it was to those moments and occasions – erotic intimacy, family relations, teaching and learning, therapy – when we are most prone to will meaning, that Farber gave his acutest attention.

In proposing 'serious' for 'sincere' Farber was, in a sense, being deliberately (or archly) old-fashioned. And by offering it to Trilling – out-Arnolding Arnold, as it were – he was also declaring an affinity. Though Trilling was neither solemn nor sanctimonious he was serious about what was then called Literature, and about literature's seriousness. Farber, one could say, was serious about psychiatry and psychotherapy in the way that Trilling was serious about literature. They both conveyed, with a distinctive eloquence, that a lot could be felt to be at stake in the writing and the talking – that is, in the practising – of such things. They want to persuade us that real candour is hard to come by; and that knowledge and method, though necessary, are never sufficient in finding the right words for things. And that when we are in search of redemption, from whatever source, we will always be looking in the wrong place. Farber, in other words, is one of the very few writers after Freud who can make us feel that to be serious about psychotherapy – which in Farber's case means to write always lucid, pointedly amused essays – is to be serious about the things that seem to matter most. So to talk about psychotherapy, like talking about literature, can be another way of talking about how one might want to live.

Quibbling about authenticity – about what the word might refer to and why, if at all, we should value it – is what psychotherapy, after Freud, has been about. And Trilling's book *Sincerity and Authenticity*, with its shrewd unease about the anti-psychiatry movement associated with Laing and Cooper, was an uncanny portent of things to come. Trilling brought out a literary and philosophical history of the vocabulary that had begun to haunt contemporary life, and one of its professional products, psychoanalysis. And he made it clear in a style pointedly at odds with the devotees of madness, a style airbrushed of hysteria, what a belief in authenticity can inure people to. That, in its own way, it was as callous to idealize the mad as oracles as it was to scapegoat them as degenerates. Within a relatively short space of time the contemporary cultural world Trilling had described was to split into the essentialisms, the willed authenticities of identity politics; and the multiple performances, the chosen provisional sincerities, of contemporary selves. Broadly speaking, the essentialists were very serious, indeed in earnest about their rights and wrongs; for the performing selves, as playful as possible, seriousness itself was symptomatic – type-casting as a repression of the repertoire. It was the complicity of such alternatives – the way they mirrored each other without reflecting enough on their images – that both Trilling and Farber were preoccupied by *avant la lettre*, as it were. Both of them, that is to say, in different ways held on to their ambivalence about the theatricality of the self. Life may be a tragicomedy of manners – and it was part of Farber's subtlety to describe psychotherapy as being more about manners than about anything else, like instincts, or passions, say, – but in the performing self it is as though there is something akin to an instinct for honesty.

Authenticity was not a good word for Farber, I think, because it is always an unconscious parody of honesty. It coerces us into believing that there is a way of being that takes the difficulty out of truth-telling. And it has, as the anti-psychiatry movement revealed to some people's cost, an unholy alliance with fanaticism. 'The truth that interests me', Farber wrote in *Lying on the Couch*, 'is problematical, partial, modest – and still breathing. It is not normally dramatic or revelatory, and its attainment depends far more on thinking hard than feeling freely. To put it another way: I think that speaking truthfully is a more fitting ambition than speaking the truth.' It is not incidental to Farber's own ambitions that a 'more fitting ambition' sounds like something out of Johnson, as does his repudiation of the romantic cult of feeling. Farber's sensibility is neither apocalyptic nor overly dismissive ('it is not *normally* dramatic or revelatory'). It makes its appeal to what was once called, in literary terms, the common reader, and in psychological terms might be called the common truth-teller. It is a fitting ambition not to be excessively ambitious in one's pursuit of truth. It is a characteristic of contemporary psychoanalytic theorists to be uncommonly punitive in their truth-telling demands ('and still breathing', of course, says something about how suffocating so-called truth-telling can be). What Farber called our 'age of the disordered will' was an age in which the will had become an instrument of self-torture; willing what cannot be willed being the most prevalent and merciless modern form of self-punishment. In Farber's three primal scenes of contemporary life – the couple in a room (at sex or therapy), the laboratory, and the party – that recur again and again as the figure and ground of his writing, it is the always uneasy, discomfiting tension between drama and honesty that absorbs his attention. It is the difference that contemporary psychoanalysis has lost sight of – a vocabulary, in fact, it cannot accommodate – between willing and choosing, between self-punishment and (relative) freedom.

Indeed, one of the reasons, I suspect, that Farber's remarkable writing has suffered such neglect within his putative profession has been the difficulty of locating him (of course, writing well and ironic hilarity, not to mention being literate, have always been grounds for dismissal in the so-called helping professions). He has made of such apparently incompatible influences a style. Out of languages at odds with each other, if not actually at war with each other – the languages of Freud, of Sullivan, of Buber; of autobiography, of existentialism, of phenomenology, of a too-much-protested-against romanticism – Farber has found a way of being at once easily accessible to his readers, and surely but subtly unusually demanding of them (his writing often makes one feel that the psychotherapist's real affinity should be with the great poet-critics like Arnold, Empson and Jarrell). It was part of his own self-proclaimed 'addiction to non-addiction' that his writing is always interesting and amusing, but never fascinating or tricky. Of a piece with his (notably few) prescriptions for the doing of therapy, one feels, reading one of Farber's essays, spoken to, but not spoken for. It is to the pleasures of consideration, of thoughtfulness, rather than the thrills of recognition that Farber is drawn. And so his chosen genre of the essay – a short story of a kind, and an implicit critique of the 'professional' scholarly article: a genre in which one can be at once informed and distracted – suits his always ambiguous affiliations. He writes from both inside and outside his profession because what he had to say as an anti-psychiatrist who was not an 'anti-psychiatrist', as an unusually radical psychoanalyst with no explicitly political agenda, and as a psychotherapist willing to be a cultural critic, did not fit precisely anywhere (even in the 1960s and 1970s when there seemed to be a place for virtually anything). The publication of his essays in *Harper's, Commentary, Salmagundi, Psychiatry, Review of Existential Psychology and Psychiatry, Journal of Existential Psychiatry, Journal of the Otto Rank Association*, and *New York Times Magazine* reflects just how idiosyncratic Farber's writing ambitions were. There is everywhere in his writing the assurance of a style, and the useful uncertainty as to the nature of his audience. Psychoanalytic writing as a mixture of theology and journalism.

But because Farber was genially at odds with his profession – rather than rancorously, which is more often the way – his radical revisions of psychoanalysis could seem like merely intelligent common-sense. His plain way with the pieties, his misgivings about the therapeutic enterprise, could sound just sensible because so much psychoanalytic writing was (and is) so portentous, even at its most sober. Indeed, it was part of Farber's style to expose, by implication and intimation, the often shady rhetoric that had created what Philip Rieff was to call the 'triumph of the therapeutic'. So, for example, if Freud's description of the unconscious makes liars of us all this must be, by definition, only half the story. 'It is in our nature to lie,' Farber writes, 'but I think I must add that it is also in our nature not to lie.' 'I think I must add' is necessarily amused, and the verb is right (elsewhere Farber refers to the 'feeling of truth-telling', which perhaps has echoes of Rousseau's 'sentiment of being'). By calling a lie 'a desecration of the given' Farber is reminding us that there are some things that redescription cannot or should not change – 'an important quality of imagination', he writes in *The Two Realms of Will*, 'in the best sense, is imagining imagination's limits' – and that, if we cannot merely by will shrug off the old language of theology then the given is as good a word as any for what was once called the sacred.

It was Farber's startlingly simple point that the will to meaning encouraged lying that made him sceptical about both religion and psychoanalysis; and that by the same token revealed the sense in which psychoanalysis was spilt religion. Psychoanalysis, he writes, 'led me to a gnostic certainty about my (clinical) discoveries, a certainty depending far more on faith than fact or reason ... gnostic certainty is ... characterized by contempt for the world'. His 'distrust of any psychological – or, for that matter religious or artistic – doctrine in which revelation is obligatory and ideological' raises a time-honoured but newly interesting question: when it comes to truth-telling what are the alternatives to revelation? How will we recognize a truth, however provisional, if it is not out of the ordinary? Farber, unusually for a psychiatrist of his time and place, wanted what he often referred to as a phenomenological account of what went on for people; it was the 'phenomen-ological venture', the 'phenomenological illumination' that he was after. It was, he wrote, a 'phenomenological injustice' when 'the principles arrive first, and any phenomena developed are at the mercy of those principles'. This is not so much a dream of unmediated experience, but a wish to be present at the event. To be at the mercy of principles is to be bullied rather than guided by expectation, to be punitively protected from experience. It refers to the cruelty involved in knowing too knowingly what one is doing.

In Farber's imaginative ordinary-language empiricism, theory must err on the side of the documentary, not the surreal. Psychoanalytic theory abolishes the experience it intends to illuminate; it is an interminable heresy of paraphrase. Psychoanalysts have forgotten, in other words, that language refers as well as confers; 'what was at first an abstraction now passes itself off as experience itself, rather than a way of talking about experience', as though our language can impersonate us. 'The experience of anxiety', Farber writes, 'has been relatively neglected in favour of its causes and especially its consequences'. It is perhaps a sign of our bewitchment that it is so difficult to imagine what might be left once we take the causes and the consequences out of the picture. And when what is left is not required to be a revelation. 'A motive cannot explain an act; the act must ultimately be judged on its own terms'; these are, of course, Farber's terms, but they nevertheless manage to confront us without needing to affront us. We may not know where its own terms can come from, but the act is illuminated by such plain prescription.

So Farber distrusts what he calls knowingly the 'pact of hypnosis' because it takes away our pleasure and our responsibility, two things he sees, unfashionably, as being of a piece. 'Qualities suggesting the "merely human", such as self-consciousness, doubt and humour ... are inimical' to that apotheosis of bad faith, hypnosis. But it is also, of course, part of Farber's intent to suggest that we can be hypnotized by Freud's description of the unconscious – the unconscious as our first hypnotist, as it were – and that psychoanalytic theory itself has not been overly hospitable to humour and doubt, to the merely human. Explanation is only there, Farber wants to persuade us, to make responsibility possible, not to obviate it. And explanation without humour and doubt is akin to hypnosis. The aim of psychotherapy is in our gaining some sense of where our responsibility might lie. The risk, in Farber's view, is that the theoretical systems that inform its practice can obscure such necessary discriminations. The 'system' of Harry Stack Sullivan, one of Farber's early mentors and teachers, 'has no room', he writes, 'for accident, risk, surprise, mystery or grace. In Sullivan's melancholy view, there seems no hope except through psychotherapy'. No room, that is, for everything in our experience that cannot be consciously willed. No room for those things it would be mad to take any responsibility for, at least until after they had happened.

Because Farber is most impressed by what cannot be arranged or engineered or calculated, he is, by the same token, a stickler for such clarity as is possible in drawing the line; the line that is the limit of our conscious will. We can only be responsible, Farber implies, by being able to recognize what our sense of responsibility is really good for (good for voting, say, or for deciding to make a pass, but not useful in relation to the weather). We have become overimpressed by determinism because we have been choosing where choice is not possible, taking responsibility for things where responsibility does not apply. We have baffled our sense of ourselves as choice-makers through a simple confusion of realms (Farber is an undeclared pragmatist in so far as he is always interested in what works where). 'The problem of will' he writes, in a passage which straightforwardly describes the whole gist of his argument, and of his project,

lies in our recurring temptation to apply the will ... to those portions of life that not only will not comply, but that will become distorted under such coercion. Let me give a few examples: I can will knowledge, but not wisdom; going to bed, but not sleeping;

eating but not hunger; meekness, but not humility; scrupulosity, but not virtue; self-assertion or bravado, but not courage; lust, but not love; commiseration, but not sympathy; congratulations, but not admiration; religiosity, but not faith; reading, but not understanding ... I can will speech or silence, but not conversation.

Farber's characteristically understated 'few examples' cover virtually the whole of our lives. It would be silly to muddle this up with hip-Buddhism, or any of the other glib pieties of the commodified 'wisdom of the east' variety. Farber simply offers us an account of what is within our reach as self-conscious agents. The fact that we can decide to go to bed, but not to go to sleep does not, in and of itself, diminish our capacity for choice; it just shows us where choice can't work. It is worth noting that Farber wants us to imagine that there is a something there that can be distorted, and distortion means twisting out of shape, specifically, as the *OED* says, 'a condition of the body or a limb in which it is twisted out of its natural shape'. The will Farber describes, that is to say, tortures something akin to the body. The appeal to nature here doesn't feel rhetorically coercive because the burden of proof here doesn't feel like a burden. There is no 'phenomenological injustice' at work, whatever else may be going on in this deftly interesting list. Above all it renders the absurdity of much of our opportunism.

Wilfulness in Farber's account is another word for impatience; when we can't let things evolve (or not) we must make them happen. We simulate what we can't wait for; we must grab what we assume will never be given. So that religion of the will that we call opportunism is a form of rage. 'In wilfulness,' Farber writes, 'one is like a man who has lost his chance to tell his anecdote to the assembled party and now waits to seize the next opportunity'. A man, in other words, on the verge of disordered manners; but a man frantic about being heard. If, for Farber, man is the animal who goes to parties it is because he is the animal who is forever wanting to turn his monologue to dialogue ('In our most interesting moments – dialogic moments, if you will – will is unconscious', Farber asserts, his arch conversational mannerism doing the work). The sovereign will is only soluble in conversation, in our engaged apprehension of others. We are relieved of wilfulness not when our wills are thwarted, but when we recognize what the sheerest will-power is unable to do. At that point, at that transitional moment, between choosing to go to bed and falling asleep, we have no choice but to entrust ourselves to something else.

In conversation, Farber implies, we entrust ourselves to the possibility of intimacy. In the battle between will and imagination, between collusion and exchange, it is 'talk at its best' that Farber promotes, in which 'honesty, equality and imagination of one's own and the other's reality prevails'. And this is no simple, blithe self-forgetting because it entails 'imagining one's own reality' (Farber's phrase-making is often so telling because it performs but it never shows off). He manages to talk about the ultimate value of people looking after each other without succumbing to the available sentimentalities. 'Real talk between a man and a woman offers the supreme privilege of keeping the other sane, and being kept sane by the other.' It is by not glamorizing sanity either, but simply observing its value, that Farber makes privilege make unusual good sense.

It would be an ominous sign of the times if Farber's patent, unembarrassed moralism was to be mistaken for high-mindedness. The fact that Farber has written some of the very best psychoanalytic essays on sexuality – 'I'm Sorry Dear', 'My Wife, the Naked Movie Star', 'On Jealousy', 'Will and Wilfulness in Hysteria' – and the best essay in the professional (and the non-professional) literature on suicide – 'Despair and the Life of Suicide' – would soon offset any presumption that Farber was merely in the business of being morally bracing. But it was against both the contagious scientisms, the languages of objectivity, and the grandiose romanticisms – the Scylla and Charybdis of contemporary therapies – that he wrote, with such unusual wit and eloquence. He wanted to keep psychotherapy as the ethical project it undoubtedly is, without recourse to spurious idealisms. And this should remain the project of any psychotherapy worth having. 'If a theory is merely experimental or, as we say, heuristic, we do well to take it to mind if not to heart, and give it a run for whatever money we risk on it,' Denis Donoghue writes in *The Practice of Reading*, 'But if it is offered to us as a creed or a vision or a doctrine, we should approach it much more sceptically and estimate the consequence of taking it to heart and soul.' It was precisely to such ordinary momentous distinctions that Leslie Farber gave his unique attention.

Prynne Collected

When the American poet John Ashbery was asked why his poems were so difficult he said that he had noticed that if you go on talking to people they eventually lose interest, but when you start talking to yourself they want to listen in. Rather than trying to understand supposedly difficult modern (or Modernist) poems, listening in might be a better description of what we should be doing with them; hearing things rather than anxiously trying to figure them out. Unlike propaganda, or political rhetoric, good poems can remind us just how difficult some things actually are to articulate, and how pleasurable it is not to have to know what's going on. So the popularity – the apparent accessibility – of poets like Larkin and Betjeman or Hughes and Heaney makes it easy to forget that the whole notion of popular poetry can also be a contradiction in terms. The modern poet may crave a wider audience, but his very success might make him wonder just how amenable, how accommodating his poetry has become.

The popular poet becomes the poet taken for granted, the poet we seem to know. Nobody gains anything from being ignored, but being overly recognized can be its own distraction. So Bloodaxe's astonishing and soberly titled 'J. H. Prynne, *Poems*' may be a mixed blessing because Prynne has managed to sustain himself as that rarest of things, a great poet who has not suffered from his relative neglect. A poet, in other words, who hasn't ended up endlessly imitating himself to satisfy the

Review of J. H. Prynne, *Poems* (Bloodaxe Books, 1999),
from *The Observer*.

market, or the taste he has created. Always publishing with small presses, and working as a lecturer and librarian at Cambridge, Prynne's uneasy poetry has never courted any kind of wilful, self-impressed obscurity; he seems simply to have followed his improbable mixture of affinities – with Wordsworth, with Pound and Eliot, with the American Charles Olson, with Chinese poetry – to write poetry that sounds at once unheard of – as full of obscure and unexpected melodies as contemporary music is – and echoing with the various traditions it is immersed in.

But what is uncanny about this poetry is that it is learned without being intimidating. Prynne never seems to be determinedly refusing to make concessions to the reader, or to be high on his high horse. It is a poetry interested in, rather than merely wary of, the easy invitations poetry can make. A sense that words too obviously combined might be flattering nonsense, 'a betrayal of sorts in a rather uncertain mile' ('Nothing Like Examples'), an evasion of the restlessness of language. 'It is a very wild and / distant resort that keeps a man, wandering / at night, more or less in his place,' he writes in 'The Common Gain, Reverted'; if we think of language as a resort, we have to be able to think of resorts as wild and distant. The idea that we are kept 'more or less' in place by wandering – that wandering is what we cannot help but resort to when we use words – is the keynote of Prynne's vagrant poetry, obsessed as it is by the difficulties of location. 'Nomads are perfect' for Prynne, because their place is to have no place: like words, they have no fixed address. And by the same token, Prynne encourages us to be nomadic readers of his poetry, to move through it without settling down.

In a Prynne poem the reader's wish to locate herself – to work out what's going on, or who is doing what to whom – is soon baffled. But the sources of bafflement are referred to along the way: 'you could say speech was the domin- / ating discretion. All discretion is a private / matter, all changes of pace and childhood' ('A Gold Ring Called Reluctance'). Speech is the dominating discretion because it is only in language that we can choose what to be discreet about; just as you can change pace, you can change childhood by deciding what not to say about it. And if discretion is itself private we may be more secretive with ourselves than we know, more well-mannered with ourselves than we suspect.

We are uniquely able 'to elect terms, / to be the ground for names' ('The Numbers'), but the pun of the title reminds us of the strange fact that we measure ourselves in language, and the lines suggest just how confounding a map made of language can be. Words, Prynne is saying here, are the ground for words, and they are chosen, 'elected' by us (and 'terms', like line endings, set limits). But also, as the punctuation implies, we are the ground for names; they are planted on us, or scattered over us. They tell us who and where we are, but on their own terms, as it were. Prynne's poetry dramatizes the prevailing wish for resounding, accurate descriptions pitted against the actuality of a language that makes its own unruly worlds. In this poetry of maps and grids, of movements and journeys, language is a means without an end, a map for no discernible country or journey. 'This idea of the end is a neat / but mostly dull falsity ...' because there is 'No resolve about places, the latch-key to / our drifting lives'. The idea of place, of location, is a latch-key for a home that doesn't exist; home as a 'mostly dull falsity'.

This sense of our grounding in language makes Prynne's poems unusually alert to the directions his words take him in; indeed, many of his most startling and compacted poems can seem like meditations on single words; at once spirited essays in etymology, and the setting of words in new sentences. But it is always his informed misgivings about purpose and direction that gives these poems their odd vertigos of sense. 'The true expansion / is probably drift', he writes in 'Die A Millionaire', but drift means driven as well as aimless, and truth wants always to be more than probable to be worth its name. This book is one of the most inventive, intelligently experimental collected poems of the century.

Christopher Hill's Revolution
and Me

At school, history books – unlike novels – seemed like the definitive form of the textbook. Even at their best these books – Dickens on the Reformation, Scarisbrick's Henry VIII – always read like unimaginative novels, badly written by people who obviously hadn't been there. As an adolescent I had never come across anyone – or rather, anyone I admired – who read history for pleasure. Real curiosity, I knew, was effortless. My friends and I would have thought it uninspired and glamourless to be found pouring over Geoffrey Elton on the Tudors when you could have been reading Keats. In history books, it seemed, good plots and interesting characters were wasted in an excess of information.

In fact, as an adolescent I only ever read history books in order to understand something else that really interested me (which was usually literature). History was like a stage-set in front of which the important things – like poems and novels and plays – happened. And just like a set it was something you registered in order to forget, to take for granted; something that could quickly become a kind of necessary tacit knowledge. History (what we then called 'background') just set the scene for the poem. The French Revolution, for example, was a pretext for a lot of my favourite literature (when John Ashbery's first book of poems, *The Tennis Court Oath*, came out I thought it was just the title of John Ashbery's first book of poems). History, in those days, was not an agent, or a force or a process, or anything aesthetically complex like a Great Work of

Literature. It was merely a subject. This, at least, is what I remember feeling while doing History A-level, but really reading, undutifully, the then Great Works of English Literature, inspiringly taught by a pupil of Leavis's, at a public school in the late 1960s. History was simply an occasion for literature.

This privileging of literature – literature as an intelligible and wholesome refuge from the vulgar mess of politics – gave us the sense, I think, that art actually redeemed us from history. It freed us to be Olympian in our judgements. Certainly my own history – in so far as I thought of myself as having one – seemed to have nothing to do with History. Until I read Christopher Hill the idea that I, or anyone I knew, was *in* History, or the idea that History was something one couldn't help but make, would have seemed absurd. As would the sense, I also got from Hill, and would later get from Freud, that all history was contemporary history.

History, that is to say, was academic; like Science, something you could get wrong and needed teachers to help you get right. Getting it wrong meant not knowing enough, or knowing what you knew too vaguely. In no sense did it seem to belong to you; and you couldn't make it yours (in that sense, I could say now, it was pedagogy as trauma). Unlike poetry or novels then (the late 1960s), and free-association later, History seemed to require information, indeed, was a form of information. Chronology, like maths, made me feel bullied. And the very idea of accumulating knowledge, and particularly information as knowledge, seemed then, as it does now, pointless. Learning things off by heart – being told what to put inside my body – always felt like a violation, and made me stubborn. What I happened to remember always seemed infinitely more mysterious and revealing than what I tried to remember. Knowledge as a medium for coercion, all unchosen knowledge, made me blank and weary with resentment.

One of the many things I was to get from Christopher Hill's *The English Revolution 1640* – which I found by chance on the floor of a secondhand bookshop when I was sixteen – was some understanding of what people used knowledge to do. Of course the idea that institutions – like the State, the Crown, the Church, a Public School – could insidiously determine what people were capable of thinking, was an idea I was more than ready for. But the sense that there were, as Hill put it, 'people whose intellectual vision was not restricted by anxieties for their own property' seemed amazing. That there was a link between money and what went on, or could go on, in one's mind, seemed to change everything; turned the world upside down in ways I was not keen to acknowledge. The romance of what one was capable of thinking, the romance of hero-worship and the cult of genius on which literature seemed to depend, lost some of its edge. For Hill censorship – property as censorship – made history what it was. And this inevitably made one wonder, as psychoanalysis does, what an uncensored life would look like. So it was something of a revelation for me – and one that my age, in both senses, prepared me for – that authoritative (in this case, religious) knowledge was like material wealth, was informed by it; and that, like money, it could legitimate forms of coercion. And often under the assumed name of law and order. What was order, or legitimacy, if it could only be sustained by intimidation? What, then, were our pictures of what these things were like? Those questions, in very different versions, began to come to life. They are, after all, the questions that become urgent in adolescence, and therefore the questions people are encouraged to relinquish.

History, Hill made it abundantly clear, as both an academic subject and a political process, had been about leaving people out. Privilege was exclusion. Hill provided in his book a setting for (of) the repudiated voices of the Civil War. It was as though he had discovered a new country in a country I thought I knew. And this country of dissenting voices Hill did not colonize; he, in the seventeenth-century meaning of the word, advertised ('To take note of, attend to, observe'). Of course, these were not my words, or quite my thoughts then, when I found this book that I was so ready to read, and felt almost as though I was re-reading. But the story Hill was telling in this brief book must have, at least in part, formulated for me what I would now also think of as an internal dilemma. This was History that worked on me; that prompted me – unlike Elton on the Tudors – to make unconscious links with my own history and present preoccupations. It seemed, despite the remoteness of its subject, also somehow simulta- neous with my own life. It was, in other words, a form of history that made me an involuntary and willing participant. It fascinated me without effort; and it was about, among other things, the value of struggle.

As second-generation Jews from Poland and Russia, my parents, very determinedly, wanted to protect their children from struggle; to make the struggle for survival, which had been the project for them and their parents, seem like a thing of the past. For my grandparents this survival was not, as it was to us, heroic; it was itself demeaning that they had had to suffer such heroism. Their history had been an insult to their often good-natured natural snobbery. So my parents – fervent socialists with a passion for the Bloomsbury group – wished they had been the beneficiaries of long-standing English wealth and culture. But they instinctively identified with the people they would never – must never – aspire to be: all those who were the potential victims of other people's privilege. Their solidarity was with the people they were trying not to be. They may have been endlessly intrigued by Harold Acton, or the novels of Evelyn Waugh, but they believed in Aneurin

Bevan. You must be just, they told their children, but you must be decadent. Selves are to be indulged, but no one is to be left out.

Not surprisingly, perhaps, my hazy knowledge of the Civil War, prior to reading Hill, led me to identify with the Cavaliers, who I associated with a film I had seen about the Three Musketeers; the connection, I think, was something to do with their hats. I imagined them as witty and strong-minded rakes, wearing glamorous clothes (mostly velvet), and laughing as they fought; ruling-class public school boys of the seventeenth century. And, of course, the word Cavalier, unlike the word Puritan, was thrilling. I remember a teacher referring to me as having 'a rather cavalier attitude' to carpentry, and my feeling rather flattered. One of my favourite poets at this time – though his was not my favourite poetry, which was a crucial distinction – was the royalist Lovelace who was known to be the most handsome man in England (though by whom, I would wonder now?). As a wishy-washy royalist, fired by these adolescent fantasies of sexual terror and class aspiration, I was simultaneously confirming and defying my parents' contradictory ideals, the psychic errands they wanted me to run for them. In my own eyes I was insouciant and affluent enough to be outrageous; but in spite of myself I was a downmarket hybrid, a Jewish public school boy. I remember having a dream around this time about Prince Rupert in which he looked rather like Groucho Marx.

It was, I can see now, a small step from these incompatible ambitions – the split ego ideals and double-binds I inherited from my family – to a virtual passion for Hill's buried heroes, Winstanley and the Diggers: and then, at a later stage, for Freud and Ferenczi, and psychoanalysis (there is no royalist road to the unconscious). 'Freedom', Hill quotes Winstanley at the end of his book, 'is the man that will turn the world upside down ...

True freedom lies in the community in spirit and community in the earthly treasure.'

It was, I can also see now, Norman O. Brown's *Life Against Death* that was, without my noticing, to link these preoccupations together for me. But as a sixteen-year-old boy, holed up in an English public school and living vicariously (mostly in the music of the time) through what we were being told was also a revolution, the first sentence of Hill's book placed me, without irony, in the vanguard of radical thinking. 'The object of this essay', Hill wrote, 'is to suggest an interpretation of the events of the seventeenth century different from that which most of us were taught in school.' As I was still at school, and had been taught nothing about the seventeenth century as yet, I thought this put me in rather an enviable position. The book seemed slightly illicit. And its brevity, I would later realize, allied it with the pamphlet wars Hill was to write about so inspiringly. By reading it I would be ahead of the field without having entered it. And the idea that England was a place that had actually had a revolution already – like France, always a more glamorous country – and the idea that history writing could be as interestingly contentious, as dramatic, as the events it tried to describe, seemed astounding to me. The word 'revolution', like the word 'cavalier', was a seductive invitation. As Hill's work seemed to show – and psychoanalysis seemed to confirm – there can be no end to the rewriting of history, because the history is the rewriting.

It is not incidental, I think, that it was the dismay I felt reading Jonathan Clark's *Revolution and Rebellion* recently that reminded me how significant Hill's book had once been for me, and how prolific his influence has, one way and another, continued to be. In Clark's sometimes persuasive brand of revisionary history – with its determined reaction to Hill in style, tone and prejudice – there is the following footnote.

Footnotes, of course, are often for the people who don't quite make it into the text; people just this side of being left out. Clark has been discussing what is, in his view, the patent misuse of the word 'revolution' when what is being described, in Clark's more knowing view, is 'rebellion':

'the English revolution of 1640–1660 was a great social movement like the French Revolution of 1789. An old order that was essentially feudal was destroyed by violence, a new and capitalist social order created in its place. The Civil War was a class war, in which the despotism of Charles I was defended by the reactionary forces of the established churches and feudal landlords. Parliament could beat the King because it could appeal to the enthusiastic support of the trading and industrial classes in town and country-side', etc., etc.,: Christopher Hill, *The English Revolution 1640* (London, 1940), p. 9. It is the simplistic nature of such writing which now seems even more astonishing than the tenuousness of its claims to accuracy.

Of course, more temperate (and generous) revisionary historians of the period, like John Morrill, have shown, for example, Hill's inability, or unwillingness, to evoke the Royalist mentality, making the enemy, so to speak, a bit unreal; or shown the uneasy mix in Hill's writing of a kind of Manichean history which at the same time has an absolute commitment to the complexity of every historical process. But this is done partly in the service of acknowledging the inspiration of Hill's work (see, for example, Morrill's aptly titled, *Christopher Hill's Revolution*); the sense in which Hill set the terms for the debate. That it was essentially Hill that was being revised is not encompassed by the superciliousness of Clark's two wearied etceteras. Clark's uncivil war with Hill, his decidedly uncertain rebellion against, or revolution of Hill, too exactly calculates the rancour it cultivates.

What Clark quotes, and then scolds Christopher Hill for, was exactly what impinged upon my sixteen-year-old self (and still does, though there are more contexts now): the simplicity of the writing – the plain style that is itself an affiliation, a claim for affinities at work – and the generous astringent passion of its commitments.

What could be more 'astonishing', in the context of this particular debate, than Clark's claim to superior knowledge? Fantasies of rigour can always be used to occlude value, or belittle specific political commitments. Clark can be too keen to use the word objective; but evidence, of course, never comes first. One of the things that Hill has always been showing is that criteria of accuracy (or evidence) are always forms of vested interest: the question being, accurate for whom? Accurate to what end? Or perhaps, more simply, what does the historian want?

Hill has always made it integral to his practice to tell us what kind of world he wants. 'It is clearly seen', he quotes Winstanley as saying, 'that if we be suffered to speak, we shall batter to pieces all the old laws ...'. Reading *The English Revolution 1640* was, among other things, a way of hearing voices, a cure for the blandness of history.

Sameness is All

It seems somehow appropriate – whatever the scientific equivalent of poetic justice may be – that the first animal to be successfully cloned was a sheep. Sheep, after all, are not famous for their idiosyncrasy, for the uniqueness of their characters. We had assumed that sheep were virtually clones of each other, and now we have also been reminded that they are inevitably – all but two of them – genetically different. Now that what was once a figure of speech has become a reality – now that cloning has become a practicable possibility – it may be timely to wonder why describing someone as a clone has never been a compliment. Whether cloning, that is to say, is the death or the apotheosis of individualism?

One of the characteristics of contemporary culture has been a longing for community, for a sufficient sense of sameness with others; and at the same time a suspicion of people's wish to believe themselves to be too similar to each other, or, indeed, identical to – overly convinced by – the images they have of themselves. From our experience of small-scale cults and large-scale fascism we have become fearful when too many people seem to agree with each other – seem to be of the same mind about something – or claim to know who they really are. Democracies, in other words, have to be ambivalent about consensus. Too little and there is fragmentation, too much and there is a (spurious) homogeneity. But with the advent of cloning – when the same has, as it were, been literalized as the identical, when the identical, at long last, supposedly exists – a whole range of political and psychological vocabularies are stopped in their tracks. Cloning, among many other things, seems to be a final solution to the problem of otherness. And, of course, the end of any continuing need – at least in the mass-production of animals – for two sexes in the task of reproduction. In one fell swoop cloning is a cure for sexuality and difference.

From a psychoanalytic point of view, one of the individual's formative projects, from childhood onwards, is to find a cure for – or, less strictly speaking, some kind of solution to – exactly these two things: sexuality and difference, the sources of un-bearable conflict. And it is this that makes children's fascination with, and interpretation of, cloning – and the whole science of genetics – so interesting. Indeed, children are instructive witnesses of the great scientific issues of the day because they usefully anthropomorphize these issues for us (for them it's all about bodies and the connections between them: about mummy and daddy and me and you). So, from the child's point of view, what might the appeal of cloning be, and what might be the conscious and unconscious fears associated with it? Since there can be no general answer to these questions – even if cloning itself radically changes our sense of what generalization might entail – I want to use two brief clinical vignettes that are suggestive and perplexing rather than exemplary: suggestive both of what these particular children are using their ideas about cloning to say and to solve; and perplexing if for no other reason than the fact that one new thing adults can do now that children can't, but can aspire to do, is clone. In other (old) words, that once again cloning, shall we say, ironizes – children have a new role model on their horizon.

An eight-year-old girl who was referred to me for school phobia – that had begun a year after her sister was born – told me in her second session that when she grew up she was 'going to do clothing'. I said, 'Make clothes for people?', and she said, 'No, no, clothing ... you know, when you make everyone wear the same uniform, like the headmistress does ... we learned about it in biology.' I said, 'If everyone wears the same uniform no one's special.' She thought about this for a bit and then said, 'Yes, no one's special but everyone's safe.' I was thinking then, though I couldn't find a way of saying it, that if everyone was the same there would be no envy but she interrupted my thoughts by saying, 'The teacher told us that when you do clothing you don't need a mummy and daddy, you just need a scientist, a man ... it's like twins, all the babies are the same.' There was so much in all this that I couldn't choose which bit to pick up, I could only apparently carry on with the conversation. I said, 'If your sister was exactly the same as you maybe you could go to school'; and she said 'Yes' with some relish, 'I could be at home and school at the same time ... everything!'

In this little girl's strong misreading – to use Harold Bloom's phrase – of cloning there seemed to be several theories afoot. First, that what she called 'clothing' was a uniformity imposed by powerful solo individuals, either the female headmistress or the male scientist. And that if specialness or uniqueness was what was lost at the birth of a sibling then 'clothing' was the last punitive act in the drama, a drama that actually begins with the parents' sexuality. You lose your place in the family when your sister arrives; then you begin to experience your school uniform as the ultimate proof of your loss of individuality. She wanted to 'do clothing' perhaps because then she would at least be the active agent not the passive victim; the appeal here is of a certain kind of omnipotence that in and of itself differentiates the cloner from the cloned. The headmistress has one unique talent – to make the children the same – but not the same as her. In other words, the scientist who clones acquires a paradoxical (and enviable) uniqueness (as though the new law of the genetic jungle is clone or be cloned).

The theory I seemed to want to introduce was that because the girl and her sister were different there was a competition (for the mother) that she had lost. Cloning, in other words, is a cure for the terrors and delights of competition. If the two children were identical they would, by definition, be getting the same things. If the parents don't have to have sex – 'you don't need a mummy and daddy' – then the child doesn't need to be preoccupied by the relationship between the parents; nor indeed, need she then see the primary relationship – the 'source' that babies apparently come from – as one between two people of similar status, and that involves difference. My patient keeps her (symbolized) parents apart, the female head-mistress and the male scientist, both doing the similar thing, but separately. She imagines one person having a mysterious talent, rather than two people doing something to each other, which they can't do by themselves. What is interestingly obscure or ambiguous in this child's account is whether, or in what sense, the cloner and the cloned are looked after – 'you don't need a mummy and a daddy'; as though the unconscious fear might be that the cloner is a tyrannical parent, oblivious or hostile to difference and the individuality of need.

It is also possible, of course, that the child is wondering whether *I* am going to clone her, remake her out of my words. What Freud called transference – the way we invent new people on the basis of our earliest relationships – was evidence for him that a kind of psychic cloning went on between people. That we unwittingly treat people as though they were the same as us (the same as ourselves or our parents). The analyst interprets to show the patient that the analyst is not the same as anyone in his past, that the patient's cloning of the analyst is his defence against the shock of the new. The analyst, in other words, contests the patient's strong wish to clone him (psychoanalysis, one could say, was a cure for cloning before cloning itself existed; the cure as precursor of the problem). Psychoanalysis calls the simulation of sameness narcissism, which it tends to treat as the saboteur of development; Narcissus wanted to be the same as himself, the same as the image of himself, a distinction he didn't have it in himself to make. From a psychoanalytic point of view, successful psychic cloning – making people, including ourselves, in our own image of them – is a denial of difference and dependence, and therefore a refusal of need. The art of self-cloning is an attempt to stop time by killing desire. Replicating myself I keep finding nothing else. I depend on something other than myself to actually nourish me.

Adolescents are preoccupied by the relationship between dependence and conformity, between independence and compliance. So it's not surprising, perhaps, that in the cultish jargon of adolescents to be called a clone is an ultimate insult. Yet it may be worth wondering exactly what is being repudiated – what longings or pleasures may be encoded in the word – in this particular, increasingly topical, form of scapegoating. Cloning, that is to say, gives us the opportunity to re-wonder what's wrong with being apparently or exactly the same as someone else. And this is a question, not only about why we may be frightened of being like other people – what it is we imagine we lose in this process – but about why we may be frightened of other people being just like us.

If cloning as analogy captures the adolescent imagination then this tells us as much about cloning as it does about adolescence. And one thing it tells us, I think, is that there is – now, for some people – a deep fear of not being a clone, of not being identical to someone, or identical to someone else's wishes for oneself (the child enacting the parents' conscious and unconscious projects being the model for this). As though we can only work out what or who we are like from the foundational belief – the unconscious assumption – that there is someone else that we are exactly like. For the adolescent the question is: if I'm not the same as someone else what will I be like? And this is where cloning comes in. The adolescent lives as if she has been cloned, and is trying and not trying to find out what else there is to her. But now, of course, she can also find a more accurate and exacting description – an unprecedented picture – of this predicament which recreates it anew. Once there were twins and mirrors and doubles; now cloning is available for adolescent consumption. Ideas about development are themselves developed by fresh analogy.

A sixteen-year-old boy given to disparaging some of his male contemporaries as clones – kids who, in his view, were rather too keen to please their teachers, rather too timid to defy their parents – mentioned one day in a session that he wanted to find a girlfriend who would be his clone: 'Just like me so we'd have lots of things in common ... anyway, girls are so good at being clones.' I asked him what that meant that they were good at, and he replied, 'Being like the people they like.' I wondered aloud whether if this was true it was because some girls picked up how frightened boys were of them. And he said, a bit too quickly, with that dazzling logic we all have recourse to when ruffled, 'Well I'm not scared of them, that's why I want a clone girlfriend.' I suggested that having things in common with people was overrated. This interested him, so after a pause I continued with this impromptu lecture that was stirring in me, elaborating what I meant – because he had asked – and ending, for some reason, with a slightly impatient question: 'Anyway, what would two people who were exactly the same do together?' I was, at this moment, genuinely confounded by this and didn't expect him to answer (it's often surprisingly difficult to work out who one's questions are addressed to). We both sat there for a few minutes and then he said, as if he was stumbling over what I'd said, 'They couldn't ask each other ... because they'd get the same answer, so they'd have to ask someone else.' I said, clearly helped by him, 'So they'd need a third person, they'd still need somebody different?' and he said, 'Yes', perking up, 'me and my clone would need you to guide us!'

The fantasy of the clone girlfriend – not exactly a rarity – was for this boy an all-purpose magical solution. A way of pre-empting what you do about, or with, the parts of yourself that have nothing 'in common' with an object of desire. What is of interest is that the (narcissistic) solution of creating absolute sameness – the clone – unconsciously kills desire. The fantasy of cloning a girlfriend is a fantasy of not needing a girlfriend. The exact replication of the self merely replicates the problem. That men must not be clones, but must clone women – one contemporary description of a war between the sexes – suggests, among other things, that men already experience themselves as having been cloned by women. The fantasy of cloning – made puzzlingly real by the actuality of it – raises the question now of what the alternative analogies are for relationship? The cloning has already happened; the problem is where we can go from here?

Cloning is for obvious, and not quite so obvious, reasons a compelling way of talking about what goes on between people. But of course the fantasies about cloning – the cultural gossip about it – are informed by wishes. Genetic inheritance, for example, is always a potential; it doesn't predict growth, but it provides (often unknowable) constraints. The environment is an essential part of the equation. The cloned sheep will be identical genetically, but they will have different histories. As my two examples suggest – though for quite different reasons given the ages of the children – cloning is used to get around history. As though in the total fantasy of cloning, history as difference is abolished. People, in actuality, can never be identical to each other. Perhaps this relentless wish for absolute identity – that even real cloning cannot satisfy – conceals, tries to talk us out of, a profound doubt about our being the same as anything. Wishes always return us to the scene of a crime.

Nijinsky's New Diary

Psychiatry has been most demeaning when it has sought to classify those people who have suffered most acutely throughout their lives from spurious classification; at its worst it misrecognizes those who have the most to tell us about misrecognition. If the psychiatrist 'Bleuler's description of Nijinsky – "confused schizophrenic with mild manic excitement" – seems exactly correct' to Joan Acocella in her useful introduction to this extraordinary book, it may be partly because we still can't find good enough analogies for what the people who disturb us most are like. To treat the so-called mad as oracles was as diminishing in its own way, as scapegoating them. Now that the agony and the tedium of so-called madness are so evident, now that its waste is recognized as often being in excess of its revelations, it may be just the right time for this first and excellent translation of Nijinsky's complete diary. Where previously we have his wife's understandably expurgated edition, we have Nijinsky here with his shames intact, as it were.

'Nijinsky', Acocella remarks, 'has become one of the most famous men of the century, but never was so much artistic fame based on so little artistic evidence: one eleven-minute ballet, Faun, plus some photographs.' The erotic mystique of choreography – its moving and placing of bodies, its relinquishing of words as the medium of contact – combined with Nijinsky's

Review of Joan Acocella (ed.), *The Diary of Vaslav Nijinsky*,
unexpurgated edition, translated from the Russian by Kyril Fitzlyon
(Farrar, Straus and Giroux, 1999), from the *New York Observer*.

inspired instincts as a dancer, had made him instantly fascinating to people; but as the diary so poignantly shows, it was this very fascination that made people so inattentive to him. Like the jumps for which he was so famous in his dancing, those long pauses that seemed to defy gravity (in both senses), his 'madness' at thirty seemed of a piece; such daring and poise could never be sustained. But this consoling myth of genius – these fantasies of hubris and punishment that makes us lump the inspiringly mad together (Nietzsche, Artaud etc) because their extreme singularity, their extreme worldliness, stuns us – is usefully exploded by even the most cursory reading of this diary. The jumps in his writing – the mixed magic of transitions, the way he moves the reader through to a climax of nonsense – are themselves a subtle commentary on the forces of progress (and profit) that had driven Europe into the devastations of the First World War. The *Diary* is in no puerile sense a case-history; begun in the immediate aftermath of the war, and recording Nijinsky's spiral into thirty years of invalidism, it is rather a dramatic monologue of a remarkable man devastated by his world. Indeed, it often sounds like *The Wasteland*, but written by Dostoyevsky.

What is most striking about this diary – and that is redolent of its authenticity – is that it is at once insistently tedious in its obsessions and endlessly fascinating in the cunning of its artfulness. Nijinsky intrigues us about himself, and puts us off; indeed, intrigues us by putting us off. As though all the time he dares the reader to be sufficiently interested in him, to find out what will happen if we follow him. The diary, in other words, is clearly written by someone who knows that those around him – mostly his wife and her parents, his daughter, and his doctor – are beginning to consider him as mad. So it is the text of a terminally scrutinized man; a man adored as a great dancer, who is gradually becoming the object of a different kind of concerned attention. It is perhaps not surprising, given the glare of specialness that he lived under, that the abiding preoccupation of the diary is about what people want from him, about the paradoxes of perfectionism. It is a book by a perfectionist, in praise of mistakes. 'When everything I now write is published, with its mistakes, I will correct it all. I wanted to have mistakes and therefore put them in on purpose.' It is part of the wonderful logic of this that he can have it both ways by acknowledging that he can't have it both ways. He tells us that he believes in his mistakes, but he will eventually correct them; though without telling us what they are.

There is a terrifying shrewdness about Nijinsky's logic in this diary. He writes like a man who has understood his audience so well that he can no longer perform for them, he can only outperform them. As though what they want from him reveals something impossible about wanting. 'I like mistakes', he writes in one of the letters that the diary turns into, 'because I want people to understand me. If I write without mistakes people will think that I am a madman.' What people 'understand' is imperfection, vulnerability; and yet now he must calculate his mistakes to assure people that he is not mad. So in this self-protective second-guessing of the audience he is no longer free to make genuine mistakes. If you don't make mistakes people give up trying to understand you, so you are mad. 'I am', he writes, 'a Napoleon who forgives mistakes.' This is the ordinary megalomania of so-called madness, but of an unusual subtlety. When Nijinsky is God in this diary, as he is all too often – 'I am God. I am the spirit. I am everything' – it is always nuanced by his interest in error, by his sense that perfectionism is a form of hatred. If God, by definition, doesn't make mistakes, then he is mad. 'I like perfecting things,' Nijinsky writes as a virtual God, 'I do not like things.' If you like

344

perfecting things, it means you don't like them. Nijinsky's life seems to have been a chronicle of people, from his mother to Diaghilev and his wife, who urged on him his own perfection. Dance was the only place, apart from this diary, that he could explore the terrible nature of their demands.

It is not, therefore, incidental that this unexpurgated translation of the diaries reveals Nijinsky's seemingly compulsive and (to him) shameful obsession with prostitutes that his wife airbrushed out of the diary she published. Having felt like Diaghilev's 'tart', and sought out prostitutes when he was touring with the Ballets Russes in Paris, the prospect of being sent to Zurich by his wife for psychiatric treatment brings one thing, above all, to mind. 'I will not be writing in Zurich', he writes, 'because I am very interested in that town. I will go to a brothel because I want to have an intuitive understanding of tarts. I have forgotten tarts. I want to understand the psychology of a tart.' Nijinsky knew that what he needed to understand – or rather, to remind himself of – was the psychology of the prostitute. And he knew that this was the key to understanding not merely his own predicament but also the mad 'materialism' of pre- and post-war Europe that he so despises in this diary. It was as though Nijinsky somehow realized that the response to him as a dancer was itself a symptom of something larger and more daunting. Once he was unable to use dancing to explore the problem his dancing had exposed, he had two options: conversion to a then fashionable Tolstoyism (spiritual vegetarian pacifism) or the (almost) muted violence of madness. His devout Tolstoyism couldn't staunch the wound created by the image everywhere of the exploited body. The diary becomes a last eloquent rant of the once-poised body finally humiliated.

'I am', Nijinsky writes, 'a simple feeling that everyone has.' Read for the simple poignancy of his predicament, or for the intricate canniness of his 'mad' logic, the diary is an

345

extraordinary work. Like a novel by Thomas Bernhard, the rhythm of its obsessions is integral to its power (the diary could itself be performed as a monologue). The struggle to articulate is always a kind of madness. Nijinsky may have had to actually go mad because there was no one in the vicinity who could even acknowledge that. 'The man who is right', he wrote, 'is the one who feels but does not understand.' That, one might say, is the question. Music and dance make one believe this to be true, but the fascism that followed on from the war made that kind of truth horrifying. Nothing could be at once more belated or more timely than this remarkable diary.

Jokes Apart

As there's nothing you can do to a joke to make it funny, except tell it well, the telling of jokes can be a testing time for everyone involved. And once they've been told we rarely have conversations about whether or not they have worked. Good art makes us think and talk and write; good jokes just amuse us. Either we get them or we don't; and when jokes are interpreted they begin to sound like bad jokes. In fact, when it comes to jokes, explanation and understanding are at odds with each other. If you get the joke you can explain it, but explaining a joke rarely makes anyone happy (you couldn't have a book called 'The Best Jokes Explained'). So the idea of someone being serious about jokes – wanting something from jokes besides what is patently on offer – is not, in the ordinary way of things, very enticing.

The joke-theorist – it is significantly difficult to know what to call such a person – has to believe that he can compete with the joke; that he can give us something as good, if not better. He has to believe that there is something we would rather do than laugh. One of the many triumphs of Ted Cohen's *Jokes* – apart from the not incidental fact that the jokes are so good that he doesn't bother to compete with them – is that it never tries to sound more profound than the jokes it tells. Cohen's amazement that there are such things as jokes – 'the fact that there is a kind of story meant to make us laugh' – and that they can work so spectacularly, and fail so dismally, has fired him to write a

Review of Ted Cohen, *Jokes: Philosophical Thoughts on Joking Matters*, (Chicago University Press, 1999), from the *London Review of Books*.

deliberately small-scale book on many subjects that are liable to make people think big. 'One of the more ponderous and depressing features of large-scale moral theories', he writes, 'is that they tell you what makes things right or wrong, good or bad, and then leave it to you to make a case about whose morality you feel strongly and try to outfit it with the theories' sanctioned reasons.' It is fitting that a book which is so finely eloquent about Jewish jokes should prefer untailored truths. Cohen gives us such a keen – and daunting – sense of what it is for a joke to misfire, implicitly likening it to what happens when a theory gets too greedy in its explanations ('large-scale'), that he makes you feel he is doing an unusual kind of philosophy. as though he has managed to turn J. L. Austin into one of the Marx Brothers.

The philosopher on jokes, and indeed the jokey philosopher, has to be mindful of the fact that the joke is always on someone. To write with the wrong kind of seriousness about jokes – or the wrong kind of unseriousness – is unlikely to inspire confidence in a reader who may already feel compromised by the fact that he is reading such a book: is he an earnest saddie, one of those people who needs an explanation for everything, and particularly his pleasure? Books that explain poems, or dreams, or even sex can add to our pleasure in these things; but when it comes to humour, those who can, do. Yet as Cohen knows, with the cunning and sureness of tone that is everywhere in this book, the misgivings we have about doing anything with jokes other than telling them is part of their appeal. Unlike poems and dreams and sex, jokes virtually instruct us not to talk about them: all we have to do is perform them properly (i.e. very well) and for that short time they give us the life we want. Cohen wants us to be intrigued by his subject but not suspicious, susceptible but not naive. *Jokes*, in other words, tells us many things about jokes, and jokes, in appropriately bold type and sensibly categorized, take up over a third of Cohen's text. It also tells us many remarkable things about intimacy, about explanation, understanding and belief, about Jews and, more or less inadvertently, about philosophers, and what Cohen thinks they should be doing with our time.

'A philosopher', he writes ruefully in the Introduction, 'has to say at least a few theoretical words. But I will attempt nothing global or universal; there will be no comprehensive theory of jokes or their purpose, not only because I have no such theory, but also because I believe there could be no such theory.' If this makes us wonder what theoretical words are, as opposed, say, to theories, it also reminds us how much philosophers in the past believed that size matters. That the reach of a theory is more a matter of what it reaches in us than of the amount of ground covered (the globe, the universe) is one of the things Cohen uses jokes to show us. Jokes, in his words, are 'devices for inducing intimacy'; and technology notwithstanding, there is no such thing as global, let alone universal intimacy. It has been the absurd fate, Cohen implies, of large-scale comprehensive theory to produce ever more inclusive forms of explanation through ever greater denials of difference. The old-style philosophical quest for universals is a quest for a world without too many differences; and that world is, of course, no laughing matter.

Fortunately Cohen's dismissal of comprehensive theory is not merely, as it usually is, an opportunity to be grand in a different manner. Reading *Jokes* makes you feel that being genial is the most profound thing we ever do – which is something jokes also make us feel – and that doing philosophy is as natural as being amused. Cohen, in other words, performs in this book what he promotes; jokes, in his account, are one of the best forms language takes, and so can show us what it might be that we want language to do for us, and what kind of calamity it is when it fails us, when we fail at it (the excruciating vulnerability of the bad comic). But to pull this off without portentousness – or the embarrassment about portentousness that can be worse – Cohen has to tell funny stories and make us think about them, without making the wrong kind of meal of it. 'The thing about German food is that no matter how much you eat, an hour later you're hungry for power.' The problem here is obvious and Cohen isn't interested in resolving it. 'If it offends one to have Germans represented in this way,' he comments, 'then the amusement may be lost altogether.' But it may not be, and the reason we are amused may be rather more interesting than the joke's overt racism. That seemingly superfluous 'altogether' notes how much there is in amusement, and what there is to lose when one loses it. 'It is a general thesis of mine,' Cohen writes, 'that a deep satisfaction in successful joke transactions is the sense held mutually by teller and hearer that they are joined in feeling.' And to be joined in feeling is different from being joined in belief, or joined in business (the consequences, for one thing, are less predictable). If a joke, when it's successful, is a transaction – an action performed, and a deal done – it may be, by the same token, a communal act – the closest some of us ever get to a so-called sense of community. Jokes tap into those affinities and recognitions between people that seem to reveal something essential about themselves, or at any rate something they can't help but value. It's this that makes humour akin to sexual desire, and makes jokes seem like safe sex. Modern people who experience themselves, for whatever reason, as 'over-controlled' are more likely to value what seems to be involuntary, like amusement and sexual desire.

Jokes and Their Relation to the Unconscious is as tentative a title, in its own way, as *Jokes: Philosophical Thoughts on Joking Matters*. But in its aspiration to be a comprehensive theory, Freud's book is by definition far more ambitious (as well as being, at the same time, a book about ambition, and about jokes as a form of ambition). But Cohen's guarded relationship to Freud – and his covert ambition to outwit him by doubting not merely his theory, but theory-making in general – is one of the many subtle pleasures of this book. (Bergson and Meredith wrote books on humour, but Freud is the only one to have attempted a kind of universal theory.) It is the amusement of influence rather than the anxiety that he is, perhaps unsurprisingly, given to. So he offers as an example of what he calls the 'slightly more intricate ... mildly hermetic joke':

Early one morning a man awoke in a state of terrible anxiety because of the dream he had been having. He immediately called his psychiatrist, and after making a special plea because of his distress he was granted an appointment that morning even though it was not the day for seeing his psychiatrist. When he arrived in the doctor's office he said: 'I had the most awful dream you can imagine. In it I raped my mother, killed my wife, and seduced my daughter, and more things worse than those. I woke up shaking and sweating, and I called you immediately. Then I had a quick piece of toast and some coffee, and ran down here to see you.'
'What?' said the psychiatrist. 'You call that a breakfast?'

Ostensibly a joke about Jewish parents, the joke is also about – on – people who have what Cohen calls 'comprehensive theories' and people who distrust these people. It works because the audience takes it for granted that the psychiatrist is a man with such a theory. As though one thing the joke is saying is: only people who have such theories can surprise us like this. This is why the joke suits Cohen's book, though it would be against the grain of the book – which is always deadpan in its insinuations – to say this. Cohen prefers jokes that don't over-protect their tellers.

A comprehensive theory, like Freud's – all jokes are sexual, all jokes are artefacts that make the unacceptable sufficiently pleasurable – is implicitly amusing for Cohen because it offers exactly the kind of predictability that good jokes trade on ('An exhibitionist was thinking of retiring, but he decided to stick it out for one more year'). People with theories like Freud's allow us to expect something of them and allow us not to take that too seriously. Jokes for Cohen constitute a sense of community simply by relying on 'an implicit acknowledgment of a shared background ... this is the foundation of the intimacy that will develop if your joke succeeds'. By taking for granted what they depend on, good jokes confirm the existence of this shared background. We only get the joke because in some sense we are in the world it comes from. If your joke misfires, or you don't get the joke, then you have either fallen out of the world or you are, if only momentarily, in the wrong one. 'I urge you to agree,' Cohen writes (his urgencies are mercifully few and far between), 'that this estrangement is very important indeed, and that it can represent a threat to one's conception of one's own humanity.' Jokes are always, however secretly, poignant because they express our longing not to be too strange to each other, or to ourselves, not to be too determinedly unique. So on Cohen's unpleading account jokes are a kind of informal politics, one of the unusually successful forms of group life (a totalitarian state is a state of canned laughter):

When we laugh at the same thing, that is a very special occasion. It is already noteworthy that we laugh at all, at anything, and that we laugh all alone. That we do it *together* is the satisfaction of a deep human longing, the realization of a desperate hope. It is the hope that we are enough like one another to sense one another, to be able to live together.

It is as though the joke does with relative ease and economy something we usually do with a great deal of resistance and effort: that is, identify with each other. And yet, as Cohen knows, this is also what makes jokes so disturbing; racism, sexism, nationalism, not to mention comprehensive theories, all thrive on a currency of jokes. But for Cohen the point to take seriously, so to speak, is that we are amused; that when it comes to humour – and, of course, sex – our preferences don't always accord with our principles. And that that might tell us something more useful than the forlorn (and often vicious) attempts to shame us out of our prejudices. Cohen's motto about all this is unsurprisingly pragmatic. 'Try remaking the world so that such jokes will have no place, will not arise. But do not deny that they are funny.' Because no theory of joking can get round the fact that jokes are often cruel, philosophical thoughts on joking matters are always, whatever else they are (or want to be), philosophical thoughts on cruelty. When jokes are not charmed verbal puzzles – 'What do Alexander the Great and Winnie the Pooh have in common? They have the same middle name' – they are stories about humiliation. Cohen is at his best about jokes that make a mockery of the idea of innocence. Indeed, if this book is a critique of anything it is a critique of the vagaries (and vagueries) of wilful innocence and, by extension, of many versions of political correctness.

Like a number of philosophers before him Cohen clearly wants to make philosophy more worldly, or even more vulgar. And jokes might be just the thing to stop philosophy turning into a campus novel. (His footnotes alone are a radical counter-cultural statement.) Something, anyway, has made Cohen a bit frantic and thus prompted him to write his own genre of confession-cum-jeremiad, but without the grandiloquence that usually attaches to these things. Cohen clearly doesn't want all theory to aspire to the condition of autobiography; he just wants to get us to worry about the right things:

It is one thing to worry over a version of eighteenth-century scepticism, and wonder whether green looks green to you the way it does to me, and what it would mean to inhabit a world in which

353

we did not experience green the same way, and what it means that we seemingly do inhabit a world in which we can't be 'sure' that we see green together. It is quite another thing to wonder what the world would be like for me if I never found the same things funny that you or anyone else find funny. I personally have no worries on account of the problem about green, but I worry and feel stricken every time one of my jokes does not reach you.

It is the way the 'it' gradually turns into the 'I' that is artful about this; it is the 'I personally' that Cohen wants to get back into philosophy but without too much of the sentimentality and self-importance that such Is usually collect around themselves these days. Though Cohen doesn't say this in so many words, a joke that fails is a form of madness. If you want to know what scepticism feels like, if you want to feel it really kick in, tell your favourite jokes to people who don't get them. The first few times this happens you can blame the audience, but imagine never finding a single person who smiled. That would be scepticism red in tooth and claw. Cohen's choice of the Biblical 'stricken' stands out in this context – and is also a clue to some of his more complicated affinities.

Not finding the same things funny that you or anyone else finds funny is, of course, a common immigrant experience. What Cohen intimates in this book is that the link between 'scepticism', as philosophers see it, and what all sorts of people call 'assimilation' may be of more than academic interest. Because at its most tendentious – and jokes are always that – *Jokes* is about Jewishness. Not about Jews as chosen joke-tellers of exemplary jokes, but rather what Jews have used jokes to do. Cohen finds a 'specifically Jewish sanction for humour' within the traditions of Judaism itself. 'Laughter', he writes, 'may be heard as the echo of faith' – and it is echoes of faith that most religions are after.

What he doesn't find, though, and this is of a piece with the argument of the book, is any discernible essence of Jewishness; anymore than he finds an essence of joking. 'Of course there are jokes that are recognizably Jewish,' he writes. 'And of course one cannot say just what the Jewishness in these jokes is.' And of course, the fact that we can be convinced by recognitions that we are unable to describe is itself a philosophical knot. Cohen claims a Biblical, 'even Talmudic' sanction for this Jewish humour he knows to be a kind of common knowledge while not being available in the forms knowledge is commonly supposed to take. The jokes this tradition 'underwrites', he writes in the language of analytic philosophy, 'may belong to a class that has necessary and sufficient conditions, but I have too much heart to attempt to formulate them.' Though many people, I imagine (and I'm sure Cohen imagines), find this a heartening claim, it wouldn't have cut much ice with the Vienna Circle. But anyone who gets the joke – who senses what Cohen means by 'heart', who likes the way he writes, whether they want to or not – will prefer his inclination to 'characterize' rather than formulate. (It is the difference, broadly speaking, between the diagnostic manual and a good novel.)

At this point in the argument, Cohen retells five really funny Jewish jokes. Each one 'displays a crazy logic ... an insane rationality, a logical rigour gone over the edge'. Just as Freud's psychoanalysis was the double of Logical Positivism, the Jewish jokes that Cohen tells are close to the heart of his chosen profession. 'Logically speaking,' he writes, knowing the phrase is virtually a contradiction in terms, all these jokes 'incorporate implausibilities, absurdities and downright contradictions. What does it mean that one *laughs* at such a thing?'

Rather than a 'logical rigour gone over the edge' it seems, in Cohen's account, that logical rigour is what you come up with after you've gone over the edge. Joking, for Cohen, is a cure – or as close as we are going to get to a cure – through wholehearted acknowledgement of 'the incomprehensible'. 'What is the most incomprehensible thing you know?' he asks, and wants us to ask; not so that we can be starry-eyed with wonder, or stupefied with terror, but so that we can acquire something which he believes the Hebrew Bible offers: a 'conception of decency in which the fully human, fully acceptable response to the mystification of the world is a laughing acceptance, a kind of spiritual embrace'. What Cohen doesn't tell us, and it does seem rather important in the circumstances, is whether in his view it is fully human to believe in the God of the Hebrew Bible. A laughing acceptance is sufficiently equivocal not to be unduly awed; and a mystification is not a mystery that one can prostrate oneself before. But 'a kind of spiritual embrace' has a jarring piety that is sufficiently at odds with the rest of the book to make one wonder who the joke is on.

Perhaps Cohen believes that the mystification of the world was perpetrated as some kind of joke by God; and that 'kind of spiritual embrace' is a calculated red rag. Some people might wonder, for example, in their logical way, how many kinds of these embraces there are and, indeed, what exactly a spiritual embrace is. Whether Cohen is veering away from or veering towards a kind of religiosity here – or that secular form of religiosity called sincerity – this is a strange moment in the book. But then the book is written, like much of the most interesting contemporary philosophy, in the crossfire between analytic philosophy and theology. And in this now traditional drama, this antagonism of languages, it is not clear what constitutes the return of the repressed. The sacred certainly doesn't seem to be a candidate. 'I am scarcely the first to feel', Cohen writes with perhaps calculated ambiguity, 'a sacred twinge in someone's laughter.' The varieties of twinge are legion.

Cohen's two points, about 'a kind of Jewish style' and the

'abiding characteristic of at least some Jewish humour', are entirely plausible, after such droll caution. That there is a Talmudic 'fascination with language and logic', and that Jewish humour has 'often been the humour of outsiders' ('often' is doing quite a lot of work here) makes the good sense Cohen wants it to. And the connection he makes is at once incisive and straightforward. 'When one has this tradition of incessant questioning and criticizing,' he writes, 'then when one finds oneself an outsider, one will deploy these techniques of criticizing and questioning when examining what is inside.' It may also be true, of course, that the aim of incessant questioning is to keep one outside: that idealizing the critical spirit keeps at bay the fears associated with being an insider. Specialness is hard work, and it is the virtue of Cohen's book to see jokes as a way of negotiating the anxieties of privilege, and especially the dire privilege of being discriminated against.

That we are capable of being amused is the really telling thing for Cohen. Everything after that, is after that. 'I insist that you do not let your conviction that a joke is in bad taste, or downright immoral, blind you to whether you find it funny.' This is not, of course, worlds away – though Cohen doesn't say so, and can't really say so because Freud has the say-so on this – from always allowing oneself to notice what one happens to be sexually aroused by. But then Cohen is not fashionably committed to the (theoretical) wonders of blindness. What he wants us to see is that what looks as if it could lead us into moral havoc may be the only thing that will give us heart.

Doing Heads

In their Introduction to the *Picador Book of the New Gothic*, Patrick McGrath and Bradford Morrow proposed a familiar kind of progress myth to help us find our way around the New Gothic; the old, or rather, original Gothic being by definition a genre in which the protagonists lost their way in horror or deranged bewilderment. 'Gothic fiction,' they wrote,

in its earliest days, was known by the props and settings it employed, by its furniture. Dark forests and dripping cellars, ruined abbeys riddled with secret passages, clanking chains, skeletons, thunderstorms and moonlight – from such material did the first Gothicists frame their tales. It's not until the 1830s and 40s, with Edgar Allan Poe, that the Gothic begins to shift the emphasis away from all this gloomy hardware and become increasingly fascinated with the psyche of the Gothic personality ... With Poe the Gothic turns inward, and starts rigorously to explore extreme states of psychological disturbance.

If the terror is all inside us now – if animism is dead, and the psyche is the terrifying modern ghost in the machine – then the ideal setting for the contemporary Gothic would not be a ruined abbey or a dark forest but a mental hospital, or a family. And the ultimate parody, or apotheosis of the novelist – or indeed of the so-called omniscient narrator – must be, as McGrath intimates so artfully in *Asylum*, the modern psychiatrist: the person who treats the madness as though it was all outside him, raring to be cured (or rigorously explored); the

Review of Patrick McGrath, *Asylum* (Viking, 1996), from the *London Review of Books*.

person who gets people to keep the madness inside – inside language, inside themselves, inside mental hospitals. After all, if he doesn't speak from a position of sanity, from where does he speak? And what exactly makes his tales better than the patients'? Psychiatrists, and their poor relatives, psychoanalysts, have always been Gothic figures trying to escape from the genre in which the characters are always shady, and authority is simply melodrama.

One of the Gothic devices that McGrath has exploited so well in his fiction – and perhaps most successfully in this riveting new novel – is to begin by speaking to the reader, as he does in the Picador Introduction, in an apparently sensible, eminently intelligent voice. This voice of patient, informed explanation – with its knowing lists, its confidence in narrative – makes the reader feel that it's more than possible to have a grip on things. Then, as the story unfolds, everyone loses their grip, and there is no way of regaining it, because all the available forms of competence and comprehension – from the theological and the medical, down to the police – are either ridiculed by events, or shown to be complicit with the horror (it is their grip that gives them the slip). These are operatic black comedies and what happens in them makes a grotesque mockery of the understanding voice (which puts the reader as critic, as opposed to the reader as spectator, in an awkward position). Gothic stories are darkly exuberant satires of the Grand Narratives, in which explanation is just more genteel respectability: Poe's Gothic, for example, is an ironic precursor of the Grand Narrative of psychoanalysis. The masterful are as frantic and deluded as anyone else, but better at convincing us – and, of course, themselves – that they are not.

'The catastrophic love affair,' *Asylum* begins, 'characterized by sexual obsession has been a professional interest of mine for many years now. Such relationships vary widely in duration and intensity but tend to pass through the same stages. Recognition. Identification. Assignation. Structure. Complication. And so on.' It was of course the novelist, rather than the psychiatrist, who originally had a professional interest in such things. But *Asylum* is witty about what the novelist can do with the psychiatrist – he can, for example, call him Peter Cleave, as McGrath does here. 'And so on' clinches the ludicrousness of the stages. But then McGrath has always been shrewd about the minor complicities that make a world, however mad; about the agreements that keep us sane. Anyone who talks like this, in a novel like this, gets what they deserve – a sexual obsession with a quite different story. It is part of McGrath's bemusing artfulness in *Asylum* that he can make the reader suffer the fate of all his characters. Everyone in the novel, that is to say, is deranged by their own, and other people's, plausibility. When anyone speaks in *Asylum* – and McGrath has an extraordinary ear for the hollows in conversation, for the lurking soliloquies – we seem to see through them in the full knowledge that they never see through themselves. And yet what we see when we see through them is the spuriousness, the sinister brashness of our own omniscience. In other words, it is of a piece with the plot's subtle reversals and doublings that we begin to resemble the psychiatrist-narrator, who gives us the gradual creeps. In an uncanny way we perform, in the reading of this book, just what it is showing us. 'We two being one, are it' was the epigraph, from Donne, to McGrath's previous novel, *Dr Haggard's Disease*. *Asylum*, every bit as enthralling as *Dr Haggard* – and the first of McGrath's novels not to have an epigraph – is not about the way people turn into each other, but about the way in which they *are* each other.

'Inversion' was Gothic's 'basic structural principle', McGrath and Morrow assure us in their lucid Introduction; 'then' – in Lewis's *The Monk*, which, along with Walpole's *The Castle of*

Otranto, is the founding text of the genre – 'as now the Gothic clearly delighted in moving to the dark term of any opposition it encountered'. This makes the Gothic sound too glibly predictable; as though it merely confirmed the logic it was defying by reversing it (priests proving to be sinners, and so on). What the genre actually revealed was that the easy reversibility of this logic exposed its fatuousness; that this logic was too unstrange, too tautological to explain anything. Or rather, to explain anything that mattered, like sex or death or corruption, the staples of Gothic fiction. To talk about contradiction, and opposites – and inversion – when faced with the bizarre or the uncanny just shows how silly our ways of talking about such things become when we get really scared. By always keeping his characters just this side of allegory McGrath shows up the absurdity of these apparent inversions. In one of his last interviews with the heroine of the book, Stella, the wife of one of the asylum's psychiatrists, who has an affair with Edgar Stark, one of the more deranged patients, Peter Cleave, the psychiatrist-narrator, makes a suggestion (after the 'terrible events' that the novel recounts, Stella is now herself a patient in the asylum): 'Before I went away I asked her to think about what it meant, to love. Be rigorous, I said. She said she would.' Her agreement, of course, is merely compliant, a secret mockery of the all-too-reasonable violence he is doing her with his professional 'help'. In this brief exchange all the familiar, topical, opposites are in place – male: female; sane: mad; professional: amateur; thinking: feeling; rigour: weakness. But these very terms belong to the official language that everything in the plot undoes. She *said* she would, but she didn't. There are the languages we speak, and the languages we act on; the languages we find ourselves living by. In *Asylum* McGrath stages, with unfailing sureness of tone, the drama that goes on in the gap between the conversations people have –

with themselves and others – and the opera of what happens. The road of excess is paved with good intentions.

What happens, with varying degrees of excess and success, in *Asylum* is that the wife of an aspiring and ambitious young psychiatrist falls in love-lust with one of the patients, who is in the asylum because he decapitated his wife. He is also an artist, a sculptor who 'does heads', inspired, taciturn and moody. He escapes to London in her husband's clothes, she follows him, abandoning husband, child and her normal self. From this, various horrors ensue, none of them entirely unpredictable but all of them shocking, which is as it should be in a novel about the pathos of predictability. The narrator's faintly camp confidence is set against the horror of events; the asylum, unlike the novel, cannot contain its characters. But then artists and psychiatrists in this novel do terrible things to people's heads. Both literally and metaphorically they cut them down to bizarre shapes and sizes.

The obvious point, implicit in McGrath's title, is that there is no asylum, no safe place that isn't also a punishment: our ways of protecting ourselves from madness or passion are ways of punishing other people. But what makes *Asylum* so compelling – both gripping and horribly funny – is McGrath's mordant knowingness about the obvious points. So the psychiatrist's account, from whose point of view we see everything, is riddled with clichés – 'Like many artists, Edgar had the soft fearful core of a child' – and with naff symbolism (snakes, broken glass, ripe fruit) that make his faintly literary ordinary language seem terrifying in its nullity and deviousness. It is McGrath's acute sense that everyone's language is the archest rhetoric, a performance bristling with intent, that makes *Asylum* so tricky and unsettling. What he catches so well is people's obliviousness to each other – their being obsessed by, but not interested in, other people; a world of frenzy and inattention in which psychiatrists want to 'rebuild' their patients' psyches ('Insight, I realized, this is what we must work toward, a moment of insight when the inherent absurdities in his thinking undermined the foundations of the delusional structure and brought it crashing down. Only then could we begin to rebuild his psyche'). But also a world in which the crass pantomime psychiatrist bears an ominous or daunting similarity to the 'passionate' woman who is the heroine of the book because she does all for love, including, in one of the most extraordinary pieces of writing in the novel, letting her young son drown. If a 'professional interest' in the 'catastrophic love affair' makes us wryly suspicious at the beginning of the book, by the end, the professional psychiatrist and the passionate woman seem perfect images of each other: his asylum is knowledge, hers is passion. And both, as eventually becomes clear, are competing for the mad artist Edgar. That is to say, they both want the same thing – Edgar's recognition. He is the unholy grail in McGrath's sly parody of a quest romance.

In McGrath's new New Gothic the old inversions collapse, and all the terms are dark. It is an absurd darkness though, not a gloomy or cynical one (the only victim in the book is portentousness). The absurdity being that to be a character – an artist, a lover, a professional – is to be trapped in a genre. That character, whatever else it might be, is always a caricature, always a deeply conventional performance art. The theatricality of Gothic is well suited to explore the tyranny, the imaginative impoverishment, that ideas of authenticity always involve (exaggeration is also a kind of freedom). In *Asylum*, true to his lights, McGrath has made out of a certain kind of pastiche an exhilarating individual vision.

Promises, Promises

In the lecture room he seemed to sit apart and be
absorbed in something else, as if the subject suggested
thoughts to him which were not practically connected
with it. He was often in the subject and out of it,
in a dreamy way.

Henry Stephens's recollections of Keats as a medical student

I want to offer a disarray of reflections on this subject because I cannot come to any interesting conclusions about it. That is to say, I don't have a line on psychoanalysis and literature, which isn't a version of saying either that reading literature is similar to the experience of analysis or that it is very different (both of which I believe). If I don't think of literature as merely illuminating or confirming the so-called insights of psycho-analysis, I'm also aware that psychoanalysis seems to be of a piece with the broader cultural conversation that seems to be going on in what I think of as literature.

For me – for all sorts of reasons – there has always been only one category, *literature*, of which psychoanalysis became a part. I think of Freud as a late romantic writer, and I read psychoanalysis as poetry, so I don't have to worry about whether it is true or even useful, but only whether it is haunting or moving or intriguing or amusing – whether it is something I can't help but be interested in. I think of literature and psychoanalysis, in other words, as forms of persuasion. 'The study of literature', the poet J. V. Cunningham wrote, 'is not in the ordinary sense to further the understanding of ourselves. It is rather to enable us to see how we could think and feel otherwise than as we do.' Similarly, psychoanalysis, through written and spoken words, persuades us to feel otherwise. It is first and foremost a rhetorical practice. And yet, of course, people practise psychoanalysis in a way we don't exactly think of them practising literature.

Psychoanalysis is itself a body of literature as well as an oral tradition, but it is also a more or less definable social practice, a therapy (albeit of relatively recent invention). You can qualify to be an analyst in a way that you cannot qualify to be a writer. And the whole question of what literature is now – of what that word itself might refer to and whether or why it should have a capital *L* – has become increasingly contentious. The debate about the canon is an attempt to understand how people arrive in a position to persuade us that something is of value.

The psychoanalytic literature is easier to define nowadays than 'literary' literature, though one hopes that this too is changing. Psychoanalysis itself, of course, has had a very powerful impact on the ways in which we read and think about literature. In the early days of psychoanalysis there were people who might be interested in a Freudian reading of Keats; nowadays they might be as curious to imagine what a Keatsian reading of Freud might sound like. In other words, psycho-analysis has gone from presenting itself as a supreme fiction – or a privileged method of interpretation – to being itself one fiction, one method among many others. So my essay, I think, is really about the 'and', about whether we should keep separating these two 'things' with a conjunction.

If there are two things, psychoanalysis and literature, and psychoanalysis is both of them and literature is not, we cannot help but wonder how we have drawn the line. Freud, it is often said now – and often said in defence, though not always in defence of psychoanalysis – is a great writer. But some of us didn't end up doing with Freud what we do with other people we think of as great writers. We may learn a lot from reading Henry James, but we don't read James to learn how to do something specific. Inspiring writers may persuade us to become writers ourselves, may indeed persuade us of the truth or the power of their vision, but they don't offer us a job. Anyone who loves what was once called Literature can teach it, write it, and, of course, read it. But people who love psychoanalysis can teach it, write it, read it, *and* practise it. Because there is a real sense – a pragmatic sense – in which we can practise what Freud writes, we can wonder, by the same token, what it would be to practise Henry James or Shakespeare, and what the effect on our reading is when we are finding out how to do something.

What we want from reading psychoanalysis, and what we want from reading the literature that isn't psychoanalysis, can be quite different – and dismayingly similar. At one end of the imaginary spectrum there is the how-to book; at the other end there is so-called great literature, the books we really like: the books we can't forget, or the books we have been forced to read or to remember. In the middle there is psychoanalysis, as literature restored to practicality – the absolute antithesis of art-for-art's-sake, of the aestheticism that was historically contemporary with the birth of psychoanalysis. We have psychoanalysis as an art, and a body of literature, that is both a refuge from the world, and an engagement with it; and psychoanalysis as the apotheosis of pragmatism, as the literature that turns all language into its use-value. We read psychoanalytic literature, we practise or undergo analysis, in order to behave differently, both personally and professionally – the will to change usurping every other possibility. We are no longer reading for the plot, we are reading, or listening, for interpretation and transformation'. A difference has to be made. In its most extreme version, psychoanalysis becomes instrumental reason. But psychoanalysis also asks: when it comes to change, what is the alternative to instruction? What is persuasion when it isn't intimidation? In clinical practice after Freud, psychoanalysis found itself with a very interesting question: what does the analyst do with the patient if she doesn't interpret or teach? The comparable question – which has been so productive for psychoanalysis, beginning, of course, with Ferenczi's remarkable innovations and inventions – never made its way back either into psychoanalytic trainings or into university literature departments. That question is: what do you do with a text – psychoanalytic or otherwise – if you don't interpret it? With Ferenczi as our example, our source of analogy, how can you, as it were, make the reading experience more mutual, or less coercive, less palpable in its design? Can the reader let herself be read by the book? In our apprehension of them books are obviously different from people; and yet we are often tempted to use them for similar things.

There was a time when people might ask, why can't I just read Freud or the psychoanalytic literature? Why do I have to have an analysis? And people in the psychoanalytic profession would smile knowingly. There is no comparable question about literature. The closest you could get, perhaps, would be, why can't I just read Milton, instead of having to read this great critic on him, or perhaps more exactly, without being taught Milton by some renowned expert? In other words, when it comes to literature there isn't really another thing you can do; there isn't something that can make the reading real in the way it is assumed that being in analysis makes all the difference to the reading of Freud (Freud, who himself only ever talked with people and read books and was never psychoanalysed). This has been the way that psychoanalysts have traditionally privileged their own position. Of course, anyone can *read* psychoanalysis, but without the additional experience of something called 'psychoanalysis', the reading will be lacking. Something has to be added to reading Freud; there is something else you have to do to be in a position to speak or write authoritatively about these texts. It is one thing to say that people who have been in analysis have a different understanding of the literature, but quite another to say that they have a better one, or indeed, a real one. After all, where does this betterness reside, and where do the criteria come from? Or is it simply the case that the initiates have produced the most persuasive readings, the most persuasive, that is, to anyone other than themselves? If I want the real benefits of psychoanalysis, apparently I must have an analysis. If I want the real benefit of literature, what do I do? No one would now say that you can only understand *King Lear* if you are an old king with three daughters, two of whom betray you. But someone might say that you cannot really understand *The Interpretation of Dreams* – cannot get the full life-transforming impact of it – unless you've been in analysis. And they might add, only in analysis five times a week with an analyst trained at a specific institute. Why can't we just read Freud and the rest of the best psychoanalytic literature? Why can't we just read literature, some of which may be psychoanalytic?

There are, I think, two questions here. First, what are the experiences that we want from reading literature or from having an analysis? Second, what do we imagine an experience is, if we think we can compare the experience of literature with the experience of analysis? Clearly, the consequences of reading literature, in so far as they can be discerned – like the consequences of having an analysis – are strikingly unpredictable. In the best sense, both experiences have uncertain outcomes, and yet we turn to them in different circumstances, and for both comparable and different reasons. Reading literature, one might say, works for us, in a different sense of 'works'. A social practice is always situated. The project is defined by its context, even if, from a psychoanalytic point of view, it is inspired by unconscious desire. At its most minimal, there is something else we want, and this something else – sexual satisfaction, relationship, development, safety, relief from suffering, whatever we imagine it is that we are in need of – is defined by the culture. The culture sets the terms. Psychoanalytic culture overlaps with the wider culture in the form of a simple agreement: what we want, one way or another, is change. But it is not the kind of change we know is happening all the time, apparently despite us – ageing, economic change, political and social strife. We want, instead, only the kind of change we want. This, one could say, might be a shorthand definition of what Freud calls the ego: the part of oneself that tries, admittedly against all odds, to dictate change, the part of the self that disavows contingency and the vagaries of desire.

Daniel Lagache (*Selected Writings*, 1993) refers to the ego as an object of 'fascination' to consciousness, and states that the analytic aim might be to 'disengage' consciousness from the ego's influence. 'The aim of analysis is achieved,' he writes, 'when where ego was, henceforth there shall consciousness be.' He is describing the way that it is as though the ego hypnotizes us with its projects. In these terms, the problem is no longer literature and/or psychoanalysis; the problem is thinking that we know what we want from either – believing that we can orchestrate our transformations.

We can't help behaving as if we know what analysis and literature are for, and we can't help but be wrong – not totally wrong, of course, but never entirely right. 'The individual is always mistaken,' Emerson writes in *Experience*. 'He designed many things, and drew in other persons as coadjutors, quarrelled with some or all, blundered much, and something is done; all are a little advanced, but the individual is always mistaken. It turns out somewhat new and very unlike what he promised himself.' There is the contingency outside, as it were, and for some of us, that paradoxical contingency within, the purposeful contingency of the unconscious, of unconscious desire. Emerson's 'The individual is always mistaken' is a witty foretaste of Freud, who made us more vivid to ourselves in our mistakes than in our competence. 'It turns out somewhat new and very unlike what he promised himself.' The things that we mistakenly turn to psychoanalysis and literature for are hints about whatever else we may have in mind.

We can't help talking today about what we have promised ourselves with psychoanalysis, and, of course, about the promise of literature, which is by definition so much more diverse, so various in the multiplicity of its voices. And we are often told, at the moment, that psychoanalysis hasn't kept its promise; is indeed so falsely promising as to be virtually over. Current debates in literary studies are about, among other things, the nature of the promise that something we once called 'literature' is now in a position to make. There is now, Frank Kermode writes in *What's Happened to the Humanities* (1997), 'much popular confusion about what is valuable in the past, and why'. And current debates about psychoanalysis are similarly perplexed, particularly about the past.

If we talk about promises now, as I think we should when we talk about psychoanalysis and literature, then we are talking about hopes and wishes, about what we are wanting from our relationship with these two objects in the cultural field. It is a question of relationships, but perhaps it also points to the drawback of making 'relationships' the primary category. I think we should make our primary category something like *moral aims*, or *preferred worlds*, what Stanley Cavell refers to (in *Conditions Handsome and Unhandsome*, 1990) after Emerson, as 'moral perfectionism', which he defines as 'some idea of being true to oneself', but which 'happily consents to democracy'. Our description of our relationships – which entails our description of what it is *not* to have one, what a good one is, and so on – depends on our moral aims, on the kind of selves and worlds we are consciously and unconsciously committed to fashioning. There can be no democracy without the notion of relationship as somehow central, but the idea of being true to oneself may involve redescribing the idea of relationship so radically that it may sometimes be barely recognizable. (The reason Cavell's juxtaposition is so striking is that it confronts us with the compatibility, or otherwise, of our moral ideals.) Democracy thrives by valuing rival and complementary interpretation. It is not equally clear what being true to oneself thrives by, or whether it could ever be subject to generalization or, indeed, formulation. Our relationship to ourselves must be inextricable from our relationship with others; but in what sense does one have a 'relationship' with oneself, or with a book, or with its author, or with a tradition? In other words, is there sufficient resemblance between these objects to make 'relationship' the right, or rather the illuminating, word?

What we actually do – or find ourselves doing – in the presence of a book or an analyst could not be more different, from one point of view. The implication of Literature *and* Psychoanalysis is that we must be using them for distinguishably different things. But how we use them depends on what I am calling here our 'moral aims', our conscious and unconscious moral projects about whose very consequences we can have so little knowledge. What or who we seek to be influenced by – to be changed by – depends on the kinds of selves (and worlds) we want to make and the kinds of culture in which we happen to live. An analysis, like a work of literature, is potentially a transformational object (and so could anything else be for any given person at any given moment). We can think of ourselves as using these objects, from a psychoanalytic point of view, as being akin to what Freud calls 'dream-work', or what Winnicott called 'object-usage'. And here what is most telling is that these are the things we have chosen to make our futures from. But one thing that is most obviously patent in the literature-versus-psychoanalysis issue is the question of the difference – a difference about which psychoanalysis has been especially preoccupied – between the presence or the absence of what was once called an 'object' and is now more hospitably (or more hopefully) called a 'person'. Where once I might have organized my sense of my life and its meaning – what Jane Austen calls in a letter my 'self-consequence' – around the absent presence of God, I might now organize my life around my relationship with other people; even around the absent presence of a different kind of author, called a 'writer', or around the relatively absent presence of an analyst. Whenever I read a book – whatever I have done prior to my reading and whatever I do subsequently – someone is communicating with me in their absence. Rather like a dream, I am hearing things, but there is no sound. Modern technology masks how truly incredible it is that people can communicate with us in their absence and after their deaths. Of course, we want something from these people who aren't really there. So what difference does a person in the room make? What difference does actually talking and listening make? To put it more psychoanalytically, what is simply reading a book a re-creation of that analysis can never be, by virtue of the presence of that so-called real other person? There is, one might say, a self one is true to in solitude, and a self one is true to in company.

We might think of children as experimenting with what is

possible in the absence of the object, of finding out what they can do, what experiences they can have, without the palpable presence of another person. Whether we talk of object constancy, the internalization of the good object, or the capacity to be alone in the presence of the mother, one way or another a time comes, ideally, when the child discovers the pleasures of her own solitude. One of the things the child might do in this solitude – through acculturation, through identification, as a refuge from persecution, as a form of daylight dreaming – is to read. And the child, if she happens to love reading, will be able to lose herself in a book. Through a kind of self-forgetting, akin to dreaming, she will have an experience that she will have to come back from, as absorbing, in its own way, as her primary relationships are and have been. Yet these reading experiences are the repetition of these earliest states of absorption, but in the absence of an actual object. The self (or selves) one is true to in solitude is relatively undisturbed by the demand of the other; impingement is kept to a minimum. This is part of what one might mean by saying that one has a relationship with the author of a book. The author speaks to you, but doesn't answer back. The author, in actuality, never speaks at all. And the demand of this person called an author seems chosen, based on a feeling of affinity. Like the dreaming experience, the reading experience is conducted in silence, unless, of course, one reads out loud, in which case, oddly enough, one only hears one's own voice. If 'literature is a relational exchange of possible states of being', then what kind of exchange goes on between a book and its reader? What can a book give us that a person can't? One possible answer might be 'the experience of a relationship in silence', the unusual experience of a relationship in which no one speaks. Our present interest in biography, in knowing about writers through interviews and live readings, is, I think, a wish to break this silence. To think about literature and psychoanalysis is to wonder what silence might be a medium for. In an analysis there is always the possibility that the analyst might speak. There is never the possibility that the author will speak.

Reading literature is a relationship conducted in silence, and yet what we ordinarily think of as a relationship is something in which people break into words together. Indeed, it is inconceivable how people could do anything together without actually speaking. Democracy, by definition, is very noisy. Yet if someone said, as one might, that he felt truer to himself in that solitary silence – sponsored and sustained as it must be by the relationships surrounding, or pre-dating, that silence – what would we make of it? If someone said that there is a quality of relationship with himself that he could only obtain in silence – through reading, not talking – what would we assume, from a psychoanalytic point of view, is being exchanged? Would exchange, or relationship, be a good and useful description of what is going on? If we think of literature and psychoanalysis in the light of Cavell's terms, 'being true to oneself' and happily consenting to democracy', we are confronted with the fact that we can only understand our relationship with ourselves in the language of our relationship with others. I might feel true to myself in silence – in the essentially meditative experience of reading literature – but to be a democrat I must both speak and believe in the value of listening to other people's spoken voices; and not lose too much of my temper when I hear what they say.

Being true to oneself was once, for the majority of people in the West, being true to God. You could speak to him, in prayer or ritual, even if he didn't reply. That is to say, there was something to be true to, or someone to be true for. Life questions were religious questions that became, or tried to become, political questions. There was a process of what the classicist

374

Marcel Detienne calls 'the secularization of language', an evolving 'contrast between two models of speech, the "magico-religious" and the "dialogue-speech" '. So for some people the question became: to be true to democracy, what kind of self does one need? This was, as it were, a psychological version of the question: what is being true to democracy being true to?

It seems that all the psychoanalytic versions of developmental theory suggest that we are instinctual or emotional fundamentalists (believers in 'magico-religious speech'), struggling to become democrats (committed to 'dialogue-speech'): or born democrats who are always prone through fear to take refuge in magic. Democracy in this progress myth becomes a developmental achievement. Being true to democracy means seeing the point of valuing rival points of view. Being true to oneself may or may not entail this.

Psychoanalysis, Lacan writes in his *Écrits*, 'is a question of recollection ... in which conjectures about the past are balanced against promises of the future'. In this balancing act, to be remembering is to be planning a future. And to call up the future is the project of psychoanalysis. So the question is not, psychoanalysis and/or literature? But rather, what are the constraints of self-becoming provided by literature in its excessive variety, and by psychoanalysis, in all its devoted and devotional repetitions? After all, we can never know beforehand what will change us or indeed what kinds of change we want. A book can speak to us and never answer back; it can conjure up the past and the voices of the dead. But we never tell a book a story. Why have an analysis when you can read?

Acknowledgements

The pieces in this book were originally published, some in different versions, in the *London Review of Books, Raritan, Threepenny Review, fort/da, History Workshop Journal, New York Times, New York Observer, Contemporary Psychoanalysis, Slate, Critical Quarterly, Salmagundi,* and *The Observer.* I am grateful to the editors of these journals for inviting me to write for them.

'Clutter: A Case History' was published in *Mind Readings,* edited by Sara Dunn, Blake Morrison and Michele Roberts. 'Sameness is All' was published in *Clones and Clones,* edited by Martha Nussbaum and Cass Sunstein. 'On Eating, and Preferring Not To' and 'Promises, Promises' were first given as panel discussions at conferences at the Allanson White Institute in New York. 'The Pragmatics of Passion' was published in *The Dead Mother,* edited by Gregorio Kohon. 'Winnicott's Hamlet' was given as a lecture at The Squiggle Foundation; 'On Translating a Person' was first given as a talk to a TRIO conference on translation at Oxford, and in a different version as the Gwyn Jones Memorial Lecture; both are previously unpublished. 'Poetry and Psychoanalysis' was given as the inaugural Guild of Psychotherapists Annual Interdisciplinary Lecture.